Love You to Death

the unofficial companion to

the ampire Diaries

season 2

ECW Press

Published by ECW Press

2120 Queen Street East, Suite 200, Toronto, Ontario, Canada M4E 1E2
416-694-3348 / info@ecwpress.com

Library and Archives Canada Cataloguing in Publication

Calhoun, Crissy
Love you to death, season two : the unofficial companion to the Vampire Diaries / Crissy Calhoun.

ISBN 978-1-77041-056-5
Also in electronic formats:
978-1-77090-031-8 (EPUB); 978-1-77090-032-5 (PDF)

1. Vampire diaries (Television program). I. Title.

PN1992.77.V34C342 2011   791.45'72   C2011-902809-3

Typesetting: Gail Nina
Text design: Melissa Kaita
Cover and color photo section design: Rachel Ironstone
Cover image: Chris Nicholls/Contour by Getty Images
Author photo: Lee Weston Photography (LeeWestonPhoto.com)
Printing: Thomson-Shore   5   4   3   2   1

Interior photo credits by page: 2: Mark Davis/PictureGroup; 4 (left): Tina Gill/PictureGroup; 4 (right), 38, 107, 210: Albert L. Ortega/PictureGroup; 16, 55, 67, 129, 145, 183: Gregg DeGuire/PictureGroup; 24: Justin Campbell/startraksphoto.com; 51: Kristian Dowling/Warner Bros. Television Entertainment/PictureGroup; 79: Evan Agostini/PictureGroup; 97, 201, 219: The CW/Bob Mahoney/Landov; 109, 217: ML / Agency Photos; 119: Charles Lucas / Agency Photos; 138: mpi30/MediaPunch Inc/PictureGroup; 154, 233: The CW/Annette Brown /Landov; 161: Justin Campbell/BuzzFoto.com/Keystone Press; 175: Dave Allocca/Starpix/startraksphoto.com; 240: courtesy Chloe Dawn; 245: courtesy Tiya Sircar; 250: courtesy Jessica Connell Lowery. *Photo insert:* 1: Albert Michael/startraksphoto.com; 2–7: The CW / Bob Mahoney / Landov; 8: Dimitrios Kambouris/VF11/Getty Images.

The publication of *Love You to Death — Season 2: The unofficial companion to The Vampire Diaries* has been generously supported by the Government of Ontario through Ontario Book Publishing Tax Credit, by the OMDC Book Fund, an initiative of the Ontario Media Development Corporation, and by the Government of Canada through the Canada Book Fund.

Canadä

Printed and bound in the United States

Contents

Introduction

In a strange way, my experience with *The Vampire Diaries* has mirrored the change from season 1 to season 2. When we met the characters in season 1, the story stayed focused, rarely taking us outside of Mystic Falls; season 2 opened the story up — strangers came to town who wouldn't know a Fell from a Bradley and, through flashback sequences, we left America and the recent past behind. Last year, I watched *The Vampire Diaries* every week with the "knitting club," but this year I watched with the raucous fandom on Twitter and saw my timeline explode with OMGs, like clockwork, just before each commercial break. Writing for Vampire-Diaries.net allowed me to share my thoughts on each episode to the site's devoted and smart readers, and it was amazing to see the comments roll in each Sunday afternoon with theories and opinions. When I met some fellow *TVD* fans in Atlanta, it turned out that they are just as passionate, clever, and hilarious in real life. And as the show's popularity has grown around the world, I've had the opportunity to connect with international fans, particularly in Germany and Poland where my first book was published in translation. Though I'm lucky to have many close friends who love the show as much as I do, there are still those who just don't get *TVD* and can't see why I would spend the time to write *two* books on it. So it's been wonderful to always have the *TVD* family just a tweet away — a community where quips about side parts, Capri Sun, and #NotNowDana are understood and encouraged.

My assumption is that if you're interested in this season 2 companion, you are a *fan* of the show. If so, I've written this book with you in mind. Its episode guide has its genesis in the posts I wrote over the course of the season for Vampire-Diaries.net. Readers of my first season companion to *The Vampire Diaries* will notice that the episodes get more attention in this volume. With such a rich, complicated, fast-paced, and fun season, and with the writers expanding the focus to include more of the secondary characters, I felt it was appropriate to lend more analysis to each of the 22 installments of *TVD*. What isn't included here is what's covered in the first volume: I didn't want to repeat the biographies of the actors, the background information on

L.J. Smith's book series, or the background of the making of the TV show for those of you who have already read season 1's *Love You to Death*.

Each episode's write-up begins with a bit of dialogue that stood out for me either because it captures the episode in a pithy few lines . . . or it was just too well written not to acknowledge. From there, I provide an analysis of the episode, looking at its main themes, the character development, and the questions it raises, followed by these sections:

COMPELLING MOMENT: Here I choose one moment that stands out — a turning point, a character standing up for herself, or a long-awaited relationship scene (. . . usually involving kissing).

CIRCLE OF KNOWLEDGE: In this section of the episode guide, you'll find all the need-to-know info — the details you may have missed on first watch, character insights, the cultural references, and motifs or recurring elements. Often, an episode's title is a play on another title (of a film, book, song, etc.); those are explained in this section.

THE RULES: Any work of fiction with a supernatural element has its own particular spin on how that world operates. Here I catalog what we've learned about what goes bump in the night.

THE DIABOLICAL PLAN: One of *The Vampire Diaries'* defining qualities is its lightning-fast pacing, so "The Diabolical Plan" tracks the various human and non-human forces at work in Mystic Falls and raises questions about what their next steps may be.

HISTORY LESSON: The only class at Mystic Falls High School that gets considerable screen time is history. History, both real and fictional, is important in this series — and for the characters' back stories, the town's history, and subtle references, "History Lesson" is your study aid.

BITE MARKS: Bite marks, stake wounds, snapped necks, and good old-fashioned slaps to the face — this section is all about the violence on the show, cataloging injuries inflicted and suffered by the immortal and mortal.

PREVIOUSLY ON THE VAMPIRE DIARIES: History repeats itself in Mystic Falls, and in this new category for my season 2 guide, I outline the incidents, motifs, and key moments that are revisited or echoed in each episode. Included at the back of the book is a quick refresher on the season 1 episodes (see page 264), which I refer to by title in this section.

MEANWHILE IN FELL'S CHURCH: Here we travel from one TVD universe to another and I draw comparisons between L.J. Smith's original plotting and characterization and that of the TV series. Because production of the TV show was underway before The Return trilogy was published, this section focuses only on *The Awakening*, *The Struggle*, *The Fury*, and *Dark Reunion*. (Fans of The Return, please don your Wings of Understanding.)

OFF CAMERA: Here we leave the fictional world behind to hear what the cast and crew have to say about filming an episode; sometimes I provide background details on a guest star, director, or other filming details.

FOGGY MOMENTS: Elena, surprised by Stefan in the cemetery in the pilot episode, tells him the fog is making her foggy. "Foggy Moments" is a collection of confusing moments for the viewer — continuity errors, arguable nitpicks, full-on inconsistencies, and mysteries that may be explained later.

MUSIC: An important part of *The Vampire Diaries* is its soundtrack, and in this section, I tell you what song is playing in each scene.

QUESTIONS: One of the funnest ways to spend the time between episodes of *TVD* is with theorizing and wondering what will happen next or what motivates a character. In this section, I raise questions about characters, plotting, and mythology for you to consider as you watch the season unfold.

Make sure you watch an episode *before* reading its corresponding guide — you will encounter spoilers for that episode (but not for anything that follows). Within the pages of the guide, you'll also find short biographies of the actors who bring the recurring characters to life as well as sidebars about other elements of the show and about its influences. After the episode guide, you'll find a chapter that looks at the season as a whole by examining one of its main recurring themes: the double. There's an interview section featuring

Q&As with two leaders of the fandom and with actors Tiya Sircar (Aimee Bradley) and Bryton McClure (Luka Martin). Finally, I've updated the timeline included in my first companion guide to include season 2's info on the past thousand years in the *TVD* universe.

If there's something you think I missed, or that I completely read your mind about, drop me at a note at crissycalhoun@gmail.com, @reply me on Twitter (@crissycalhoun), and/or stop by my blog at crissycalhoun.com. For my season 3 posts, head on over to Vampire-Diaries.net.

xoxo
Crissy Calhoun
July 2011

Never a Dull Day on The Vampire Diaries

"The second season is always scary because you never know — are they still going to like you? Are they going to get tired of you? Are they going to get over you? But [the audience has] been just as enthusiastic." So said Julie Plec, midway through season 2 of *The Vampire Diaries*. Coming in to their sophomore year, show creators Kevin Williamson and Julie Plec had finished the first season on a high note, one that promised fans that they'd return to Mystic Falls in September to be treated to the juicy repercussions of Damon kissing "Elena" on her front porch and the sure-to-be delightfully evil Katherine Pierce, live and in the flesh.

Though major awards eluded *TVD* (as they do all shows on The CW), *The Vampire Diaries* was a fan favorite, the highest-rated program on its network, and increasingly a critical darling. It landed on "best of the year" lists on *Entertainment Weekly*, CNN, TelevisionWithoutPity.com, Fearnet. com, E! Online, Zap2It.com, BuddyTV.com, and IGN.com; it received People's Choice and Saturn Award nominations and won seven Teen Choice Awards. The *New York Post*'s PopWrap, in naming *TVD* the best show of 2010, wrote, "Scoff if you will, but for my money, no show on television has better pacing, plots, or performances than The CW's *Vampire Diaries* . . . which achieves the near impossible task of seamlessly crafting a series that is at once a comedy, a thriller, a drama, and a character piece. The world Kevin Williamson and Julie Plec created is lush, rich, and filled with amazing

personalities — characters that are in good hands with the excellent actors who have assembled to bring this tale to life."

While season 1 focused on introducing the audience to the world of Mystic Falls, its vampires, witches, and founders — with the spotlight primarily on Elena, Stefan, and Damon — season 2 promised to open up that insular world both to new characters and to those patiently waiting in the wings. Explained Julie Plec, "One of Kevin's and my disappointments in the first season was that as much as we wanted to bring a deep, rich life to the secondary characters, a lot of them ended up getting sidelined to make room for the core story — for what we call the 'power of the three.'" Kevin Williamson agreed. "You want your secondary characters to evolve and to be layered. We wanted to do everything with them that we were able to do in season 1 with Damon, Elena, and Stefan. Michael Trevino hung in there last year; he was frustrated. There were about six episodes where he said two lines. I kept telling him that this year would be 'The Year of the Wolf' and that he would eventually become a multi-layered character that people would root for, care about, and be traumatized by. And boy, was he ready." Michael

Trevino enjoyed watching the fan reaction to his character change as Tyler was given more screen time and depth in season 2. "The whole fan reaction in season 1 was . . . 'I hate this character.' . . . Now I get sympathy, because we see the humanity in him. Because he is just this kid, at the end of the day. It's fun to see fans change a little bit and feel sorry for Tyler, because in season 1 there was no way anybody was feeling sorry for him." With the large ensemble cast, it was still necessary to leave out a few characters from time to time (most cast members, with the exception of the main three, were in 17 of the 22 episodes), but Matt Davis, Sara Canning, Kat Graham, Zach Roerig, Steven R. McQueen, and, in particular, Candice Accola were given meatier plot lines in season 2 along with Trevino.

Though Paul Wesley reevaluated his approach to his work heading into season 2 ("I realized, this is a marathon, not a sprint, so I'm preparing myself for the long run"), the season looked most different for Nina Dobrev, who would be playing Katherine Pierce, as well as Elena Gilbert, with much more frequency. That change meant Nina was always working, always on set filming one or the other of her characters. "It's almost like I've developed split personality disorder myself," said Nina. "It messes with your head when you have to go back and forth so often between these two people. But it's cool and it's fun . . . both characters feed different parts of my cravings; I'm in love with both my characters."

The series stayed in Georgia to shoot, benefiting from the state's tax incentives, and episodes were filmed on location in Covington as well as in studio just outside of Atlanta. Marcos Siega stepped down as co-executive producer at the end of season 1, but many of the core crew from the first season stayed on to keep the look and feel of the series consistent. J. Miller Tobin came on board to serve as producer for season 2. A director with extensive experience in episodic TV (*Oz*, *Numb3rs*, *Terminator: The Sarah Connor Chronicles*, *Make It or Break It*, and a handful of CW shows like *90210*, *Life Unexpected*, *Melrose Place*, *Supernatural*, and *Gossip Girl*), Tobin was also in the director's chair for season 1's "The Turning Point" and "Isobel." Also on board for the first 15 episodes of the season was John Shiban, best known for his work on *The X-Files* (with an Emmy at home as evidence of that) as well as *Supernatural*, *Torchwood*, and *Breaking Bad*, among other series. Production on season 2 began in July, and over the nine months of filming, there were a few unexpected hiccups: Paul Wesley was in a cast for an ankle injury, Ian Somerhalder had walking pneumonia for two months, Nina Dobrev threw

out her back, an unusually snowy winter (for Georgia) delayed shooting, and even Kevin Williamson injured himself on a set visit.

But that didn't stop the show. Debuting in September with a killer first episode back, the pace was set with "The Return," and that pace kept up straight through to the show's finale in May 2011. And, with the popularity of Twitter and other online social media, the creators knew immediately just how the fandom had responded to any plot twist or character development. "One of the greatest things about this experience is that our fan base is very vocal. The community runs very deep and they're very, very supportive and that's good," said Julie Plec. The fandom's support extended to the other projects affiliated with *TVD*; cast members could be sure of enthusiasm for their projects outside of the show as well as for their philanthropic endeavors (see sidebar opposite).

One of the most interesting *TVD*-related projects for the fandom was The CW's new series *The Secret Circle*, which was developed by Kevin Williamson and picked up for the 2011–12 TV season. Another Alloy Entertainment project based on novels written by L.J. Smith, *The Secret Circle* is not a spin-off of *TVD*, rather it is a separate universe that happens to be inhabited by witches. (So don't expect Bonnie Bennett to show up in Chance Harbor.) For those fans who are concerned that between writing *Scream 4* and executive producing *The Secret Circle*, Kevin Williamson may have less time for Mystic Falls,

TVD Do-Gooders

The *TVD* family — fans, cast, and crew alike — channel their passion and use the strength of their community to raise awareness for worthy causes such as these:

- ScreamForaDream.net: A group dedicated to raising awareness by engaging the vampire fandom communities and starting projects that encourage the world's youth to speak up for what they believe in.
- PositiveWomen.org: A U.K.-based group that aims to empower and educate communities in Swaziland affected by HIV/AIDS by providing real, practical support.
- TheTrevorProject.org: An organization dedicated to providing crisis and suicide prevention services to LGBTQ youth.
- ItGetsBetter.org: A grassroots campaign against bullying and isolation, which began with a video that gave the message "It Gets Better" in response to a spate of suicides among gay youth in America.
- TapProject.org: An initiative from UNICEF that asks restaurant patrons to donate money for the tap water they normally drink for free. The funds raised are used to bring clean and accessible water to children around the world who normally go without.
- InvisibleChildren.com: An organization that, through the power of media to raise awareness, seeks to stop the abduction of children for use as soldiers in Uganda.
- TurntheCorner.org: An organization dedicated to raising awareness about Lyme disease and supporting research and education relating to tick-borne diseases.
- ISFoundation.com: Ian Somerhalder's foundation strives to collaborate with other nonprofits in the areas of habitat, environment, and energy and to encourage youth participation and innovation.
- DoSomething.org: Striving to encourage a culture of volunteerism, this organization inspires and empowers youth to take action.

the showrunner assured the *Hollywood Reporter*, "I'm not going to step away from my vampires. I'm too invested at this point; it's too much of a family for me to walk away from, but there's room in our day for me to help guide *The Secret Circle* along the way."

When *The Vampire Diaries'* second season was mapped out early on, the creators considered the long-term direction of their hit show and they took steps to write the mythology and introduce characters in a way that best set the stage for the seasons to follow. "It's much more *Dark Shadows*," said Julie. "It's a gothic horror, soap, genre, character piece. It's really hard to write, by the way. The world is small, but it can keep growing and expanding on itself

Meet the Writers

Asked by the *Hollywood Reporter* what the biggest challenge is in being a showrunner for a TV show, Kevin Williamson said, "The deadlines. TV goes so fast; you're filming one [episode], you're editing one, you're prepping one and you're writing one all at once. You've got your hands in seven different episodes all at one time. It's hard to juggle from time to time, particularly if one has a hiccup. Julie and I wanted to make an epic show and, you know what, it takes a lot of epic work." Helping Kevin and Julie deliver such an epic show is a team of writers. Writing for television is a collaborative process that involves many minds working together. As Andrew Chambliss told io9.com, "There's nothing like working with a room full of talented writers to break story, find solutions to script problems, and oftentimes split writing duties to get a script written quickly." Here's a brief introduction to those writers whose names appear with "written by" credits in season 2 of *TVD*.

Andrew Chambliss ("Under Control," "Founder's Day," "Katerina," "The Dinner Party," "The Last Day"): Served as executive story editor on season 2 and is the "vampire rules" expert in the writers' room. Andrew was the story editor and a writer for *Dollhouse* (where he worked with Liz Craft and Sarah Fain) and he wrote for *Spartacus*. He worked on *Crossing Jordan* and *Heroes* and was a staff writer for *Bionic Woman*. Andrew studied screenwriting at NYU and became interested in writing for TV while working as script coordinator for *Law & Order*. His first writing credits were for *Heroes* comics, and he's since worked with Joss Whedon on season 9 *Buffy* comics. For Andrew, "Writing 'good' vampires is actually a lot more interesting than writing 'bad' vampires. They're in constant [self-]conflict."

Elizabeth Craft and Sarah Fain ("Plan B," "The Descent"): Writing duo Craft and Fain went to Kansas City's Pembroke Hill school together and their professional careers have been intertwined since. Coauthors of a Y.A. fiction series (*Bass Ackwards and Belly Up* and *Footfree and Fancy Loose*), Craft and Fain have written for Kevin Williamson's *Glory Days*, Joss Whedon's *Angel* (where they served as executive story editors in its fourth season) and for *Dollhouse*, *The Shield* (where they also had producing credits), *Women's Murder Club* (a series they created), *Lie to Me*, and they also worked on the development stages of *The Secret Circle* project for The CW. They joined *The Vampire Diaries* in season 2 as consulting producers. It's "the first show we've worked on that didn't have a [weekly] 'case' of any sort to it," explained Craft. "It's fun. I think we're learning a lot, because you don't have that case to hang your hat on, plot-wise. It's a learning experience."

Mike Daniels ("Kill or Be Killed," "By the Light of the Moon," "Know Thy Enemy," "The Sun Also Rises"): Joined *TVD* in season 2 as coproducer and writer after working on The CW's *One Tree Hill* as a writer and executive story editor. His favorite death (when asked in a live tweet during "Masquerade") was Lexi's in "162 Candles." Tweeted Daniels, "I was like, What the heck just happened? 'Cuz I was just a *TVD* fan writing for *One Tree Hill* way back then."

Caroline Dries ("Miss Mystic Falls," "Isobel," "Memory Lane," "The Sacrifice," "The House Guest," "The Sun Also Rises"): A supervising producer of *TVD*, Dries has writer and story editor credits on *Smallville* and writer and producer credits on *Melrose Place*. Her favorite character to write for is Katherine. There's a challenge she finds in writing for *TVD*: balancing the nonsupernatural story elements with the supernatural ones — the stakes are always higher and characters more likely to die in the supernatural plots, but the human elements are what ground the show.

Turi Meyer and Al Septien ("As I Lay Dying"): This writing duo joined the show at the end of season 2 as writers and consulting producers once *Smallville* came to its end, a show they'd worked on as writers, story editors, and producers since 2005. They've also written for *Andromeda* and *Mutant X* and wrote the horror movies *Sleepstalker* (which Meyer also directed) and *Leprechaun 2*. Septien directed an episode of *Buffy*, three *Angels*, and two *Smallvilles*. Septien described *TVD* as "a wonderful fit for us. We had worked in the past with Caroline Dries and that was a lot of fun to come into a room with her again. You know again, it's a world that we know. Our past was in horror movies. Six years on *Smallville* where there's a strong love story. We kind of felt this was a great show to move into from that, so it exploited what we do. And we've enjoyed the time [on *TVD*] and are happy to be coming back [for season 3]."

Michael Narducci ("The Last Dance," "As I Lay Dying"): Another season 2 addition, Narducci also serves as executive story editor. He was a writer and executive story editor for *Medium* and writer on USA Network's *The 4400*. He joked on Twitter that Caroline Dries "keeps him in check."

Brian Young ("Family Ties," "History Repeating," "Unpleasantville," "A Few Good Men," "Isobel," "Brave New World," "Rose," "Crying Wolf," "The Last Day"): A *TVD* veteran, Young served as season 2's story editor. The first episode of television he wrote was for *Kyle XY* with Julie Plec. Brian's favorite moment of the season, when asked during the "Masquerade" live tweet, was Caroline's "Hi, Mom" in "Kill or Be Killed."

and you can introduce new elements in due time. And there's always a great high-stakes emotional roller coaster happening."

When asked what it was that appealed to audiences about *The Vampire Diaries*, Paul Wesley expressed what *he* finds appealing about it. "There's a good balance of humor, evil, darkness and light, and the characters are not one-dimensional. The show also has amazing cinematography and an awesome score. It becomes addictive, even for people who aren't into the genre." For the creators, crew, actors, and audience, Nina's quip during the 2011 TCA press tour was bang-on: "It's never a dull day on *The Vampire Diaries*."

The past is never dead. It's not even past.

— William Faulkner

Episode Guide

Season 2
September 2010–May 2011

CAST: Nina Dobrev (Elena Gilbert/Katherine Pierce), Paul Wesley (Stefan Salvatore), Ian Somerhalder (Damon Salvatore), Steven R. McQueen (Jeremy Gilbert), Sara Canning (Jenna Sommers), Kat Graham (Bonnie Bennett), Candice Accola (Caroline Forbes), Zach Roerig (Matt Donovan), Michael Trevino (Tyler Lockwood), Matt Davis (Alaric Saltzman)

RECURRING CAST: David Anders (John Gilbert), Lauren Cohan (Rose), Trent Ford (Trevor), Daniel Gillies (Elijah), Randy Goodwin (Dr. Jonas Martin), Bryton James (Luka Martin), Taylor Kinney (Mason Lockwood), Marguerite MacIntyre (Sheriff Liz Forbes), Michaela McManus (Jules), Joseph Morgan (Klaus), Dawn Olivieri (Andie Star), Gino Anthony Pesi (Maddox), Tiya Sircar (Aimee Bradley), Lisa Tucker (Greta Martin), Susan Walters (Carol Lockwood)

✤

Damon: I just need the truth, just once.
Katherine: Stop. I already know your question and its answer.
The truth is I've never loved you. It was always Stefan.

2.01 *The Return*

Original air date: September 9, 2010
Written by: Kevin Williamson and Julie Plec
Directed by: J. Miller Tobin

The aftershocks of Founder's Day ripple through Mystic Falls as the Lockwoods mourn the mayor, Caroline's friends rally to save her life, and Damon is rejected by the woman he's been chasing for 145 years.

With an opening sequence that feels plucked from a horror movie, "The Return" picks up in the same moment the previous episode left off with the frantic, high-stakes and high-emotions energy of the Founder's Day finale of season 1. The remaining tomb vampires are dead, but the lone vampire missing from the tomb — Katherine Pierce — proves she can raise more hell than the rest of them combined. Katherine's reappearance in Mystic Falls is already yielding interesting consequences for Stefan, Damon, and Elena but this episode reaches past the three core characters to promise compelling storylines in season 2 for those who received less attention last season.

With only two scenes, Susan Walters as Carol Lockwood puts in a great performance as the grieving widow and the confused mother of a violent son (perhaps chillingly reminiscent of the late mayor for her). Her grief is mixed with anger: who is responsible for the mistake that led to Richard Lockwood's death? Carol understandably wants someone taken to task for it, but Liz Forbes isn't able to explain what happened. She was against the plan in the first place, and it unfolded against her will. Nor can she explain why Richard reacted to the Gilbert device. Like Carol, Sheriff Forbes needs help as she tries to balance personal tragedy with the supernatural fallout, not realizing that the friend she turns to is the opposite of what he seems, or that her two worlds are about to collide as her daughter is on her way to becoming a vampire.

Katherine and Stefan have a little chat by the pond on the Lockwood property. The Lockwood estate scenes are filmed at a private residence in Covington, GA.

Help comes to Carol in the form of Mason Lockwood, the chilled-out surfer and "black sheep" of the family who's returned for his brother's funeral. While no *Vampire Diaries* character is ever as simple as he or she first appears to be, Mason offers Tyler hope: a way to overcome the rage that sometimes consumes him. In this regard he is the opposite of Tyler's father. Mason calls the blinding rage they all share the "curse of being a Lockwood," and he seems to have it under control. Tyler's grief confuses him: he hated his father but is angry with him for dying and leaving him. The love/hate relationship he had with his father can never be resolved. As he did after Vicki was discovered dead, Tyler finds a brief moment of connection with Jeremy, no stranger to loss. The contrast in how the boys deal with their loss, and how they felt about their fathers, builds on the tense dynamic between them explored since the pilot episode. As the series opened, Elena and Jeremy were children who'd lost their parents; "The Return" begins with Tyler as the grieving son, a position that foreshadows his increased importance in season 2.

Though his real father is dead, Jeremy confronts one of his father figures, his uncle John Gilbert who claims to hold the same values his brother Grayson did. But John is also responsible for Anna's death. While Elena describes John as seeing "the world with such hatred," he escapes being strictly a villain when he gives Jeremy his ring — a selfless act of love for a man so filled with hate. Besides protecting Jeremy from a death with supernatural causes (something that comes in handy sooner than either could have guessed), the ring is a symbol of family and a reminder to Jeremy that he's a part of the Gilbert legacy, just as Tyler is a Lockwood whether he likes it or not. Jeremy's resurrections bookend "The Return" and leave open the question of how the shaky sense of self that plagued him in the first season will develop from this point on.

A season ago, the brothers Salvatore could be reduced to the "good" brother and the "bad" brother. Now it's more a question of which one is holding it together and which one is falling apart. Stefan acts as a quick-thinking, confident leader while Damon's need for emotional release after the not-Elena kiss overwhelms his ability to control his destructive and vindictive instincts. Damon's final act of the episode creates chaos. But Stefan manages chaos, rather than creating it, by being the most intense version of himself: from literally slapping some sense into Jeremy, to scaring Uncle John straight out of town, to playing along with Katherine in order to see what her game is, to sensibly backing down when Damon puts up his dukes. Even when he feels himself giving over, Stefan refuses to fight or be goaded into an action he'd regret by Damon or Katherine. In the past, Stefan has been protective, violent when he deemed it necessary, manipulative for a greater good, and willing to engage in psychological warfare; but Stefan the Return Edition is somehow even more . . . *Stefan* than he has ever been before. He's on top of his game, and it keeps him from falling prey to Katherine the way his big brother does. Stefan's history with Katherine makes him react emotionally to her — he comes close to losing his cool when he professes his hatred for her — and the sparking intensity between them makes Katherine's claims that he once loved her believable. But could he turn from hating her back to loving her?

Like Stefan says to Damon, "how we respond to [Katherine] will define us." Consider Damon defined by his response. It takes the back-to-back heartbreaks that he suffers from Katherine and Elena to bring out the beast in him again; Elena was wrong to fear that Katherine's return alone would do it. Despite realizing early in the episode that Katherine played him and that he had kissed her, not Elena, Damon stays on his best behavior. He continues to play the town hero, coming to the aid of Sheriff Forbes, and seems genuinely concerned and willing to help; he mediates her conflict with Carol

Lockwood, telling them, as his brother later tells him, "We have to stick together — trust each other"; and he saves Caroline's life with his blood, a redemptive act considering how he abused her at the beginning of season 1. But as hard as he tries to be good, Damon still itches for a fight with his brother, and though harsh, Bonnie's matter-of-fact assessment of his fake persona isn't far off the mark. The old Damon is there, lurking beneath the surface, ready to snap. What Damon is unable to handle is the hurt he feels as he's rejected by the two women he's loved.

While Elena worried that Stefan confronting Damon for kissing her would set Damon off, it's her words that start his unraveling. She sees his character so clearly and she correctly anticipates what will happen, but she fails to understand that she holds just as much power over him as Katherine does. The fact that Damon cares so much about Elena and Katherine is important to Stefan; it's the humanity in him that they have been trying to draw out. With Katherine at the Salvatore mansion, Damon echoes his brother by saying that they can have this defining moment, and he asks for her true feelings, leaving himself entirely emotionally vulnerable, instead of doing what she's interested in — just having hot vampire sex. What Damon calls the "beauty of eternity" is also the pain of eternity — to pine for some-one for an inhuman length of time only to hear he was never loved. He's rejected by the woman who represents his past, Katherine, and again by his hoped-for future, Elena. What Elena feels for him, what Damon means to her, is not what Stefan means to her, and nothing shy of that is what Damon wishes he could have from her. Why should he be "better than this," as she insists he actually is, why should he play bodyguard and make himself vul-nerable when he's only answered with rejection? In "Founder's Day," Stefan admonished Damon for doing good but wanting something in return, and here Damon seems to reject being his most human self when the only payoff is hurt.

At the Lockwood mansion, Bonnie told Damon that the good he's done doesn't undo the bad: Damon acts in accordance with that, the destructive force in him rising to control him. Damon's desperation turns to violence as he's overwhelmed with feeling, though ironically he tells Jeremy that the answer to his pain is to become a vampire so he can "flip the switch" and *stop* feeling. Though Stefan tries to blame Damon's unforgivable act of killing Jeremy on Katherine (an idea Elena immediately rejects), Damon himself once told Stefan that he alone is responsible for his actions ("Blood

Brothers"). Like killing Coach Tanner in "Friday Night Bites" or feeding Elena his blood and threatening to turn her in "Children of the Damned," snapping Jeremy's neck was completely in keeping with the Damon who arrived in Mystic Falls but so unlike the Damon who laid bare his feelings to "Elena" on the Gilbert porch in "Founder's Day." His fall is swift and shocking, but utterly believable.

Taylor Kinney as Mason Lockwood

Just like his onscreen counterpart, Taylor Kinney is an experienced surfer — but luckily he doesn't share the Lockwood propensity for raging out. Born July 15, 1981, outside of Philadelphia, Pennsylvania, he grew up with the "pipe dream" of being a stunt man, but the self-described "country boy" never truly thought a career in film and television was plausible. "I grew up kicking around the woods, riding dirt bikes, playing football, climbing rocks and all that good stuff," said Kinney. While studying business management at West Virginia University, Taylor took a theater class and got into the acting scene, appearing in *A Streetcar Named Desire* and *Fallout*. His first major TV role was as Luke Gianni on *Fashion House* (2006), a soap starring Bo Derek and Morgan Fairchild. After appearing in episodes of *What About Brian* and *Bones*, he was cast in NBC's short-lived series *Trauma* (2009–2010), playing Glenn Morrison, a rookie EMT, and he guest-starred in an episode of *CSI: NY* in 2011. Taylor's also been on the big screen in films *Furnace* (2006), *White Air* (2007), *Diary of a Champion* and *Scorpio Men on Prozac* (both 2011). But it's his role as Mason Lockwood on *The Vampire Diaries* that's got him the most attention so far. "Ever since [I was] a kid, [I wanted] to play a supernatural character or an action hero," said Taylor, "so I jumped at the chance and it happened really quickly. I met with people on Tuesday and then I flew out [from L.A. to Atlanta] on Thursday and was shooting by Friday." Admittedly, Taylor had a lot of questions on that first day about who was a vampire and just what exactly that meant on this show: "It was trial by fire, but I got so into it." Part of the adjustment to working on *The Vampire Diaries* was realizing how beloved the show is and how passionate the fans are. "It lifts your spirit," he said. "It makes you want to give more to the characters. I think everybody feeds off that — I know certainly the cast does. The fans are huge in terms of what it means to tell stories and to do what they're doing on *Vampire Diaries*." Of his "black sheep" character, Kinney sums him up simply: "Mason is a good guy, but he does bad things sometimes. I dig him."

Elena has survived nearly losing Jeremy twice in 24 hours. This and her new "no more lies" policy promises a closer relationship for the Gilbert siblings this season. Frankly, Elena can use all the love, support, and allies she can get with her evil look-alike roaming around town. In Katherine and Elena's close encounter at the Gilbert house, Katherine is in control: she taunts Elena but leaves her alive. Katherine intentionally plays the part of Elena, while Elena is mistaken for Katherine by her own father. Not only do the two look the same, they also feel the same way about the Salvatore brothers. Though Katherine has no problem kissing Damon despite not loving him while Elena would "never do that," both girls choose Stefan as the one they'll always love. Is either being honest about her feelings — does Katherine actually love Stefan? Does Elena actually hate Damon?

What is certain is that the writers haven't lost their appetite for a good cliffhanger. In a jaw-dropping final scene, Caroline becomes a vampire's pawn once again, after being used by Damon, Logan Fell, and Isobel last season. Her human life is over, all to be a part of Katherine's game, and she dies thinking that Elena killed her. A fascinating character from the beginning, Caroline has so far been on the edge of the supernatural world, and when she wakes up she'll be a part of it. We know from last season that a human's personality is intensified in her change into a vampire. Assuming she completes the change, what kind of vampire will Caroline be? How will she act around Matt, her mother, Elena, Bonnie, or Damon? Katherine being back in Mystic Falls has already had game-changing effects on *The Vampire Diaries*, and this new game with no rules has only just begun.

COMPELLING MOMENT: Jeremy coming back to life cradled in Elena's arms. Beautifully acted by Steven R. McQueen and Nina Dobrev.

CIRCLE OF KNOWLEDGE:
- No Jenna or Alaric in this episode.
- The title of the episode refers to the return of Katherine to Mystic Falls, the return of the show after its summer hiatus, and the second series of Vampire Diaries novels by L.J. Smith, also entitled "The Return."
- The sequence that opens the episode was slightly modified from last season's cliffhanger "Founder's Day." A few details were added — Jeremy is said to be holed up in his room, Jenna's left to deal with the fire department, and Stefan's replies to Elena on the phone are now audible (the lack of which in "Founder's Day" made the scene just a touch awkward).
- The title card font is slightly different from season 1's.
- Elena's reaction to Jeremy's disappointment that he isn't a vampire — "Why would you want that?" — indicates how she feels about the idea of turning, without requiring a big relationship talk with Stefan.
- At the Gilbert house, Stefan knows he's embracing Katherine, not Elena, by her necklace; he quickly glances down at it.
- In the hospital, Caroline seems excited that MTV's reality show *Jersey Shore* is on, a program that actress Candice Accola admitted to watching (as she told *TV Guide Magazine*, "My shame is *Jersey Shore*").

- Notice how both Katherine and Damon snack on fruit at the Lockwood mansion as they banter with Stefan and Bonnie respectively. Two of a kind . . .
- Damon calls his brother "Fabio," referring to the male model Fabio Lanzoni who graced the covers of hundreds of romance novels in the '80s and '90s and is seen shirtless more frequently than both Salvatore brothers combined.
- "Brother, don't worry. Our bond is unbreakable," Damon said to Stefan. Judging by Stefan's immediate excuses for Damon after he (temporarily) kills Jeremy, that bond seems as strong as Damon believes it to be.

THE RULES: Uncle John explains to Jeremy that the Gilbert ring doesn't protect against natural death or injury, which was a lingering question after season 1 and explains why Grayson Gilbert died in the car crash even though he had his ring on. Unlike Damon, Katherine is able to withstand Bonnie's brain-pain spell because she's a much older and therefore stronger vampire. Damon suggests that the ability to heal involves advanced knowledge of witchcraft (but it's unclear how he would know when Emily Bennett learned that kind of spell).

THE DIABOLICAL PLAN: The return of Katherine to Mystic Falls promises a new diabolical plan that will drive the action of the season, just as Damon's return in the pilot set off events that led to the opening of the tomb.

HISTORY LESSON: Damon refers to the passion between him and Katherine as the "rockets' red glare," a phrase pulled from the "The Star-Spangled Banner," which the poet Francis Scott Key originally wrote in reference to the explosions in the Battle of Fort McHenry, part of the War of 1812 between the Americans and the British.

BITE MARKS: Katherine cuts off Uncle John's fingers and stabs him in the gut. Stefan wallops Jeremy. Katherine and Stefan slam each other into the walls of the Gilbert living room; Katherine gives his arm a good twist. Stefan chokes John and force-feeds him his blood. Bonnie does her brain-pain spell on Damon. She tries it on Katherine too, but that vampy vamp is too strong and pins Bonnie against the wall. Katherine stabs Stefan in the gut with a handy wrought-iron candle holder. Tyler's anger boils over and he shoves his mother, before he's pinned down by his uncle Mason. Damon forcibly kisses Elena and then snaps Jeremy's neck, killing him. Katherine smothers Caroline to death with her hospital pillow.

PREVIOUSLY ON THE VAMPIRE DIARIES: Like "The Return," season 1 episodes "You're Undead to Me" and "Bloodlines" begin with slightly modified versions of the final scenes of the preceding episode. Katherine's recap to Bonnie of who's who in Mystic Falls is reminiscent of Isobel's to Elena in "Isobel." In the flashback in "Lost Girls," Katherine interrupts the boys' game of football, saying, "Who needs rules?" and, after revealing herself to be a vampire to Stefan, tells him that in the future she has planned for her and the two brothers, there are "no rules"; in "The Return" she reminds Stefan that this is her credo. After Elena finds out that Damon "killed" Isobel, she's betrayed, hurt, and without faith in him while Stefan tries to explain his behavior ("A Few Good Men"), just as he does here with Elena as they wait for Jeremy to come back to life. The final scene of the pilot also took place in the Mystic Falls Hospital only instead of Caroline in the bed it was Vicki Donovan.

MEANWHILE IN FELL'S CHURCH: The thin line between love and hate exists between Katherine and Stefan in the book series too: in *The Fury*, she confronts him, saying, "I know who I hate most now, and it's you, Stefan. Because I loved you best." Elena tells Damon she hates him at the beginning of *The Struggle* and, after he threatens her sibling, says to herself, "Damon wasn't capable of kindness. Or of caring for anybody but himself."

OFF CAMERA: Katherine's fashion sense differs from Elena's, a wardrobe choice meant to help viewers see the two characters as individuals, as well as help Nina Dobrev get into the very different mindsets of her two onscreen personas. "The clothes, accessories, hair, and all those seemingly superficial details really help me transition and embrace whichever role I'm playing," said Nina. "For example, if I'm rocking a pair of Converse, I can sink into Elena, but if I'm wearing some edgy boots, I naturally begin not only walking [like Katherine] but I also feel like Katherine." The idea that Damon would snap Jeremy's neck came from the master of horror Mr. Kevin Williamson; early in the story-breaking process for season 2, Williamson pitched the twist to Julie Plec, whose jaw dropped at the idea. They both realized that if she had such a visceral reaction to it, the audience would too, and they could start off the season in high-stakes mode.

FOGGY MOMENTS: How did Stefan know that Jeremy was not transitioning into a vampire? The way that Bonnie approached "Elena" to vent about Damon seemed out of character since Bonnie and Elena's friendship is so strained when it comes to the Salvatore brothers. The conversation felt inserted as the way for the writers to let Katherine in on the news that Caroline has vampire blood in her system.

MUSIC: The morning after Founder's Day, Bonnie arrives at the hospital and talks to Matt while Gemma Hayes' "Out of Our Hands" plays. At the Lockwood mansion, an instrumental cover of "How to Save a Life" by The Fray (whose "Never Say Never" was featured in the pilot episode) is audible in the background when Bonnie and Damon talk, and a cover of The Script's "Breakeven (Falling to Pieces)" plays as Bonnie faces off with Katherine; both are performed by the Piano Players Tribute. Jeremy talks to Tyler about his father to Hurts' "Wonderful Life." Mads Langer, whose songs were also in "You're Undead to Me" and "162 Candles," makes another appearance on the soundtrack with "The River Has Run Wild," which plays as Tyler loses control in his father's office. OneRepublic and Sara Bareilles' "Come Home" provides the soundtrack to Damon's outburst in Elena's bedroom. A Sara Bareilles' song, "Gravity," was also playing during Stefan and Elena's first kiss in "The Night of the Comet," an infinitely more romantic moment than Damon's attempt here in "The Return."

QUESTIONS:
- As Damon says, whoever Katherine wants dead is dead. So why did she attack John Gilbert but not finish him off?
- What are Katherine's "other plans" for Elena?
- Why did she decide to turn Caroline into a vampire?
- What exactly did she mean by "game on" — should the Salvatore brothers expect Katherine to target more innocent victims?
- Whose blood will Caroline use to complete the transition — a friend's, a stranger's? Or will she choose not to become a vampire and actually die?

Stefan (to Caroline): When you feel the blood rush in, you tell yourself that you're gonna get through it, that you're strong enough. No matter how good it feels to give yourself over to it — you fight it off, you bury it.

2.02 Brave New World

Original air date: September 16, 2010
Written by: Brian Young
Directed by: John Dahl
Guest cast: B.J. Britt (Carter), Terri James (Nurse)

Caroline wakes up to a changed world, while Elena tries to ignore her supernatural problems for a day as she organizes the Mystic Falls High School carnival with Bonnie. Damon is intrigued by the secret the Lockwoods are keeping.

A carnival is a fittingly riotous backdrop for an episode that puts the characters on a quest for normalcy even as they navigate the unknown. Bonnie and Elena's attempt to organize the chaotic carnival in Caroline's absence is paralleled with higher-stakes supernatural secrets and violence. After the intensity of "The Return," Elena's request to have a no V-word, no D-word normal teenage-girl day was welcome — if entirely unsuccessful. In the process, "Brave New World" offers an element of winking playfulness that goes beyond *The Vampire Diaries*' usual witty banter. In some season 1 episodes, B-stories were almost completely disconnected from the main drama. But the cohesiveness here felt like a strong shift in direction, fueled by new character match-ups, a strategy that cements the idea that, in Mystic Falls, everyone's fates are deeply interconnected.

Though no one else wakes up to a world as changed as Caroline's, everyone is asking questions and encountering new and unknown entities as the once-familiar now becomes unpredictable. Bonnie questions Elena about why Katherine looks *exactly* like her and about what's happening between her and Damon, while Jeremy turns to Stefan with his questions (even Stefan doesn't know why vervain is poisonous to vampires). For her part, Caroline doesn't know how compulsion works ("but it's brilliant"). The bigger questions plague them too: why is Katherine back? Why was Caroline turned into a vampire? What secret is Mason Lockwood keeping? For Caroline, there are a million unknowns as she discovers what it means to be a vampire. The source of much of this anxiety is Katherine, the invisible (for now) puppet master. Her one sadistic act upsets them all, and Caroline, Elena, and Stefan all feel personally targeted.

Waking up alone and confused, Caroline comes to realize what has happened, and she sees its life-altering implications over the course of the day as her transformation takes place. Instead of rehashing the Vicki Donovan story arc, the writers chose to explore a different part of the transformation process. The key decision that Vicki faced in "Lost Girls" — to feed on a human and complete the change or to choose death — is one that Caroline makes (by feeding from a blood bag without knowing the implication of her action) before the title card. All alone in her transition, Caroline faces the horror of feeling her body becoming foreign to her and no longer under her control. Coupled with her new urges and hunger, Caroline's experience shows us the personal side of this vampire thing, and paints a frightening picture that has little to do with fangs or blood-veined eyes. Besides her overwhelming desire for blood, what Caroline deals with are the physical limitations and the powers of a vampire — sunlight bad, compulsion awesome. Though these parts of *The Vampire Diaries* lore are familiar, Caroline's process of discovery feels entirely fresh, because transitioning is so driven by the person experiencing it. Since the pilot episode, Candice Accola has portrayed Caroline in an endearing way that takes viewers from funny to painful in a single beat, and here Candice bravely takes her character to yet another level. She's still the same Caroline, just "more" and "different," as Matt describes her to Bonnie. But this heightened version of the human Caroline now has supernatural-sized problems thanks to being in the wrong place at the wrong time. In this way, she's just like Carter, an innocent bystander first beaten up and then killed.

Tyler is on his own search for answers about how not to "lose" himself in rage and about who his uncle is. Like Tyler, the audience is in the dark about this new supernatural force in Mystic Falls. Even the Salvatore brothers don't know what's going on; only Mason does, and he's being very guarded with Tyler, asking questions but offering no answers. Why isn't Mason more forthcoming with Tyler? Is he lying to protect him or is there a darker, selfish reason for his deceit? Whatever his motivation, Mason is repaid in kind for his cageyness as Tyler retrieves the mysterious moonstone from his father's secret safe and keeps it.

Instead of coming right out and asking Mason about the Lockwood secret like Tyler does, Damon opts for a little observation and experimentation. All the while, Damon maintains his usual self-awareness, understanding precisely what effect he's having on Stefan and Elena. Though he toys with Stefan, he also proves to him that the Lockwood secret is worth investigating. There's a delightful irony to a vampire being elected the head of an anti-vampire council, but Damon is actually not a bad choice for the job. It's the logical culmination of his efforts to protect Mystic Falls (both in earnest and in self-interest) from rogue vampires, and he's uniquely well positioned and capable of getting rid of supernatural threats to the townsfolk. He knows who attacked John Gilbert and he has a chance, in league with his brother, to win against Katherine. In his capacity as head of council, his resolve to kill the new vampire — Caroline — is an appropriate decision; of course, he's motivated by self-preservation, not by a desire to protect the townsfolk of Mystic Falls.

Jeremy threatens to expose Damon but finds that, even with his ring, he's no match — just as both brothers warned him — and more importantly his heart isn't in for vengeance. He tries on his father's legacy of being anti-vampire, but Jeremy realizes it's not who he wants to be. Despite the appeal of having firm and absolute beliefs, especially after his unhappy drifting in season 1, Jeremy realizes that killing Damon won't solve his problem. And he doesn't believe in the inherent evil in all vampires; he's not like his father and uncle. Just as Damon and Stefan threw off their father's belief system by being "vampire sympathizers," Jeremy decides not to be a hater or a slayer. And though Damon first rejects the role of big brother to Jeremy ("Sorry I don't have any milk and cookies to offer you"), he then makes a "better" choice, letting Jeremy know that he faced the same struggle with his own father. It's unexpectedly soon for an empathetic moment between these two, after all, fewer than 24 hours ago, Damon *killed* Jeremy. However, Jeremy's choice not to seek revenge and Damon's attempt to reach out, however tentatively, seems like the first narrative step toward getting Damon back in the good graces of viewers.

Despite much being in flux in "Brave New World," the characters don't hesitate to make judgments and place blame. After apologizing multiple times for biting her nurse, Caroline is overwhelmed by the scent of Carter's blood and kills him (apologizing first) and calls herself a murderer and a monster, judging her own actions. After Bonnie realizes that Caroline is a vampire and sees Carter dead, she decides all of it is Damon's fault and she wants to act as his judge, jury, and executioner. Bonnie's ultimatum in "Founder's Day" was that if Damon spills innocent blood, she'll take him out, and from Bonnie's perspective, it's a pretty safe assumption that Damon turned Caroline. He's abused Caroline in the past, and the night previous he snapped Jeremy's neck. Even when she's told that this wasn't Damon's doing, Bonnie continues to feel she would be justified if she killed Damon, to prevent him from doing further harm and to punish him for his past crimes. Fueled by the raw emotion of discovering that her best friend is a vampire, Bonnie pins it all on a clear and easily defeated enemy. It's Elena (who earlier in the episode expressly points out that they're human) who steps in and saves the vampire she said she hated, telling Bonnie, "This isn't us. This can't be us." They aren't coldhearted slayers; they have to act humanely. Unlike her father and Damon's, Elena believes that an eye for an eye will make the whole world blind.

Damon isn't at fault for Caroline's current suffering, but she does take him to task for the crimes he committed against her last season — she remembers it all now she's no longer human. Responsibility comes up in another way too with Caroline: her peers feel responsible for her fate, and Stefan, Damon, and Elena meet to discuss what to do about her. Damon considers the situation from a position of cold calculation and thinks she's a liability who could tell, or worse, lose control like Vicki did. Stefan concedes that killing Caroline might be the logically correct thing to do, but it's not the moral choice. Unlike Bonnie, Elena still sees Caroline as a person: her identity hasn't changed in Elena's eyes, even though she's now a vampire. Elena will step in front of a stake-wielding Damon to save her. Seeing Elena make that choice and being able to help Caroline gain control of herself, Stefan changes dramatically in his attitude. He goes from frustrated and defeated by Katherine's actions to a man resolved to fight on, refusing to accept that Caroline's fate will be any more tragic than it already is.

While all is far from forgiven, the Gilbert kids decide not to seek revenge on Damon, although Damon suffers a non-lethal punishment (being lit on fire) so it doesn't feel as if he's completely getting away with murder. When Elena steps in front of Caroline to save her, she not only proves again how brave she is, but she also demonstrates the teensiest bit of faith in Damon. He doesn't kill Caroline because of how much she means to Elena, but he does try to pin all of Caroline's future wrongdoing on Elena's conscience.

For a vampire who once told Stefan, "My actions, what I do, it's not your fault. I own them. They belong to me," Damon should know deep down that Caroline — and every other creature in Mystic Falls — must ultimately take responsibility for her own behavior and its consequences.

Meanwhile, it's clear Caroline feels the weight of what she's done. Her new life as a vampire — wearing leather and heavy eye makeup to fit the part and enjoying her vampire powers — loses its appeal after she kills Carter. She's lost control and is terrified of the darkness that roils inside her, of its power to kill and to ruin her life. Thankfully, she has Stefan to teach her to be stronger than her instinct to kill. He tells her to "fight it off, bury it." Control is an issue Stefan struggles with, as we've seen, and it's evident he's empowered by his ability to help her. In helping Caroline, he reminds himself that the way to survive is to never stop fighting, no matter how hopeless things seem.

In their brave new world, they have to hold on tighter to what is knowable and what makes them human (whether or not they're actually human). Though Caroline can no longer wear the vervain necklace that symbolized Elena's friendship, their relationship is reaffirmed by Elena's actions, as she literally protects her from a vampire the way the necklace once did. And just as Caroline's terrified of losing Bonnie and Matt because of what she is, Matt admits that he's terrified of losing her. His declaration of love strengthens Caroline's resolve and faith in her ability to control herself. Now that there's a second human-vampire relationship, it will be interesting to see how Matt and Caroline's story plays out compared to Stefan and Elena's.

Surrounded by death and undeath and various horrifying threats, Elena moves from an overt form of denial into a near breakdown (repeating "I'm fine" unconvincingly) in parallel scenes at her locker that bookend the episode. Stefan sees it, and his grand romantic gesture is just what Elena needs. He's remembered why it is he fights, what gives him the strength to not give up, and he reminds Elena that in spite of the chaos, they can't forget to live their lives. There are sweetness and romance in "Brave New World," which are just as much cornerstones of *The Vampire Diaries* as are the scares and plot twists. What always prevents these moments from being sappy is the darkness and sadness behind them: Stefan and Elena have a perfect moment, but it's one stolen from an otherwise terrifying day and it's colored by the knowledge of what's to come. When Matt tells Caroline he's falling in love with her, he also reminds us how much he has already lost and how little he has left. While Caroline is able to stop herself from vamping out (the old

Caroline determination comes in handy), she simply can't experience the joy of what should have been an uncomplicated moment with her boyfriend. And the question stands between them: Matt is in love with a Caroline who is now gone — can he love the new Caroline?

COMPELLING MOMENT: Stefan helping Caroline clean up and calm down in the bathroom. He knows exactly what to say to her: by showing her that he can control his bloodlust and stay "human," he helps give her the strength to do it herself.

CIRCLE OF KNOWLEDGE:
- No Jenna or Alaric this episode.
- The social calendar in Mystic Falls is pretty jam-packed. The Mystic Falls High carnival is just two evenings after the Founder's Day celebration.
- More pop culture references in this episode than usual: the Teenage Mutant Ninja Turtles get a shout-out as do *The Simpsons'* Bart and Homer and the Twilight Saga's Jacob Black.
- In this one, perhaps more than in any other *TVD* episode, the writers were throwing winks at the audience. Damon's talking-animals joke foreshadows some half-man, half-beasts. Team Jacob shirts are a hit at the carnival. Damon declares that werewolves don't exist. Bonnie says that Caroline will kill them if they don't do a good job, Elena makes a crack that Caroline isn't human, and Matt calls Caroline "killer." And Jeremy says "epic."
- A great comedic cut between the scene where Stefan worries about what Damon could be up to in his disturbed state and the reveal — Damon's having tea with Carol Lockwood!
- One of the lingering questions from "The Return" was addressed: Carol Lockwood and the rest of the Council believe it was a loose tomb vampire who was responsible for the Uncle John Incident, and they've wisely put Damon Salvatore in charge of tracking that vamp down.
- A popular gemstone in jewelry and other adornments throughout human history, moonstone is native to the U.S., Mexico, Brazil, Australia, Myanmar, Madagascar, India, Sri Lanka, Norway, and Switzerland. Its name comes from its unique shimmer (called "adularescence"); the Ancient Romans believed the stone was made of captured moonbeams. Various qualities have been ascribed to moonstone, depending on the cultural tradition — that it can bring the wearer fertility, pleasant

dreams, or greater understanding. In supernatural tales, there is often a connection between lycanthropy and moonstone: the stone is said to possess mystical power that encourages a human to shift into a wolf.

THE RULES: Caroline exhibits all the traits of a transitioning vampire: she's hungry for blood, her senses are heightened, and her personality is more intense. Through the arm wrestling duel, we learn that Mason, the "Ambiguously Supernatural Mystery Uncle," is stronger than a human but not as strong as a vampire. (Mason does beat Stefan in the matchup but Stefan doesn't use all of his strength, just more than he should have to. In the hallway, Stefan tells Damon, "It wasn't that kind of strength [meaning a vampire's] but it was more than a human.") When Mason attacks Carter in the parking lot, his eyes "glow" (like Tyler's did post–car accident in "Founder's Day") and his fighting style is just a tad more animalistic than Brazilian martial arts moves.

THE DIABOLICAL PLAN: Damon's new "obsession" is to discover the Lockwood family secret, and it's Tyler's too. He knows his uncle is lying to him about the fight with Carter and about his interest in the moonstone. The question of why Katherine chose to turn Caroline is raised a few times: Stefan and Elena each feel Katherine did it to hurt them; Caroline also takes it personally (understandably). Damon is the only one who doesn't interpret Katherine's action as an attack directed specifically at him — and he's likely on the right track. Her "game on" message reminds the whole lot of them, indiscriminately, what she's capable of and it may or may not be part of an endgame that Katherine has yet to reveal.

BITE MARKS: Caroline chokes the nurse before feeding on her. Damon puts Jeremy in a chokehold, takes his ring, and throws it at his forehead. Carter and Tyler fight, Mason joins in to break the boys apart. Caroline attacks Carter, killing him. Stefan punches a snack stand. Damon attempts to stake Caroline, but Elena steps in the way. Bonnie uses her brain-pain spell on Damon before lighting him on fire, intent on killing him.

PREVIOUSLY ON THE VAMPIRE DIARIES: Elena and Stefan tried to ignore their supernatural problems and be "normal" in "There Goes the Neighborhood" by going on a double date with Matt and Caroline; they

Brave New World

The phrase "brave new world" comes from Shakespeare's *The Tempest*, but is perhaps better known as the name of Aldous Huxley's 1932 novel. In Shakespeare's play, the words are spoken in the final scene by Miranda, daughter to Prospero — "O brave new world / That has such people in't!" At the outset of the play, Miranda's knowledge and the scope of her world is very limited, but once a ship crashes onto the island where she and Prospero live, Miranda is exposed to men (she'd never seen a European man other than her father), learns of things she never knew existed, and discovers secrets of her past that her father has kept from her. Her exclamation is one of naive wonder, humorous because of the commonness of what seems strange to her eye. In a similar way, Caroline discovers a world that's been just outside of her knowledge, kept secret from her by her parent, that she will now be a part of. Like Miranda, she finds it both terrifying and wondrous (as she chatters at the nurse, marveling at her new powers). Caroline also discovers secrets of her own past: as Damon's compulsion wears off, she remembers what he did to her.

Huxley's novel *Brave New World* is set in an imagined future where social stability has been orchestrated through genetic engineering and conditioning to hatch people who are happy and easily controlled. Though there are advantages in the new world that seem appealing, the price is soullessness, a theme that's echoed in Caroline's experience. She has new powers and strengths, but she's no longer human. Caroline was turned by Katherine, in a seemingly random and cruel act, and will live or die based on the decisions her friends make, and so she suffers from the total lack of personal freedom and self-determination that's a hallmark of *Brave New World*'s society. In the novel, those whose individuality hasn't been entirely crushed, like Bernard Marx and Helmhold Watson, have a different understanding than the rest of the folks in their community; they feel alien and alone and are able to see a perspective that's incredibly clear and removed from the established one. In *The Vampire Diaries*, there is a similar separation between those who are in on the secret of the supernatural (who often feel alone and forced to hide who they are or what they know) and those who have no idea there's anything beyond their understanding. In "Brave New World," Caroline moves from one side to the other, as the world she has always known is snatched away and another is revealed — the familiar is made strange through her new senses and knowledge. *Brave New World*'s John or the "Savage," a man who grew up separate from this "ideal" society in a "Savage Reservation" is brought to London where his false illusions are shattered. With bitterness he thinks of the phrase "brave new world" after having seen the terrors of that new society. After Caroline attacks and kills Carter, her perspective on her new state of existence is equally changed. Continuing to mimic John's trajectory, both Stefan and Caroline resolve to fight to overcome the odds against them. Ultimately, John is unsuccessful, but Stefan and Caroline may yet succeed: there was "the possibility of transforming even the nightmare into something fine and noble. 'O brave new world!' It was a challenge, a command."

were much more successful than they are here. In that episode, Elena said she refused to live every moment in fear, a sentiment that Stefan echoes while they are on the Ferris wheel. Stefan tells Damon he's glad Damon's not snacking on sorority girls, a reference to the last time Katherine threw Damon off-kilter. In "A Few Good Men," Damon fed on college girls and got drunk, but in "Brave New World," he decides to investigate the Lockwood secret instead. In both episodes, Stefan is protective of Damon; knowing his "volatile" brother too well, Stefan discourages people from confronting Damon — Elena then, Jeremy now. Bonnie flirts with Carter over a karaoke speaker in this episode and the night ends badly for him; in "Children of the Damned," she and (undercover vampire) Ben McKittrick went on a karaoke date that ended with kidnapping. Don't mix karaoke and romance, Bonnie Bennett! Damon reminds Stefan and Elena about the night Vicki died at the school's Halloween party in "Haunted." Bonnie first discovered she could set water on fire in "You're Undead to Me," a trick she uses on Damon in the parking lot. In addition to the moonstone, Richard Lockwood also kept his piece of the Gilbert device in that floor safe; he took it out in "Lost Girls." Damon and Caroline first met in the second episode of season 1; he charmed her and then attacked her. In this second episode of season 2, he tries the same tactic, calming her down and then going for the kill. Elena stood up to Damon for Caroline in the school parking lot in "Friday Night Bites," objecting to his insults because Caroline is her friend; here Elena saves her friend's life by standing up for her.

MEANWHILE IN FELL'S CHURCH: In *Dark Reunion*, a similarly frustrated Stefan tries to manage his wild-card brother: "A familiar surge of irritation welled up in Stefan. Why did Damon always have to be so difficult? Talking with him was like walking between land mines." In *The Fury*, a newly turned Elena reveals what she is to her two best friends, Meredith and Bonnie, and Bonnie is at first sickened by the idea of her best friend being a vampire. Though Jeremy isn't a character in the book series, his search for purpose is something Elena struggles with from the beginning. In *The Fury*, as she reads through her diary's past entries, she realizes that "all I can see is that I was searching for something, for someplace to belong. But this isn't it. This new life isn't it." In *Dark Reunion*, Bonnie is resolved to not let evil go unpunished; that same determination fueled Bonnie's attack on Damon in the parking lot.

OFF CAMERA: John Dahl, who directed this episode, was also at the helm for "Friday Night Bites" and is an accomplished film and television director. Kevin Williamson considers Caroline becoming a vampire one of the "game-changing" moments of season 2. He called up Candice before she'd read the script for "The Return" to let her know that Caroline would die but not stay dead.

FOGGY MOMENTS: Mason makes a joke about Grandma Lockwood passing Tyler on her walker, but then later tells him that the moonstone was passed down to Mayor Lockwood from his parents, which seems to imply that Grandma is dead. Are Tyler's paternal grandparents alive? Caroline needs to work on the lies she compels people to tell: what will that nurse's husband think when she tells him that he's the one who bit her? How did Caroline get into her house? Newly turned Caroline would need her mother's invitation to get into the Forbes house, but she mentions to Matt at the carnival that Sheriff Forbes isn't home. Was Sheriff Forbes home earlier to let Caroline in after she left the hospital? Was that who Caroline left the voicemail for as she was packing her things?

MUSIC: The Mystic Falls High carnival is set up to "Animal" by Neon Trees (who also had a song in "Isobel"). Glasvegas's "Geraldine" plays while the carnival is in full swing. Damon observes Tyler and Mason Lockwood arm wrestling to Silversun Pickups' "Currency of Love," a track featured on *The Vampire Diaries: Original Television Soundtrack*. (The Silversun Pickups also had a song in the pilot episode.) Faintly in the background, Andrew Belle's "The Ladder" is playing when Caroline meets up with Matt at the ring toss. A show favorite, OneRepublic (who have had songs in the pilot, "Blood Brothers," and "The Return") is featured once again with "All This Time" as Caroline overcomes her impulse to bite Matt, and when Stefan wakes up Elena for a romantic surprise.

QUESTIONS:
- What is keeping Mason Lockwood from telling his nephew the truth?
- Once the shock of discovery wears off, will Bonnie be able to be friends with Caroline now that she's a vampire?
- Where is Katherine hiding while her game plays out?
- Will Caroline consider telling Matt the truth or will she hide the fact that she's a vampire from him as Stefan did from Elena?

❀

Damon (to Elena): You have every right to hate me. I understand.
You hated me before and we became friends. It would suck if
that was gone forever. So, is it? Have I lost you forever?

2.03 *Bad Moon Rising*

Original air date: September 23, 2010
Written by: Andrew Chambliss
Directed by: Patrick Norris
Guest cast: Courtney Ford (Vanessa Monroe)

Alaric, Damon, and Elena hit the road to Duke University on a fact-finding mission while Stefan teaches Caroline how to be a vampire (and not kill the person you love most in the world). The full moon reveals the Lockwood secret.

Far from turning into *The Werewolf Diaries*, this episode managed to balance the introduction of new mythology with the things at the core of the show: the relationship between Elena and the Salvatore brothers, the tension between the human and supernatural elements in Mystic Falls, and unexpected twists. Add in beautifully filmed scenes in the forest, great song choices, and the return of Alaric, and "Bad Moon Rising" keeps the bar high as it explores friendship and forgiveness, curses and choices.

As Alaric tells Vanessa, Isobel *became* her research. The supernatural world has a way of taking over a character's existence. It's happened to Elena, Alaric, and Bonnie as well as to the vampires — and Alaric warns Vanessa to walk away from it while she still can. Alaric's "baggage," as Jenna terms it, is less burdensome by the time he's back from Duke. Isobel compelled him to move on (just four days ago in *TVD* time), and Alaric feels she is merely his past now. Alaric grabs hold of the very human Jenna, deciding to embrace the good parts of life instead of only being wrapped up in the bad, like loss, unfinished business, and new threats in town. The balance he finds is something that eludes the other characters in "Bad Moon Rising" who are overtaken by the power and pull of the mystical in Mystic Falls.

The story of werewolf lore is revealed in parallel plotlines: one investigates the legends while the other bears witness to the present-day manifestation of the curse. As with the vampires on *The Vampire Diaries*, a knowledge of history is intrinsic to understanding the present for the werewolves. In the cellar of the old Lockwood property are the claw marks of Tyler's ancestor, the dark hidden past that no one in his family told him about. That room holds secrets of both supernatural and human violence with its chains and cell doors. Woven into the existing show mythology, the werewolf legend is bound to the others with the Sun and Moon Curse, pitting wolves against vampires, and putting witches in the center trying to control them all.

It's difficult to pull off a werewolf plotline: the special effects (whether cheesy or impressive) often take attention away from the story. By not showing the actual man-to-wolf morph, "Bad Moon Rising" provided a full-moon scare without dipping into corny monster-movie territory. Mason's actions in preparation for his transformation suggest he's a "good wolf." He makes sure Tyler and company will be out of the woods when he'll be a threat to them; he locks himself up in a chamber that's clearly been used for that purpose before; and, when he hears Tyler and Aimee approaching, he hightails it out of there, improvising by trying to use his Bronco as a cage. He tries to minimize the damage he might cause, but once the change begins, Mason has no self-control. Vanessa makes the distinction between the curse of the werewolf and the choice a vampire has: a werewolf changes on the full moon no matter how hard they struggle against it; a vampire always has access to self-control whether or not they choose to exercise it. To compare the two, Mason and Caroline are both fighting the violent beasts inside them, but Caroline's willpower can win out over her inner monster while Mason's transformation is involuntary and torturous. (On the other hand, Caroline has to practice self-control every day, while Mason can relax until the next full moon.)

Just like the Aztec magic-wielders of yore, the witches of Mystic Falls (historical and present) make protecting human life their number-one priority by trying to keep the supernatural troublemakers in check. Time and again, Bonnie makes decisions that are ethical but come off as overly righteous. Her initial reluctance to allow Caroline to walk in the daylight and her stipulation that if Caroline harms anyone the daylight ring will be de-activated are reasonable and understandable (who would knowingly encourage murder?), but the coldness with which she treats her former best friend makes it difficult to sympathize with her. How can Caroline prove to Bonnie that she's more than just a killing machine if Bonnie doesn't give her the chance? Kept at a distance by the writers' storytelling choices, Bonnie is often a problematic character. She's emotionally isolated, a powerful witch trapped between the supernatural world that is increasingly populated by her best friends and the human world that is under constant threat from those same unpredictable forces. Bonnie's distanced herself from Elena because of her closeness to Stefan and Damon, the failed tomb spell, and the violence she's witnessed in both brothers. In "History Repeating," Caroline came to accept that being a witch was real to Bonnie, but for Bonnie to accept Caroline as a vampire, she needs to be able to trust Caroline. It's interesting that while Bonnie doesn't yet have faith in Caroline, Bonnie does trust in Stefan, agreeing to make the daylight ring for Caroline only because she's under his care. The daylight ring acts to protect Caroline from the sun, but it also symbolizes the tentative bonds of trust that now exist between Bonnie, Caroline, and Stefan.

Though Bonnie is right to be cautious — Caroline feeds on Matt that very night — it doesn't matter what time of day Caroline should be allowed to roam free but how vigilant Caroline must learn to be and the sacrifices she must make in order to stay more human than monster. Caroline now has a dark side to her otherwise sunny disposition. With the daylight ring, Bonnie gives Caroline the freedom to live a more normal life: she can stop dodging Matt, she can go on a bunny-hunting expedition with Stefan and curb some of her cravings, she can go to Tyler's party and have fun. It's a promising turn, and one that is fun to watch thanks to the energy between Candice Accola and Paul Wesley as their characters develop their friendship and banter. But, as Caroline says, her entire personality is killing her. Everything that made her who she was is now amplified. She not only has to keep her desire to kill in check, she has to bottle her jealousy, competitiveness, and neurotic impulses, simultaneously repurposing her control-freak tendencies toward managing her vampire personality. "Bad Moon Rising" shows Caroline's learning curve as Stefan teaches her to fight against her instincts — not to be jealous of Aimee with Matt, not to use compulsion impulsively, not to lick that tasty, tasty tantalizing blood from Matt's wrist. After Caroline gives in to her vampire desires and hurts the person she cares about the most, she makes a heartbreakingly selfless choice, one that Stefan himself doesn't have the strength to make. Manipulating Matt for his benefit by playing the part of the jealous drama-queen girlfriend, she gets him to dump her instead of using compulsion to end things. And it has to hurt a little bit to know that Matt was that close to breaking up with her. Trapped first by the sun and then

The Gilbert house, a private residence in Covington. Standing in front of the house, it's possible to see the courthouse's clock tower in the town square.

by her instinct to kill, Caroline's new existence is isolating, as she loses her relationships with Matt and Bonnie. But all aspects of Caroline's personality have been amplified in her transition, not just her jealousy and insecurity but also the best parts of who she is. It may be cold comfort, Caroline, but walking away from someone you love in order to protect them makes you a lot deeper than a kiddie pool.

Stefan tells Caroline that it won't get any easier, that she has to work harder. It's advice that Damon could heed if he wants to avoid hurting the person *he* loves . . . again. On Founder's Day, Elena said to Damon, "Don't make me regret being your friend," and just a few days later she's withdrawn her friendship from him for killing her brother (whether there's a "huge asterisk next to that statement" or not). The road trip to Duke wasn't as successful a Damon-Elena bonding experience as was the one to Georgia in "Bloodlines," because here there is no open communication between the two. Damon lies to Elena about seeing the Gilbert ring on Jeremy, hoping to lessen his crime and get closer to forgiveness, but Elena doesn't believe him. She wields her influence over him to protect Vanessa from Damon's wrath, and he calls that manipulation. The thin line between an honest threat and manipulation and the question of how friends should be treated are issues of contention between Damon and Elena, which remain unresolved by the episode's end. She tells him that "Friends don't manipulate friends; they help each other" and, in their final scene on the porch, Damon throws the comment back at her, feeling she used him to get info on Katherine. Did she use him? Elena certainly implies the possibility of future friendship between them, but she made no secret of the fact that, because of his actions, she no longer considers him a friend. Damon killed her brother in a fit of rage and, as he finally admits on the porch, did not know that Jeremy was wearing the magic Gilbert ring. An arrow in the back, the Petrova book, and his heartfelt apology aren't enough for Elena to forgive him, and she tells him their friendship is gone forever. Setting this conversation on the porch made it such a heartbreaking echo of Damon's epic moment with Katherine-as-Elena in "Founder's Day"; though only one of the look-alikes is in each scene, the other's presence is undeniable. Is Damon right: does Elena have more in common with Katherine than her looks?

Besides being dead ringers for each other, Katherine and Elena hold power over Damon thanks to his capacity for loving them. His actions are often driven by what he believes one or the other wants from him, and he feels manipulated by Elena in a way that reminds him of Katherine. The lengths to which Elena will go for information about Katherine shows just how curious she is about how and why they look identical. Elena seems as obsessed as Tyler is with discovering the truth about the Lockwood curse, and their search for answers may lead them into dark and dangerous situations. If a doppelgänger's mission is to "torment the people they look like" and "undo their lives," as Vanessa explains portentously, what lies ahead for Elena now that Katherine has re-resurfaced in Mystic Falls? Katherine outdates Elena by centuries: is Elena the doppelgänger who will torment and undo Katherine's life? Since it's safe to assume on a show like this one that it will not turn out to be a genetic coincidence that they are identical, will Elena be taken over by whatever mystical lineage exists in both her and Katherine or will she be able to hold on to what makes her an individual and human?

COMPELLING MOMENT: Mason Lockwood struggling through his change, clawing at the ground and groaning. It didn't take Taylor Kinney long to fit right in on *The Vampire Diaries*, and it's not just because he looks good in chains. (But it helps.)

CIRCLE OF KNOWLEDGE:

- No Jeremy in this episode.
- "Bad Moon Rising" is an often-used title for songs, albums, TV episodes, and books. The Creedence Clearwater Revival song was used in *An American Werewolf in London* as David waits for his first transformation to take place.
- Damon refers to Mason as "Lon Chaney" and to Tyler as "Lon Chaney Jr." The elder Chaney did appear in a now-lost short silent film as "The Wolf" (*The Lamb, The Woman, The Wolf*, 1914), but the "Man of a Thousand Faces" never appeared on film as a werewolf. His son played the famous Wolf Man in five Universal Pictures horror films. In the first, *The Wolf Man* (1941), Lon Chaney Jr.'s character, Larry Talbot, is bitten by a werewolf played by Béla Lugosi, a legendary actor more famous — to Damon and the rest of us — for his role as Dracula in the 1931 film.
- As far as Jenna knows, when Alaric takes Elena along to Duke it is his first act of opening up about Isobel with her; she doesn't know Alaric actually arranged for the two to meet in "Isobel." (In "A Few Good Men," he wasn't ready to talk about Isobel with Elena.) Also unbeknownst to Jenna is the fact that, for Elena, the trip is less about finding out what her birth mother was like than about finding out why she looks identical to Katherine.
- Stefan and Elena have taken to responding to Damon in kind: when he goads them, they simply fire back. Here Elena macks on Stefan to irk Damon and to remind him of which Salvatore brother she has chosen.
- Based on a map we see in "Rose," the drive from Mystic Falls to Duke University would take around four hours.
- Vanessa refers to Scandinavian skinwalkers. An old Norse tradition among warriors was to wear the skins of slain animals — like wolves — to intimidate their enemies (as well as protect the wearer from the bitter cold). Legend also told of warriors who could transform into those animals, had access to demonic powers, and terrorized the peaceful. Outlaws, the godless, the mad, and those prone to fits of rage were thought to be under demonic possession or to have the ability to shapeshift, and this in turn fostered superstitions about werewolves. In *The Book of Were-wolves* (1865), Sabine Baring-Gould writes, "Among the Scandinavian nations there existed a form of madness or possession, under the influence of which men acted as though they were changed

into wild and savage brutes, howling, foaming at the mouth, ravening for blood and slaughter, ready to commit any act of atrocity, and as irresponsible for their actions as the wolves and bears, in whose skins they often equipped themselves."

- The Maréchal de Retz, or Gilles de Laval (1404–1440), was an historical figure executed by hanging for the gruesome murder of children (reports on the number vary from 40 into the hundreds). After a distinguished military career, the French knight retired; reportedly his interest in the occult led him to make human sacrifices for the devil while in "wolf" form. Though there is now some debate as to whether he was actually guilty of these crimes or if he was persecuted in a manner analogous to the Salem witches, the legend of Maréchal de Retz tells of both a serial killer and a werewolf.

- In the Nahuatl language (what is commonly called Aztec), *tona* means sun (Tonahtiuh is the sun god) and *metztli* means moon (Metztli is also the name of the moon god). There is a Mesoamerican legend that one god threw a rabbit (*cihtli*) in the face of the other so it would not shine as brightly, and that is why the shape of a rabbit is visible on a full moon. A literal translation of what Vanessa calls the Curse of the Sun and the Moon, which sounds like *tona cihtli metztli*, may be "sun full moon."

- Dear Tyler, taking a girl to a creepy underground chamber in the dead of night is also on that "Steps to Becoming a Serial Killer" list.

- Damon informs Elena that Katherine's originally from Europe and her name was Katerina Petrova. That last name is one of the most popular in Bulgaria, where according to traditional naming conventions a surname takes a gender-agreeing suffix (that is, Petrov for men, Petrova for women). When Katherine gave herself an Anglicized name (perhaps when she came to America?) she chose the last name "Pierce," similar to her birth name but with the added pun about the piercing fangs she has as a vampire.

THE RULES: Though we've known about daylight jewelry since the pilot episode, here we see the magic take place (somewhat anticlimactically) as Bonnie creates a daylight ring for Caroline. The spell comes from Emily Bennett's grimoire and draws its magic from the sunlight. As the witch who spelled the ring, Bonnie has the power to render it inert, which she says she'll do if Caroline hurts anyone. Mason's transformation from man to wolf is defined as a curse; it's not voluntary or controllable like vamping out can be. On the night of a full moon, Mason shifts into a wolf, returning to his human state by morning. Werewolves hunt vampires and, according to legend, their bite kills.

THE DIABOLICAL PLAN: The gang goes into research mode to find out more about werewolves and doppelgängers. Katherine shows up in Caroline's bedroom — what is her plan for her?

HISTORY LESSON: Carol describes the architecture of the old Lockwood mansion, which is seen in "Memory Lane," as antebellum (which translates from Latin to "before the war"), a term that describes the period leading up to the American Civil War (1861–1865) when neoclassical architecture was popular in the Old South; the large-columned square façade of a plantation house is typical of that style. The "freaky underground cellar," as Tyler calls it, is a reminder that the Lockwoods were slave owners in 1860s Virginia, a state that had particularly strict laws and practices when it came to governing enslaved people, in part because of the importance of the slave trade to its economy. In the whole of America, there were four million African-Americans held in slavery in 1860, according to the U.S. Census.

The Aztecs, who were primarily situated in central Mexico (as in nowhere near Virginia), had established a thriving culture by the early 1400s, when Vanessa says the shaman made the curse; after the Triple Alliance was made between warring peoples in 1431, the empire reached its height at the end of that century, shortly before the conquest of the Spanish.

BITE MARKS: Damon gets an arrow in the back from Vanessa, who intended it for "Katherine." Alaric shoves Vanessa to disarm her. In wolf form, Mason jumps on Stefan, knocking him to the ground. Caroline bites Matt on the wrist and neck, feeding on him. Both Caroline and Stefan briefly tussle with wolf-Mason.

PREVIOUSLY ON THE VAMPIRE DIARIES: Stefan encourages Caroline to see Matt as a way to connect her to her humanity. Compare that with Damon's suggestion that Vicki go see Jeremy in "Lost Girls"; his motivation was to get her to feed on him. This is not the first time Elena has tricked Damon: in "Fool Me Once" she and Stefan lie to him about the plan to open

Werewolf Lore

Legends of men turning into animals have been a part of human storytelling for as long as history's been recorded. In Ancient Greece, the story of Lycaon told of a misbehaving cultist who tested the god Jupiter by trying to trick him into eating human flesh. Lycaon's punishment was banishment as a half-man, half-wolf creature.

The first major werewolf picture was 1941's *The Wolf Man*, directed by George Waggner during Universal Pictures' monster movie phase from 1923 to 1960. Starring Lon Chaney Jr. as Larry Talbot, the story tells of a son who returns home after 18 years because his brother has died. As the younger son, Larry was left out of the family legacy but now that his older brother is gone, he tries to pick up the mantle of the "good son." The family has a history of being plagued by lycanthropy. But Larry thinks nothing of the poem a pretty local woman, Gwynn, recites to him as she sells him a walking cane with a silver wolf's head on it marked with a pentagram, which she identifies as the sign of the werewolf: "Even a man who is pure at heart and says his prayers at night may become a wolf when the wolfbane blooms and the moon is full and bright." In the spooky, foggy forest on the night of a full moon with that wolfbane in full bloom a rampaging werewolf (Bela, a Gypsy man, played by Béla Lugosi) kills a young woman and bites Larry before he's able to beat him to death with his cane. Larry's wounds heal miraculously but the police and his doctor question him about the murders in the forest: there was no dead wolf found, only Bela's corpse. Larry insists it was a wolf, so he's labeled "mentally disturbed," and he has no one to turn to but the old Gypsy woman, Maleva, who warns him that he will turn too. The full moon (which inexplicably lasts more than one night) rises and Larry finds himself growing hair and getting wolfy. The next morning he realizes he's gone on a rampage as a wolf man. He begs his father to lock him up as the authorities set traps for the vicious animal terrorizing the town. His father, still believing it is simply a "mental quagmire" that Larry's in, takes the cane at his son's insistence and it comes in handy later, when father has to kill son with it, saving Gwynn from his attack. Larry Talbot's body returns to human form and he is hailed a hero, supposedly dying as he protected Gwynn from the wolf. Only in death can Larry find, in the words of the wise Maleva, "peace for eternity."

Because of *The Wolf Man*'s success, poor Larry Talbot was resurrected for four more movies where he was paired up with other Universal monsters. In *Frankenstein Meets the Wolf Man* (1943), Larry is brought back to life by moonbeams shining on his corpse (pesky grave robbers get their comeuppance). But he wants to die again to get rid of the werewolf curse, so he goes in search of Dr. Frankenstein — of course, why wouldn't you? The same themes are explored with Larry's character: the split within a man between a moral person and an uncontrolled killer, his melancholy at facing this horror, and others treating him like a madman when he tries to tell the truth.

Along with other stories and movies, *The Wolf Man* popularized the werewolf lore that persists today — transformation on the full moon, silver is the only way to kill a werewolf, the transformation is painful and horrifying, and a human surviving a bite will result in another werewolf. Movies like *An American Werewolf in London* (1981) played with those well-established tropes, dropping the idea that silver is deadly to werewolves, for example, but keeping the pentagram as the sign of the beast. In the Kevin Williamson–penned werewolf movie, *Cursed*, a brother (Jesse Eisenberg) and sister (Christina Ricci) are bitten by a werewolf and can only reverse the change by killing the "head" werewolf, who is the alpha because he was born with the curse.

Parts of "Bad Moon Rising" play on horror movie conventions with Mason warning partying teenagers to clear out by nightfall and the cocky and clueless Tyler playfully asking his uncle, "What happens after dark?" Shots of the sun setting, the full moon and the fog, and teenagers partying and making out all alone in the creepy forest build to Mason's transformation, a painful, torturous process beyond his control. Being a werewolf is indeed a curse. Despite Mason's precautions, he comes close to killing someone; the fury and violence of a werewolf stands in striking contrast to the deliberateness with which a vampire behaves, a trait we've grown accustomed to on *The Vampire Diaries*. As Damon says it's "not good" for the vampires that the Wolf Man thing is true — the most powerful creatures in Mystic Falls now have a natural enemy capable of taking them out with one bite.

the tomb; he forgives her but warns her, "Fool me once . . ." As it does with "Aimee Freaking Bradley," Caroline's jealousy reared its head in "There Goes the Neighborhood" when she admitted to feeling second-best to Elena in Matt's heart. In "Let the Right One In," Elena calls Damon a "self-serving psychopath with no redeeming qualities"; she has similar words for him at Duke. Tyler lost his temper and fell into a rage on nights of full moons in "The Turning Point" and "Under Control."

MEANWHILE IN FELL'S CHURCH: Matt is fed on by a girl he loves in *The Fury*. In *Dark Reunion*, Stefan does research into the history of Tyler Smallwood's family and discovers their secret: the original Smallwood in Fell's Church was a werewolf.

OFF CAMERA: "Bad Moon Rising" aired on the night of an actual full moon. This episode marks director Patrick Norris's first effort for *The Vampire Diaries*; his résumé of television credits includes *Chuck*, *Friday Night Lights*, *Parenthood*, *Gossip Girl*, and *The O.C.* as well as Kevin Williamson's previous shows *Dawson's Creek*, *Hidden Palms*, and *Wasteland*. Courtney Ford, who plays Vanessa Monroe, is best known for playing Christine Hill in the "Trinity Killer" season of Dexter and landed the recurring role of Portia Bellefleur on season 4 of *True Blood*. The werewolf sequences were filmed with real wolves playing the part of Mason in animal form. In an interview with Candice Accola for cwtv.com, Kevin Williamson quipped, "There's no such thing as a Meryl Streep wolf," so the crew had to get what they could out of the four-legged performers, as well as use fake wolves, and make enhancements in postproduction as necessary. Some viewers were confused about how Katherine got into Caroline's house, something Julie Plec cleared up on Twitter: "The Sheriff invited her in thinking she was Elena before going to work. But the scene didn't make it into the episode."

FOGGY MOMENTS: Is Aimee Bradley any relation to Amber Bradley ("Miss Mystic Falls") or were they short on surnames in the writers' room? Vanessa hands Elena a box of files and books, saying it contains details on Katherine's arrival in Mystic Falls in April 1864, but the file folders are marked "Mystic Falls 1500–1599" and "Mystic Falls 1600–1699." If the Aztec shaman really did put a curse on vampires and werewolves 600 years ago, does that mean that up until circa 1400 all vampires could walk around in daylight and all werewolves changed at will? Why doesn't Tyler act like an ass on this full moon like he has in the past? Why does wolf-Mason leave Stefan alone after knocking him down when he crashes out of the Bronco? If a werewolf's primary instinct is to kill vampires, it seems odd to ignore the one lying right there in front of him.

MUSIC: Matt knocks on Caroline's door and gets no answer to Meiko's "Under My Bed"; the lyrics relate particularly closely to the scene's action. Stefan asks Bonnie to make a daylight ring for Caroline while "In Your Skin" by Lifehouse plays at the Grill (where, in "Founder's Day," another Lifehouse song played). The Asteroids Galaxy Tour's "Fantasy Friend Forever" plays at the swimming-hole party. Caroline arrives at the party while the Duke Spirit's "Send a Little Love Token" is on. Night falls to "Changes" by Stars (who also had a track in the pilot). Matt and Caroline break up and Damon and Elena talk on the porch to A Fine Frenzy's "Ashes and Wine," their second song on the show following one played in "Lost Girls" at the Grill.

QUESTIONS:
- How could Tyler stare down wolf-Mason and get him to stop his attack? Does that mean he's the alpha to Mason? Or does Mason retain some or

all of his humanity while a wolf, enough that he recognized Tyler and understood his command to back off?

- Since Caroline attacked Matt, will Bonnie take away her daylight ring?
- Katherine conveniently waited for Caroline's most vulnerable moment, post-breakup, to show up in her bedroom. What does Katherine want with Caroline? A new best friend to wreak havoc with? A pawn for games with the Salvatore brothers and Elena? A little of both?

❄

Katherine: Go ahead, Stefan. Torture me. Keep me captive; drain me of my blood until my body turns to dust. It will never change the truth. I never compelled your love. It was real and so was mine.

2.04 *Memory Lane*

Original air date: September 30, 2010
Written by: Caroline Dries
Directed by: Rob Hardy
Guest cast: Simon Miller (George Lockwood), Evan Gamble (Henry), Brad James (Tow Truck Driver)

Jenna hosts a barbecue, unwittingly providing Damon with an opportunity to get to know Mason Lockwood and Caroline the chance to distract Elena while Katherine spends some quality time with Stefan reminiscing about 1864.

With a tight, smart script, "Memory Lane" provides some answers while raising even more questions. It's playful with the boozing, banter, and Pictionary but complicates season 2's story arc as the ancient vampire-werewolf grudge breaks into new mutiny. And Stefan's understanding of his past changes as Katherine makes him remember one very important thing: he fell in love with her in 1864 and it was real. Though she's appeared in flashbacks and raised hell in "The Return," this episode reveals just what a fascinating and layered evil vampire ex Katherine Pierce truly is. Long may she and her doppelgänger be the rope in the Salvatore brothers' tug-of-war. This episode would have crumbled if given to a lesser actor than Nina Dobrev; she gives two distinct performances in her scenes as Katherine, Elena, and Katherine *and* Elena.

Stefan finds himself asking the same crucial question of Katherine — why is she back? — that he was asking Damon at the beginning of season 1. Damon's return to Mystic Falls (as he revealed in "History Repeating") was motivated by love and revenge; Katherine insists she's back for Stefan. Stefan refuses to believe that, but the last moments of "Memory Lane" lend credence to her insistence that she loves him. Her logic — that, since he loved her before he knew she was a selfish, self-serving, violent, treacherous vampire, he still loves her or could love her again — is faulty. But she's successful in manipulating Stefan's feelings by forcing him to remember what she once meant to him. Meanwhile, at Katherine's behest, Caroline is making Elena reexamine her relationship with Stefan. Though Stefan and Elena realize what Katherine and Caroline are up to, the truth in their words remains. A hallmark of a great insidious, devilish character is the ability to take the truth and use it as a weapon in order to meet his or her own ends, which is something that Katherine does expertly both in the dream she creates for Stefan and the problems she points out that are inherent to Elena and Stefan's relationship. Almost proud of her villainy, Katherine freely admits her past misdeeds. From Stefan's point of view, there's nothing she holds sacred, no one she wouldn't betray — based on what he already knew of her character and what she now confesses to him about what really happened in 1864. He sees her as a monster of self-interest.

It's not surprising that Stefan has a hard time believing what Katherine tells him. But she's not the only one playing a game in "Memory Lane." The episode is chock-full of characters toying with and faking out each other. Stefan engages in an intense face-stroking session with Katherine and tells her what he imagines she wants to hear from him. Little does he know that she's faking it too, the vervain doesn't hurt her, and she plays prisoner willingly. Though Mason is wise to his game, Damon (and Alaric) puts on a friendly, pun-filled show at Jenna's barbecue, playing get-to-know-the-werewolf. Damon pretends to agree to a truce with Mason. Following Katherine's "do it or die" instructions, Caroline tries to destroy the stability of Elena's relationship with Stefan and keep her away from him so that Katherine can have her uninterrupted one-on-one time with him. And Elena and Stefan put on a performance at the Grill for Caroline, so she will report back to Katherine: everyone has to believe their fight was real in order for Katherine to buy it. But the ultimate fake out of the episode belongs to Katherine, who reveals that she was in on the Great Vampire Purge of 1864. She betrayed all 26 members of her "vampire family"

The Old Lockwood Mansion, seen in the flashbacks in "Memory Lane."

and made a deal with their enemy, George Lockwood (who himself tricked the Founder's Council into believing vampires were responsible for the brutal deaths around town), to fake her own death. Katherine didn't need to be saved by the Salvatore brothers — she was already saving herself.

All that trickery has the strange effect of making the sincere moments in "Memory Lane" more profound. Caroline's "I really am sorry" to Elena felt like an apology for her betrayal rather than for her snippy behavior. Elena and Stefan's reunion in her bedroom after their faux fight is packed with more emotion than usual. And most surprisingly, in flashback, Katherine promises Stefan, who died trying to save her, that they will be together again. Katherine *is* capable of love — and that, combined with her proven capacity for betrayal, manipulation, and murder is going to make this season *very* compelling.

As a counterpoint to the duplicitous vampires, Mason Lockwood comes across as a stand-up, straightforward guy: he has no interest in a war with the vampires and he only keeps secrets from Tyler to protect his nephew from becoming obsessed with the curse. In a cruel twist, the werewolf gene makes the Lockwoods prone to violence and rage blackouts, which in turn makes them all the more likely to take a human life and trigger the curse. From the description that Henry provides in the flashback, it seems that a werewolf's victims are more brutally ravaged than those of a vampire. The vampire-werewolf relationships in "Memory Lane" — the one present and evolving, the other a key part of Katherine's history — show that it is possible for these natural enemies to forge a successful bargain. Damon makes a deal with Mason Lockwood that he has no intention of keeping, but Katherine keeps hers with George Lockwood, to both their benefits.

Damon may not know quite what he's gotten himself into with Mason Lockwood, but, for the time being at least, focusing his attention on the lycanthrope issue has successfully kept him from thinking about either doppelgänger. He shows restraint in how he handles Katherine outside the Grill, refusing to play the mouse to her cat, proving there's nothing quite like an ancient supernatural feud to keep your mind off your evil ex. But in the flashback the more vulnerable human side of Damon comes out as he asks Katherine, "Is my love not enough?" In that one question we see the desperation that has fueled his actions since 1864 — to save her from the Council, to get her out of the tomb, to prove himself the better choice over his brother — and we see the source of the hatred he's felt for his brother in Katherine wanting Stefan too. But now Damon exhibits self-control, seemingly resolved not to get jealous over Katherine and Stefan; by contrast, it is Stefan who's riled up by her admissions and threats in the Salvatore dungeon.

Katherine is successful at needling Stefan because he's left himself open to attack, unlike Damon who has had enough of being vulnerable after "The Return." Katherine preys on Stefan when he's asleep — at his most unguarded — and manipulates his dream to play out his fear of losing Elena to Damon, of seeing himself replaced in her life by his own near double. In letting him chain her to a chair she can easily free herself from, Katherine gives Stefan a false sense that he's in control of a situation (a classic con artist move). He's actually just as vulnerable as he was before he imprisoned her, which she shows him when she turns the tables on him in an instant. Stefan once thought of Katherine as an angel but there was a devil inside, and here she proves that she's still capable of hiding her true self beneath a false persona. The question is where does the truth begin with Katherine? Is she just a game-playing puppet master or does she love Stefan?

Stefan tells Katherine that the appeal of being with Elena is that he doesn't have to pretend, he can just be himself. But for now, at least, that will be limited to private moments as Stefan and Elena fight at the Grill in an effort to convince Katherine that her threat is taken seriously. But could a fake breakup turn into real distance between the lovebirds? While Caroline was simply parroting back to Elena what Katherine told her, "all that mortality stuff" should strike a chord with Elena because it's absolutely going to become an obstacle if she and Stefan stay together — and if she stays human.

COMPELLING MOMENT: Katherine kicking free from her restraints and showing Stefan that she was never playing by his rules. Bad ass.

CIRCLE OF KNOWLEDGE:
- No Bonnie, Jeremy, or Matt in this episode.
- Katherine's stories about 1864 aren't the only trips down memory lane in this episode: Jenna and Mason also reminisce about their high school days together.
- In Stefan's dream, Katherine says to him the same thing she did when he lay dead in 1864: "I love you, Stefan. We'll be together again, I promise."
- In the flashback, Damon offers a toast to George Lockwood's service in the Confederate army, which raises the possibility that George triggered the werewolf curse when he killed someone on the battlefield.
- While the product placement for Caroline's car was heavy-handed in this episode, it was better integrated than the awkward "Bing" moments in season 1.
- Perfect fodder for a game of Pictionary with a werewolf, the Academy Award–winning 1990 film *Dances with Wolves* stars Kevin Costner (who also directed it) as a Civil War army lieutenant who befriends a wolf while stationed at a remote Colorado outpost. This earns him the nickname "Dances with Wolves" from the local Sioux tribe. The violent clash between the Sioux and the army forces him to choose between the two cultures.

- In keeping with the game theme of the episode, Jenna makes her guests play Pictionary and threatens Guitar Hero.
- In "Blood Brothers," Katherine didn't fight with her captors as they put her back in the cart, though her bonds were loosened and it had been a while since she had been poisoned. Her inaction makes sense in light of her revelation to Stefan: she wanted to be captured.

THE RULES: Katherine reminds us that because Stefan subsists on animal blood, it's very easy for her to get in his head and manipulate his dreams. It is possible for a vampire to build up immunity to the poisonous effects of vervain. Katherine confirms that a werewolf bite is fatal to a vampire. Mason says he has no control over his actions while in wolf form. Silver doesn't have any special effect on werewolves. Taking a cue from L.J. Smith's *Dark Reunion*, human blood must be spilled in order to activate the latent werewolf gene.

THE DIABOLICAL PLAN: Damon arranges for Jenna to have a barbecue so he can prove that Mason Lockwood is a werewolf; he's successful in that but fails to kill him. If Katherine's telling the truth (big if), then her diabolical plan is to spend time with Stefan while Caroline plants doubts in Elena's mind, and it worked. The question Stefan asked Katherine in "The Return" — why she wanted the tomb vampires dead — is answered. Those vampires could reveal to whoever Katherine is running from that she didn't die in 1864.

BITE MARKS: Katherine throws Stefan across his room when he tries to lunge at her. She gets a vervain dart in the back and some fresh vervain sizzling on her skin courtesy of Stefan; he also chokes her when she threatens Elena. Katherine throws him again, then stakes him in the leg. Caroline grips Elena's arm hard. Damon stabs Mason in the gut with a silver knife, to little effect. Mason shoves Tyler into the wall.

PREVIOUSLY ON THE VAMPIRE DIARIES: Fittingly, Katherine and Stefan's trip down memory lane is accompanied by a ton of references to previous episodes of *The Vampire Diaries* so viewers share in that familiar feeling of history repeating. Beyond the flashback to 1864, which revisits events seen from a different perspective last season, "Memory Lane" reprises many elements and themes: the "intimacy of the near touch" dance ("Miss Mystic Falls"), another vampire-controlled dream sequence ("Family Ties"), talk of Katherine's

no-rules credo ("Lost Girls," "The Return"), someone reading Stefan's diary without his permission ("Friday Night Bites"), a vervain dart stab-in-the-back ("Miss Mystic Falls"), Henry the Friendly Tomb Vampire ("Blood Brothers") in 1864 garb, another guest in the Salvatore dungeon ("You're Undead to Me," "Blood Brothers"), references to the ubiquitous founders' parties ("Family Ties," every episode in the second half of season 1), and the idea that love and hate rise from the same emotional source ("The Return"). In "Friday Night Bites," Stefan says in voiceover that Damon is a monster with no humanity left while Damon is shown caressing a sleeping Elena. Here he says Katherine is incapable of love while she reminisces about a moment shared in 1864 with Stefan. Is Katherine just as capable of love as Damon turned out to be?

MEANWHILE IN FELL'S CHURCH: In *The Fury*, Katherine explains to Stefan (and Damon) how she faked her death back when the Salvatore brothers first turned. In the opening chapter of *The Struggle*, Damon threatens to destroy everyone Elena loves if she won't yield to his will, the way Katherine does here to Stefan.

OFF CAMERA: An actor as well as a photographer, Simon Miller plays George Lockwood, which marks his second role on The CW; he played Patrick Roberts in season 3 of *Gossip Girl*. His other credits include the film *Between Love & Goodbye* and a guest role on *CSI: Miami*. The beer Mason and company drink at Jenna's barbecue is Heisler, a fictional brand supplied by prop company Independent Studio Services to various film and television productions; it's the same brand that Elena and Damon were drinking at Bree's Bar in "Bloodlines."

FOGGY MOMENTS: Strange that Katherine superimposed the words "Lockwood Mansion, 1864" in Stefan's dream. . . . Also, Katherine asks Stefan why he came back to Mystic Falls, but in "Bloodlines" Stefan tells Elena he returns to Mystic Falls every decade or so — is it really so surprising that he returned to his hometown? Elena leaves Caroline, a newly turned vampire who's been talking about her blood cravings all day, alone with the innocent tow truck guy. Not very neighborly, Ms. Gilbert. Mason spent the afternoon drinking at Jenna's and then drove to the Mystic Grill? Let's assume that old werewolf gene also gives him an extremely high alcohol tolerance.

MUSIC: Katherine and Stefan dance in his dream to Haydn's Quartet for Strings in C Major, Op. 76, no. 3 (also known as "Emperor"). Damon surprises Elena at the Grill; playing in the background is Collide's "Rock On" (originally recorded by David Essex). The guests arrive at Jenna's barbecue to Ballas Hough Band's "Together Faraway." Howls' "Hammock" (a track on the season 1 soundtrack) plays as the gang plays Pictionary. Caroline shows off her car's fancy song ID feature with Goldfrapp's "We Radiate" (which is also on the soundtrack). Caroline listens in on Stefan and Elena's argument while Tyrone Wells' "Time of Our Lives" plays; Wells also had a song in "The Turning Point." Katherine remembers the promise she made to Stefan in 1864 to Sara Bareilles' "Breathe Again." (Sara Bareilles' songs played when Elena and Stefan shared their first kiss in "Night of the Comet," and when Damon confronted Elena in "The Return.")

QUESTIONS:
- When Stefan touches the vervain to Katherine's cheek, it sizzles her skin, but she tells Stefan it doesn't hurt her anymore. How far does Katherine's vervain immunity go?
- Who did Mason kill in order to unleash the Lockwood curse? How did Mason know that Damon was a vampire (or even that vampires exist)? Is there a separate founders' journal for Lockwood wolves?
- If "how" Katherine and Elena look alike isn't the right question, what is?
- What or who was Katherine trying to dodge by faking her death in 1864?
- What does the moonstone do and how did Katherine have it in the first place? Did George Lockwood want it for the same reason that Mason wants it now?
- Why has Stefan kept Katherine's portrait?
- Damon's attempt to kill Mason with a silver heirloom fails, and Katherine says werewolves are not "easy prey." How *does* one kill a werewolf?
- Did Stefan and Damon die for nothing or did they die for love?

❀

Caroline (to Liz): Look, I know that we don't get along, and that you hate me, but I'm your daughter and you'll do this for me, right?

2.05 *Kill or Be Killed*

Original air date: October 7, 2010
Written by: Mike Daniels
Directed by: Jeff Woolnough
Guest cast: Courtney Cummings (Lemonade Girl), Justin Greer (Jimmy), Jason Guiliano (Deputy Jess), Kevin Nichols (Deputy #2), Maiara Walsh (Sarah)

At the Historical Society Volunteer Picnic, the tension between Mason and the Salvatore brothers comes to a head, and Sheriff Forbes learns why Caroline's been acting differently lately.

This episode opens with the threat of an alpha-male showdown but it is the women of *The Vampire Diaries* who actually deliver the ass kicking. Liz Forbes nearly kills our beloved Stefan and Damon; Caroline takes Mason down in a display of utter awesomeness; Elena whacks a deputy with a two-by-four; and Katherine is masterminding more schemes than anyone realizes. Katherine doesn't show up on screen until the end, but her influence guides the characters: she drives Stefan and Elena to fight, Mason to search for the moonstone, and Caroline to spy. And whatever her plan for Mason is, it began at least a year ago when she triggered his curse by compelling his friend to fight him to the death.

Though the end reveal that Mason and Katherine are together is a surprise twist, there have been many clues and moments of foreshadowing to tip viewers off about what's to come. Mason and Katherine arrive in Mystic Falls at the same time. In "Memory Lane," Katherine reveals she's dealt with a Lockwood in the past and once possessed the moonstone, which connects her to Mason's plotline. In that flashback, she says she wouldn't come to Mystic Falls without knowing who's in town, so she must know Mason somehow. Also, Mason is aware that the Salvatore brothers are vampires but is cagey about how he knows. In this episode, Mason specifically threatens to snap Elena's neck, just what Katherine said she'd do in "Memory Lane." The biggest clue came in Mason's flashback: a friend attacks him in a parking lot and just won't let up. Just a few episodes ago in "Brave New World," Damon

pulled this very trick, compelling a guy to attack Tyler in order to provoke a wolf attack. That a vampire was behind Jimmy's determined assault should be no surprise and, before we see her smirking in the final Florida flashback, it's clear that the most likely candidate is Katherine. Yet with all the other things going on in Mystic Falls, it was still hard to see that Mason-Katherine lip lock coming.

But as always on *The Vampire Diaries*, as soon as one answer is revealed more questions pop up to fuel the fast-moving plot that keeps connecting the characters in new and trickier ways. Mason is already on the Salvatore brothers' hit list, what will happen once they find out he's with their ex? While Katherine's connection to Mystic Falls' resident wolf answers a lot of questions about Mason, it raises even more about Katherine, the moonstone, and why she'd intentionally create a werewolf. A werewolf could be a powerful minion to have and an occasional weapon against other vampires, but Katherine puts herself at risk too, should Mason ever . . . you know, bite her. It makes a good deal of sense why Mason was dodging Tyler's question about the moonstone: he can't tell Tyler that Katherine wants the stone; Mason may or may not know what she wants it for. Like Uncle John before him, who got most of his insider information from Katherine (via Isobel), Mason likely only knows as much as Katherine wants him to. It doesn't seem like he's aware that she deliberately turned him by compelling Jimmy to fight to the death or that Stefan and Damon are her creations too.

Once again, Tyler and Jeremy act as foils for each other's character. They each begin this episode trying to find out more about the supernatural world, but both are shut down by their respective family members. Mason gives Tyler a bit of information but not the whole werewolf story, warning him to stay out of it, but Tyler wants to know more. Jeremy finds out about the Lockwood curse but Elena wants to protect him from supernatural dangers, so she forbids him to get involved. Both boys feel quite rightly that they are innately involved: Tyler carries the wolf gene, and Jeremy wears a magic ring that's already saved his life once. The "freak show" and "damaged goods" were at each other's throats last season, but here Tyler fights his natural instincts and he responds to Jeremy's friendliness at the Grill and later even confides in him (after choking him a little bit) about the Lockwood curse. The darkness inside Tyler has always frightened and confused him, but now that he knows he could become a "scary demon wolf thing," he's even more afraid. As Jeremy reveals that he knows his secret, Tyler is shown through the grate of the study window, a visual echo of the trap Tyler's in because of the curse that rages inside him. His momentary wish that Sarah would die (so the werewolf gene would be activated) changes Tyler's attitude to his family's secret, his legacy, and Mason. For Tyler, being a part of the supernatural world takes him further away from who he is, makes him lose his self-control and his identity. No longer interested in using the moonstone as leverage for information about the curse, and resolved not to become something darker and more violent than he already is, Tyler hands over the moonstone to Mason. By the end of the episode, Tyler wants out while Jeremy still wants in. For Jeremy, being in the "we" that Elena says he isn't a part of would mean being included and having a purpose — and that's important enough to him that he'll go against his sister's will and warning. And while Jeremy keeps initiating a friendship of sorts with Tyler, he is also keeping secrets from him. He fibs when Tyler asks how he knew about the Lockwood curse, choosing to hide the fact that Elena told him and that vampires also exist.

Those already in the thick of Mystic Falls' secrets explore how to deal with a threat in "Kill or Be Killed" and they ask the moral question is it acceptable to kill in order to protect oneself? In "Brave New World," Damon thought killing Caroline was the best option while Stefan and Elena vehemently disagreed. After Mason puts vervain in Damon's lemonade, Stefan agrees that Mason is a big enough threat that he needs to be taken out; his attempts to call a truce and to threaten him had failed, their handshake was empty, so it comes down to the base strategy of "kill or be killed." In a decision that catches Damon off guard, Stefan believes the threat Mason poses to their secret identity and to their lives justifies killing him. Compare that to later in the episode when Damon is threatening Liz; Stefan, Elena, and Caroline won't let him kill her — but Damon wouldn't do it, anyway. The courtesies extended to an enemy (Mason) are different than those for a friend (Liz), even one who's denying that friendship. Damon finds a solution — an enforced peace — that spares her life. By deciding to erase her memory, Damon ensures that Liz will no longer pose a threat to them. She and Damon will be "friends" again, though Damon is unlikely to forget Liz's willingness to torture and kill him.

What is most elegant about "Kill or Be Killed" is how easily the writers took a supporting character who's never been front and center and placed her in the thick of the action and at the heart of the story. We've watched Sheriff Forbes struggle to keep her town safe over the past year, we've seen her develop a friendship with and dependence on Damon, and we've seen her clash with her daughter. In "Kill or Be Killed," we see how unenviable her position is. She tries to be a good parent by generally protecting her daughter (and everyone else) in her role as the town's sheriff, but she alienates Caroline by seeming to consistently choose her work over her daughter. She's unwittingly befriended a sometimes-murderous vampire in her crusade against vampires.

No wonder she can't believe Mason's accusation that Damon's fooled her into believing he's one of the town's greatest allies. In keeping with the "kill or be killed" philosophy of the episode, once Liz has proof, she acts decisively and quickly, luring the brothers into the woods to question them and then kill them, without considering why exactly Damon would have helped her in the past. The base strategy has no room for the consideration of more complex notions, like a useful enemy or dangerous friend. But learning that her own daughter is a vampire — who feeds on her deputy right in front of her — takes the fight out of Sheriff Forbes. Everything about this situation is heartbreaking: Liz betrayed and humiliated by Damon's deception; Damon hurt by Liz's resolve to torture and kill him; Liz realizing that her daughter is a vampire; and perhaps most awfully, Caroline hearing her own mother ask to die rather than keep her secret.

Liz is one of the few living or present parents on *The Vampire Diaries* and her relationship with Caroline has been marked by mutual snippiness since they first appeared on screen together. Even so, Caroline's fear of her mother actually hating her is strong enough that she hesitates before saving Stefan and Damon, because she'd reveal what she is. And Liz is attentive enough to have noticed the recent changes in her daughter. Both have been forced to keep secrets from each other in the past, and this has bound them in a pattern of bitchiness and misunderstandings. Following Caroline's particularly monstrous vampire debut for her mother, the distance that existed between mother and daughter at the beginning of the episode has grown chasm-wide by the end — a daughter dead to her mother, feared by her and treated like a monster.

In the look that Damon gives Caroline as she stands outside the cell door, broken at her mother's words, and in his statement to Liz about how wrong she is that her daughter is "gone," we see Damon find a kinship with and connection to Caroline, one they've not shared in the past. Damon's own father rejected him for being a vampire sympathizer and, in the end, killed him for it; he knows what it's like to be at total odds with a parent who's madly hunting vampires. Damon's decision to spare Liz is not self-motivated: he won't kill someone he considers a friend — and his choice doesn't go unnoticed by Elena. This Damon Who Was Her Friend makes another appearance in "Kill or Be Killed": instead of trying to take advantage of the fight between Stefan and Elena, Damon helps her to resolve it. In "Bad Moon Rising," Damon tried to chip away at Elena's wall of hatred by being his usual cocky self, but it backfired and she called him a "first-rate jackass." This is the way to do it, as Elena makes explicit to him. She responds to the good in him, not the self-serving or manipulating attempts to win her over. For a vampire whose refrain last season was that he doesn't have any friends, Damon now can count a fair number of them (on a good day) between Elena, Stefan, Liz, and Alaric, and he is mending relationships with Jenna, Jeremy, and even Caroline. The value that Damon places on his friendships, like his with Liz in this episode, increases the esteem that Elena holds him in. Her responses to his actions teach Damon how to be human, whether or not she's intentionally trying to have this effect on him.

And in Damon's wise words, "Relationships are about communication," and Elena and Caroline's becomes a lot healthier when Caroline admits that she's been spying for Katherine. Just as Damon seems to have forgiven and Liz will have forgotten their mutual betrayal, Caroline and Elena patch up the gulf that lies between them. Always admirably empathetic, Elena understands why Caroline has betrayed her and Stefan (nothing scarier than death threats from Katherine Pierce). Katherine must be taken seriously — and Elena admits to herself that that also means Stefan needs to be less vulnerable to the danger Katherine poses.

Nothing makes for more boring television than a couple blissfully in love. The *TVD* writers have carefully kept Stefan and Elena's relationship from becoming stale with uninterrupted sweetness; at the same time, they never force conflict for conflict's sake. Their struggle to stay together in spite of Katherine trying to tear them apart feels real and honest. From their coded "I love yous" in their faux fight to their real fight over Stefan's decision to drink human blood again, their romance remains interesting enough that it still works as an important keystone of the show.

Though *The Vampire Diaries* isn't shy about killing off characters, there's a sense that the main three will survive. Nonetheless, seeing Stefan shot, vervained, and still as death was more than a little unsettling. His bunny-blood diet has been his downfall time and again; this season and last, every vampire who takes Stefan on knows to take advantage of it. He and Damon are right: Stefan needs to be stronger in order to fight Katherine and to protect himself, Elena, and the rest of the town. Stefan's emotional nature, his humanity, and his refusal to drink "the people blood" are his personal strengths, but these turn into potentially fatal weaknesses when he's up against a vampire who hasn't forsaken her nature, as Katherine put it in

"Memory Lane." Like Mason realizing that he is outnumbered and physically outmatched and seeking an ally in Sheriff Forbes, Stefan recognizes his weakness and finds a solution: a little bit of human blood every day. As Damon explained to Elena in "Miss Mystic Falls," Stefan never learned to control himself on human blood, and, as we saw in season 1, his last attempt turned him into a lying, violent vampire drunk on blood. After his faceoff with Katherine in "Memory Lane" and his near death in "Kill or Be Killed," Stefan decides to try to level the playing field and accept the risk of that happening again. But he doesn't do it without Elena. Her decision to be a part of Stefan developing control of his bloodlust brings in an integral element of Stefan and Elena's relationship from the book series. Elena offers Stefan her own blood, and it's a smart move on her part. By being his blood supply, she knows he'll be as careful as possible when he feeds, terrified of hurting or killing her. Both symbolically and literally, she becomes the source of Stefan's power and strength. The way he vamps out while drinking her blood but returns to his human face as he kisses her brought to mind their first night together in "The Turning Point" — but here their connection feels even stronger and more intimate.

COMPELLING MOMENT: "It's you and me, Stefan — always."

CIRCLE OF KNOWLEDGE:
- No Jenna, Alaric, Matt, or Bonnie in this episode.
- The episode's title applies to the situation Mason faces in the parking lot: if he hadn't killed Jimmy, Jimmy would have killed him. The idea of "kill or be killed" is set up in opposition to what Damon calls Stefan's usual "'Give Peace a Chance' crap" (a reference to the John Lennon–penned song from 1969).
- Matt hasn't been around since "Bad Moon Rising," but Jeremy mentions that Caroline's attack on him has been blamed on a wolf.
- R.I.P. Nameless V5 Deputy (Kevin Nichols) and Deputy Jess (Jason Guiliano), who have been kicking around Mystic Falls since "Lost Girls" and "162 Candles" respectively. You served your town well.
- Damon and Katherine think alike and often use the same strategies. Both compelled a man to attack a Lockwood in a parking lot, both enjoy the "play dead in the road" trick for luring a victim, and they use minions to help execute their plans.

THE RULES: Mason explains that the family's werewolf curse is triggered by any death at a Lockwood's hands: accidental or intentional, it doesn't matter. There is a parallel between how vampires and werewolves are created: both require a personal sacrifice and taking life or life force from another, and the soon-to-be-supernatural must be "chosen" in some way — by another vampire, or through family legacy. On a full moon, without restraints and sedatives, a werewolf will kill anything in its path.

THE DIABOLICAL PLAN: Jeremy goes on a solo mission to find out more about Tyler and the Lockwood curse. Elena and Stefan put on their faux fight for Caroline who is acting as Katherine's proxy. Outnumbered and weaker than the vampires, Mason Lockwood decides to get the Mystic Falls P.D. on his side and outs the brothers to Sheriff Forbes, whose attempt to kill Damon and Stefan is thwarted by Caroline and Elena. Mason turns out to be doing Katherine's bidding, getting the moonstone for her. Why did she trigger his curse?

BITE MARKS: In flashback, Jimmy attacks Mason and Mason accidentally kills him. Damon chokes on some vervain-spiked lemonade, courtesy of Mason Lockwood. Tyler shoves Jeremy against a wall and chokes him. Sheriff Forbes and her deputies shoot Damon and Stefan with wooden bullets multiple times and inject them with vervain. Mason puts Elena in a chokehold, and Caroline kicks his ass. Elena smacks Deputy Jess with a handy wooden board. Caroline bites one deputy and uses him as a shield when the other one tries to shoot her; she knocks the second deputy to the ground, killing him. Tyler accidentally pushes Sarah down the stairs.

PREVIOUSLY ON THE VAMPIRE DIARIES: In "The Turning Point," after reading Johnathan Gilbert's journal, Jeremy begins drawing vampires; at the Career Fair later that same episode he discovers that Tyler also draws supernatural creatures. Jeremy first demonstrated his investigative abilities in "There Goes the Neighborhood" when he forced Anna to reveal her supernatural status, like he does with Tyler here. In "The Turning Point," Logan Fell kidnapped Caroline and threatened Liz that he would turn her; here that nightmare possibility has become a reality for Liz. Elena first fed Stefan her blood in "Let the Right One In." In "Under Control," Damon argues that there's nothing wrong with drinking human blood as long as a vampire's not killing someone (e.g., drinking from blood bags) and that they need their strength to battle tomb vamps; here, Stefan makes the same argument to Elena. Trudie Peterson is pushed down the stairs in "A Few Good Men," but unlike Sarah, she dies.

MEANWHILE IN FELL'S CHURCH: The werewolf lore revealed in *Dark Reunion* states that "you can have the werewolf virus all your life but never even know it because it's never activated"; the key to activating it is to "kill and taste fresh blood." In the TV series, any death at a potential werewolf's hand can cause the change; in the books, it has to be a deliberate human sacrifice. After the sacrifice, the werewolf will turn on the next full moon. In *The Fury*, both Salvatore brothers are near death as an enemy tortures them in an underground room. As Mason points out to Liz, the wave of vampire crimes started when the Salvatore brothers came to town; in *The Struggle* the same argument is made by the Fell's Church townsfolk who blame Stefan for crimes they have no proof he committed. Like Stefan and Elena do at the volunteer picnic, Meredith and Bonnie stage a fight in *Dark Reunion* to trick their adversary.

OFF CAMERA: When it comes to biting a fellow actor, Candice Accola told AssignmentX.com, "I'm so my mother's child in safety first. Most of the time, you're meeting that person that day. It's like, 'Hi, I'm going to be biting you.' So you let them feel the teeth, and I make sure that my mouth is closed. It's kind of more just like a peck — it's like I'm trying to give them a hickey as opposed to really bite their necks."

FOGGY MOMENTS: In the flashback, Mason's eyes turn wolfy after he kills Jimmy, and Mason tells Tyler that any accidental death, like in a car wreck, can trigger the curse. After the car accident in "Founder's Day," the paramedic examining Tyler opens his eye and it's an amber wolf eye. Was Caroline actually dead but just for a moment? Was it because Tyler himself was close to death? Despite having super vampire hearing, neither Stefan nor Damon hear Liz and her two deputies approaching in the forest before they are ambushed. It seems like a convenient oversight that Deputy Jess wasn't ingesting vervain, so Caroline could take a bite without being poisoned. Also, what will the cover story be for those two dead police officers? Who told Katherine that Mason set up the Salvatore brothers to die? After all, the two deputies are dead, Liz is in the dungeon, and Caroline's curled up on the couch. Does Katherine have more minions in town than Mason and Caroline, or did Mason tell her in an earlier, unseen conversation?

MUSIC: Mason's Florida flashback is set to the Smashing Pumpkins' "The Fellowship," which is featured on the soundtrack. Elena and Jeremy talk werewolves to Trent Dabbs' "Counting Sleep." "Superhuman Touch" by Athlete is on as the Historical Society's volunteer day gets underway. Jeremy approaches Tyler at the Grill with the Rifles' "Sometimes" on in the background. Caroline talks to Elena about her problems with her mother while The Fast Romantics' "Cool Kids" plays. "Punching in a Dream" by The Naked and Famous provides the background music to Stefan and Elena's faux fight. The girls have a dance party at the Lockwood house to Sky Ferreira's "Obsession," which is also on the soundtrack. Title Tracks' "Steady Love" is heard when Damon approaches Mason by the lemonade table. Sarah and Aimee barge into the Lockwood study to New Politics' "Yeah Yeah Yeah" and Sarah is okay after her tumble down the stairs while The Pass's "Colors" plays. Damon and Elena talk and Elena gives Stefan her blood to "I Need to Know" by Kris Allen.

QUESTIONS:
- Did Mason get involved with Katherine willingly, or did she compel him?
- Forget the moonstone: what secret files are on those floppy disks in Mayor Lockwood's safe??
- Will Katherine realize Caroline confessed to Elena and punish her or Matt?

> *Katherine: I will always know, Elena.*
> *I will always be one step ahead of you.*

2.06 *Plan B*

Original air date: October 21, 2010
Written by: Elizabeth Craft and Sarah Fain
Directed by: John Behring

Across the pond toward the Lockwood mansion. The pond is home to a swan, named Steven after Mr. Steven R. McQueen, who is fiercely territorial (be warned).

In preparation for the annual masquerade ball, Carol Lockwood once again enlists the help of the entire Mystic Falls population. Katherine proves that messing with her master plan has dire consequences.

While pushing its mythology forward episode after episode, *The Vampire Diaries* never puts plot points ahead of emotional impact. The writers twist the plot with purpose: to challenge characters in new ways. In "Plan B," new revelations about the moonstone take a backseat to the consequences of retrieving it. Damon has killed his double in Mason, Jeremy and Bonnie faced impossible moral dilemmas, and Stefan and Elena are punished for disobeying Katherine. By delivering such an intense, shocking, and emotional episode on a regular week in the season, the show promises to truly terrify its viewers and break their hearts as it builds for the next 16 episodes toward its finale.

It's been a while since Damon's allowed himself to kill anyone (well, a while for a killer vampire) and he relishes ripping out Mason's heart. Not unlike his heart-to-heart with Alaric before (temporarily) killing him in "A Few Good Men," Damon tells Mason he sees himself in him — a guy who has fallen for Katherine, is willing to do anything for her, and earnestly believes that she wants to live happily ever after at his side. In killing Mason Damon doesn't just rid them of a sworn enemy, he tries to hurt Katherine and, most importantly, to destroy that part of himself that was made a fool by falling for her back in 1864. In part, Damon's focus on Mason since "Brave New World" has been his way of distracting himself from the presence of Katherine, the woman he loved who didn't love him back . . . for a century and a half. The discovery that Mason is who Damon was 145 years ago allows Damon to mock and destroy that "stupid" part of himself, the part that believed her lies and put so much at risk and lost so much, the part that put him on the path he's still on as an emotionally confused vampire in love with a girl who loves his brother.

Like Damon (and like almost every other character on this show), Mason is neither solely good nor bad. He did some shady things (other than setting up the Salvatore brothers to be killed, his threat to snap Elena's neck comes to mind) but he truly loved Katherine and his last words show how earnest he was about protecting his nephew from the curse, as he begs Jeremy to help Tyler avoid this fate. Taylor Kinney brought an easy charm to the show — take his bemused reaction to seeing Stefan alive at the Lockwood mansion. The always-smiling (except when being brutally tortured) surfer-turned-werewolf will be missed as Mason's name is added to the long and growing list of men who die for their unrequited love for Katherine.

As a Gilbert who can't help but involve himself, Jeremy's resolve to be part of the supernatural adventures is tested by the horror he witnesses in "Plan B." Like his big sister who can't stand being out of the loop (Elena has never been as impatient and frustrated as she is in this episode), Jeremy doesn't listen when he's told to stay out of it, even though his presence is questioned by Damon, Alaric, Elena, and Stefan. In his bid for independence from his sister's rule, Jeremy shows enthusiasm and skill at research and during his reconnaissance with Tyler. And yet he's clearly troubled by the gruesome torture scene he stumbles upon and that he has unwittingly participated in by bringing Damon the wolfsbane. Though he tries to discourage Damon from torturing Mason any further, ultimately, he walks away, leaving Damon alone to do what he does best. His sister's warnings about the dangers of this world and, in particular, of being a party to one of Damon's schemes have now become reality. Jeremy's in an unenviable position: he's a friend to Tyler and (presumably) wants to protect him from the Lockwood curse, but he also knows exactly what has happened to Mason and he must keep it a secret from Tyler. While Jeremy's not responsible for these events, he certainly is complicit. Interestingly the violence that Katherine commits against Jenna doesn't scare Jeremy off, instead it strengthens his resolve to hold on to the new identity he's building for himself. With Elena at the hospital (in one of their rare and heartwarming moments of sibling closeness), he comforts her with a chilling vow to make Katherine pay. Compare that to his retreat when Anna was taken away from him in "Founder's Day," followed by his decision to give in to his melancholy. The new Jeremy Gilbert wants to fight back. Will he also adopt Damon's kill-or-be-killed philosophy?

As the resident "morality police," as Damon calls her, Bonnie must also decide what evils are necessary in the name of good. She's been estranged from her best friends because of their closeness to the vampires, and without Grams, she's all alone surrounded by secrets and danger with no one she can truly confide in. When Elena forces a heart-to-heart, Bonnie seems firm: there are "sides," you must choose one, and Caroline is "lost" to her. It's refreshing to later see a side of Bonnie that's something other than "judgey" and closed off; this glimpse of her struggle between her beliefs and her friendships helps to round out the character and humanize her. Though she is at first standoffish with the Salvatore brothers, telling them she won't help them hurt Mason and Katherine, she is convinced to cooperate when Damon points out that the "bad guys" pose a threat to Elena. Bonnie's firm anti-vampire stance softens when her best friend is at risk, and she trusts what Stefan and Damon tell her to be the truth. For Bonnie, Elena's safety is worth putting aside her moral reservations. Also, in part for Elena's sake, Bonnie reaches out to Caroline, inviting her along on the moonstone-in-the-well adventure, and taking that necessary first step to rebuilding the bond between them, just as she did with Elena in their conversation at the Lockwood estate. Bonnie proves to be a helpful ally: with her magic, she easily disables Mason, gets information from him, and figures out where he's hidden the moonstone. She also walks away after helping Damon with the (creepy) drop cloth without asking what

he's about to do to Mason. Could this be the beginning of a tentative alliance between the Salvatores and Bonnie?

Since the pilot episode, Caroline Forbes has always yearned to be loved and admired. Here she tries to make things right with Bonnie and with her mother, despite being rejected by both for something she neither chose nor can change. Caroline takes the tiny opening Liz gives her to share what she's been going through in a frank and honest way. She admits she wants to kill but she's fighting her instinct, and she seems justifiably proud of herself for the self-control she's built in a short amount of time. Liz sees how amazing Caroline is — how brave and perseverant Caroline is — and she acknowledges that, even if her daughter is a vampire, she is still alive. What a huge moment for Caroline: better than winning Miss Mystic, better than Matt falling in love with her, this love and recognition could go a long way to bringing Caroline peace. Mother and daughter finally realize that, despite outward appearances, they're not all that different at their core; Caroline is very much her mother's daughter. But, just as love and trust turned out to be mutually exclusive concepts for Mason with Katherine, the final scene between Caroline and Liz reveals how complicated their situation is — Liz's love for and trust in her daughter isn't enough. Of course, since this show is terribly cruel, the breakthrough in communication between the Forbes women is one only Caroline will remember. As with her choice to end things with Matt in order to keep from harming him, Caroline makes the choice here (to compel her mother to forget) that she believes will best protect those she cares about — the Salvatore brothers as well as her mother. Compelling her mother through tears with a cover story about making salty soup and bickering so that "all is right in the world," Caroline proves once again to be so much more than she's given credit for. Caroline makes another hard decision that puts the greater good over her personal happiness. At least she'll always know that her mother does love her, no matter what, and wants nothing but to keep her safe, a marked change from just one episode ago.

Elena and Stefan have always known that their relationship is dangerous: Stefan's very nature puts Elena at risk and the destructive forces in Mystic Falls tend to take issue with their coupling. Last season, they each tried to push the other away to prevent harm, but neither could hold their resolve for long. They believed that together they could overcome whatever dangers arose. But Katherine is relentless and focused, and her punishments are swift, brutal, and unpredictable. At the beginning of the episode, Elena asks Stefan what he thinks will happen should Katherine find out they are only fake-fighting; by episode's end she has her answer and knows that Katherine's won. In an incredibly sad breakup scene, Stefan knows there is no argument he can raise to save their relationship. If being together means that others could pay for that happiness with their lives, Elena and Stefan have no moral choice but to be apart, no matter how deeply they love each other. They feel responsible for what happened to Jenna; in fact, their first reaction isn't anger at Katherine, but with themselves. If they hadn't persisted in seeing each other, Jenna wouldn't be in the hospital. While Katherine is obviously to blame for Jenna stabbing herself, anyone would feel as culpable as Stefan and Elena do in this situation.

So far this season, Stefan has been so much more dynamic than the brooding, humorless vampire Damon once mocked; he's been everything from more ruthless and violent to playful, funny, brotherly, and passionate. This more nuanced Stefan still stays faithful to the character Paul Wesley created last season, thanks to a consistently strong performance. In "Plan B," he gives us a broken Stefan, and seeing him cry over losing Elena was too heartbreaking for words.

The little in her life that Elena felt she had under control is now gone and with it she loses hope, yielding to Katherine's demands. And if Katherine "always gets her way," with Mason gone, that can mean nothing good for her two new targets, Matt and Tyler.

COMPELLING MOMENT: The jaw-dropping shock of Jenna stabbing herself.

CIRCLE OF KNOWLEDGE:
- Neither happy couple rolling around in bed at the beginning of the episode knew that those were their final moments together. By the end of "Plan B," Mason is dead and Elena and Stefan are over.
- The way Elena describes Damon's M.O. to Jeremy — he uses people and those people end up dead — is just how Damon thinks of Katherine.
- Damon is glad to see that Mason feels pain and isn't a "Beastmaster," referring to the 1982 cult classic movie whose title character communicated telepathically with animals and was "born with the courage of an eagle, the strength of a black tiger, and the power of a god."
- "Snakes. Why'd it have to be snakes?" Damon calls Jeremy "Indiana Jones" (the adventurer character made famous in four films starring

Harrison Ford in the role) for involving himself in their moonstone scheme, but it's Elena who has the true Indy moment: searching for a hidden artifact in a well full of vicious snakes.

- Notice how Stefan just tosses the hard-won moonstone to his brother, who pockets it. Their relationship is markedly different from last season, where Stefan would never willingly have handed over to Damon an object of supernatural significance, especially not if Katherine was after it. With a common enemy, the boys have rebuilt so much of their brotherly bond. It warms the heart.
- The phone conversation between Damon and Katherine showed just how talented a villain Ms. Pierce is, even when taken by surprise. Her last jab — "Give my love to Stefan" — shows she can out-Damon Damon any day of the week.
- Carol Lockwood comments to Tyler that Matt hasn't been around lately. The boys were estranged after Tyler made out with Matt's mom and then beat him up in "Under Control," but the accident in "Founder's Day" buried the hatchet between them.
- Though Jenna survives, Katherine was following through on the threat that she made to Stefan in "Memory Lane": "I'll kill everyone that she loves while she watches."
- Katherine compels Matt, even though we assume Stefan got Matt on vervain as he said he would at the end of "Bad Moon Rising." Seeing as Katherine easily got Aunt Jenna off vervain and under compulsion, we can assume she did the same with young Mr. Donovan.

THE RULES: Since Katherine appears to enjoy licking blood off Mason's neck, it seems a vampire can drink the blood of a werewolf. According to the Aztec legend, the shaman limited the werewolf's shifting to the full moon by sealing it with the moonstone, which makes the stone a likely candidate for unsealing it. With the lunar tie lifted, a werewolf could turn whenever he wanted to, or never at all (according to Mason). Wolfsbane is poisonous to werewolves: it burns and sizzles the skin and consuming it leads to unpleasantness. Damon confirms what we assumed after Mason's swift recovery from the knife in the gut in "Memory Lane": werewolves heal quickly. According to Damon (though it's unclear how he knows this), a vampire cannot compel another supernatural creature (e.g., Katherine could not compel Mason). One surefire way to kill a werewolf and pretty much any other living creature: tear out his heart. With

Damon and Jeremy are not the first to use wolfsbane as a poison: it got its name from the Ancient Greeks who called it *lykotonon*, or wolf slaying, because they tipped their arrows with the plant when hunting wolves. Legend had it that the deadly plant, known as the "Queen of Poisons," was created by Hecate from the foaming saliva of the multi-headed monster-hound Cerberus. Most commonly found in the mountainous areas of the northern hemisphere, there are over 250 species of *Aconitum*, the most deadly (to humans, not just werewolves) being monkshood — a name sometimes used interchangeably with wolfsbane. Jeremy specifically mentions *Aconitum vulparia*, which is a yellow flowering plant (seen in "By the Light of the Moon") rather than the buttercup-blue of monkshood. Some legend suggests that wolfsbane encourages the werewolf to shift (like in *The Wolf Man*, see page 42). But it has also been identified in folklore as a repellent, hung on the door of a home or grown around a house to ward off werewolves (and sometimes vampires as well), and as way to prevent or reverse the shifting from human to wolf (as in the film *Ginger Snaps*) or to allow a werewolf to maintain his human rationality while in wolf form (as in the Harry Potter series). In the world of *The Vampire Diaries*, wolfsbane is to werewolves as vervain is to vampires.

just a touch, Bonnie is able to sense more than just whether someone is a vampire — she gets visions but isn't able to get direct answers to specific questions. Bonnie explains that when she disables a vampire with the brain-pain spell, she's actually repeatedly causing aneurysms from which the vampire quickly heals from then suffers again.

THE DIABOLICAL PLAN: Discovering the importance of the moonstone, Damon, Stefan, Jeremy, and Bonnie track it down and Elena finally retrieves it from the well. Damon tortures Mason for information but finds he has no more to give. When Damon tries to gloat over ruining her "master plan," Katherine reveals that while Mason might have been her plan A, she has an alphabet full of alternatives.

BITE MARKS: Bonnie disables Mason with a brain-pain spell; Damon knees him in the head to knock him out. Damon chokes Jeremy. Damon tortures Mason with a hot poker and wolfsbane, and finally he kills him by ripping his heart out. Exposed to so much vervain, Stefan passes out in the well, his skin burnt and blistered. Elena cuts her hand to feed him her blood. Compelled by Katherine, Jenna stabs herself in the gut.

PREVIOUSLY ON THE VAMPIRE DIARIES: Damon used a similar move to dispatch Bree in "Bloodlines," reaching into her chest and crushing her heart; here he tears Mason's out. In "You're Undead to Me," Elena decides the risk Stefan poses to her family is too great and she can't see him anymore. In "History Repeating," Stefan breaks up with Elena for the same reason. Here they both realize that the danger their relationship poses to their loved ones is too high.

MEANWHILE IN FELL'S CHURCH: Mrs. Flowers runs the boarding house where Stefan stays in the book series, rather than a charming B&B; the gang thinks she's a dotty old lady but learns there's more to her than meets the eye. Bonnie mistakes a vision of Katherine for one of Elena in *The Fury*, as Bonnie does in "Plan B" when her psychic moment shows her Mason and Elena kissing. Though generally less "judgey" in the books, Bonnie is still tentative about Damon, but she acknowledges that he is the lesser of two evils in *Dark Reunion*: "She knew he was dangerous; not as bad as Katherine had been, maybe, but bad." In *The Struggle*, Stefan is trapped in an abandoned well (by an enemy, he doesn't jump in willingly) and is rescued by Elena, Bonnie, Meredith, and Matt; Elena feeds Stefan her blood to revive her starving vampire boyfriend. In *The Struggle*, Damon compels Elena's Aunt Judith and it freaks Elena out (though book-Damon doesn't make Judith stab herself as Katherine does to Jenna). Like Katherine with her plans A through Z, Elena of the book series also valued a solid plan B whether she was planning school events, getting a boy, or figuring out who the evil Power was in Fell's Church.

OFF CAMERA: Of his onscreen lady love, Taylor Kinney told the *New York Post*'s PopWrap blog, "Nina as Katherine — she works it. What card doesn't she hold? What doesn't she know? She's got everything by the balls and has fun doing it. Even when she gets worked up over something Damon does, or she doesn't get her way, there's that smirk that makes you think she still knows something the rest of us don't." Filming that torture scene, however, was a little less enjoyable for the actor, as he told AOLTV.com: "It was like a marathon. I was in that chair for maybe 10 hours that day. They blocked it out over three separate pieces. We just shot the shit out of it. It was like an all-day thing. I slept for about two days afterwards." The scene where Jenna stabs herself, said Sara Canning, "was really messy. Really, really messy. But partially because with the blood you never really know what's going to happen. There was someone lying behind the counter and actually controlling it. We actually did everything in two takes, which is really not a lot when you're doing a stunt. We tried to get it right off the bat, because you only have so many resources, whether it's wardrobe or blood or timing. So it was really fun to shoot."

FOGGY MOMENTS: Caroline helps Bonnie lay Stefan on the ground but her hands don't sizzle from touching his vervain-drenched clothing.

MUSIC: This episode features the return of artists whose work has been on the show before, opening with The Script's "This = Love." (An instrumental cover of a Script song played in "The Return.") Volunteers set up for the masquerade ball at the Lockwood estate to "Tighten Up" by The Black Keys, who also had a song in "Friday Night Bites." Matt and Tyler talk about Caroline while The Temper Trap's "Science of Fear" plays; the band's first time on *TVD* was in "Lost Girls." Carol tells Tyler that Mason's gone and Stefan and Elena break up to "Wires" by Athlete, who also had a song in the previous episode.

QUESTIONS:
- Wolfsbane foaming in the mouth of a werewolf or a vampire sizzling in a well full of vervain? Which is the grossest moment on *TVD* since the Eye-Gouging Incident in "There Goes the Neighborhood"?
- What does Katherine need a werewolf for? (Other than for bed sport.)

- Mason hides the moonstone somewhere even Katherine would be hard-pressed to find. He tells her he doesn't trust anyone, but does he have a reason not to trust Katherine specifically?
- Will Elena and company finally tell Jenna what's really going on in Mystic Falls? It seems like the best way to protect Jenna is to tell her about Katherine and what she's capable of. Either that, or keep the secret and kill Katherine. . . .

❁

Jeremy: It's not just you anymore, Elena. She's messed with all of us — she has to be stopped.

2.07 Masquerade

Original air date: October 28, 2010
Written by: Kevin Williamson and Julie Plec
Directed by: Charles Beeson
Guest cast: Jackie Prucha (Ms. Flowers), Maiara Walsh (Sarah), Natashia Williams (Lucy)

An elaborate kill-Katherine plot is afoot at the masked ball, but Katherine has her own game in play.

Usually at masquerades, characters hide their true identity or self behind masks (think Romeo and Juliet at the Capulets' ball, free to fall in love), but at this masked ball most characters — united against a common enemy — are more grounded in their identities and purpose than ever. Katherine, posing as Elena, and her involuntary minions (Matt and Sarah, under compulsion) are the only ones who play into the usual masquerade antics.

Because everyone is deeply invested in defeating Katherine, their very unity made for what felt like an "event" episode, though one that is less emotionally driven than usual. There were so many shocking moments, quotable lines, twists and turns, new connections, and handsome men in suits in "Masquerade." But perhaps most impressive of all was how the writers managed to let so many characters share the spotlight in such a short amount of time. With the audience and Elena in the dark about how the plan would play out, "Masquerade" had the feel of a great caper film. Under Stefan's leadership, the gang's plan was clever and their misdirection believable as everyone played his or her part flawlessly. Well, almost everyone. The underused Alaric may have been able to take on a house full of tomb vamps last season, but now he can't even keep an eye on Elena for an evening.

Jeremy tells his sister that she's naive to think that everything will be back to normal if she just does what Katherine's asked. As she retreats into her human cocoon with Matt and Jenna and Jeremy and Alaric (her master plan is to take care of her aunt, order pizza, and watch bad TV), Elena is trying to reestablish the order of her universe, to shut down the chaos. Jeremy asks her what they're going to do, and she replies, "Make lunch." For Elena, the priority isn't justice or revenge, or personal happiness, it's the safety of her family. What she says to Matt about "so much . . . that will never work" in her relationship with Stefan may be about how far from "normal" they could ever be, regardless of Katherine. At the end of "Masquerade," Elena pushes Stefan away, telling him she needs to feel that her family is safe and that she is safe before she can be with him again. With her aunt just home from the hospital, with her brother joining the fight against Katherine without her knowledge, and with her body riddled with the injuries inflicted on her vampire twin, Elena's reluctance to leap right back into the relationship that introduced all things supernatural into her life is understandable. She's shell-shocked. Of course, after she's nabbed in the driveway, we remember that it's not just her relationship with Stefan that has put her in danger — it's who she is, who her parents are, her bloodline, the town she lives in, and almost every single one of her friends. What she said to Stefan in "The Turning Point" is truer than she realized then: "I know that you think you brought all this bad stuff into my life, but my life already had it. I was buried in it." Trouble was there before Stefan came into her life, and, to a degree, that fact becomes ever clearer as Elena learns more about her bloodline. Whoever she chooses to be with — a human, a vampire, or no one at all — there's no escaping the dangers in Mystic Falls. There is no quick fix, no escape from the darkness in Elena's life.

Lucy's spell that binds Katherine and Elena together made the tie that exists between them explicit just for duration of the episode. Besides being an incredibly clever way for Katherine to protect herself, it also foreshadows that the look-alikes share something far more significant than their appearance. As that tomb door closes, Katherine says that Elena is in danger and, as

the doppelgänger, she must be protected. From Elena's perspective (and consequently the audience's), Katherine is *her* doppelgänger. But Katherine was born first, which makes Elena the copy, the doppelgänger. What that means for Elena remains to be revealed, but it's a safe bet that both Elena's kidnapper and Katherine herself have a better understanding than we do yet of how they are connected, let alone what power or threat comes from that tie.

The doppelgänger issue — if Elena is in some way more than just a visual copy of Katherine — also further complicates the Salvatore brothers' already messy feelings for Katherine and Elena. Just as Elena's presence is felt when the boys can't attack Katherine without hurting Elena, Katherine's presence has always been a haunting image imprinted on the brothers' relationships with Elena. When Damon, Stefan, and Katherine are temporarily bound in that room by a spell, we see very clearly the emotional tie between the three,

one that binds them for eternity and would be there even if the brothers had actually killed Katherine. In filming this sequence, the director has almost always positioned Katherine in between the brothers to visually reinforce her role in their relationship: she drove them apart. They loved her and died fighting to save her; now they both risk their lives to protect Elena, another woman they both love, who has the power to either unite or divide them. As a master manipulator, Katherine knows how best to play with these tensions: she tries to hurt Damon by mocking his love for her and teases him by offering him a way to kiss Elena by kissing her. She takes the opposite approach with Stefan, trying again to convince him that she really does love him (which has the nice added effect of hurting Damon). It's a twisted situation.

But the Salvatore brothers united aren't so easily defeated. They've fought side by side before, but this fight is more emotionally significant than past battles. As Stefan says to Bonnie, this is about more than getting Elena back. Damon and Stefan's love for Katherine is what tore them apart; by fighting against her together, the brothers become closer than they've been in a century and a half. The brothers see Katherine's tactics for what they are but that doesn't necessarily render her strategy ineffective. Damon gives Stefan a pep talk when, with Aimee's death on his conscience, he wants to quit, and Stefan stops Damon from hurting Katherine (and Elena) when she taunts them about both loving the same woman. Never mind that a dead Katherine would drain a whole lot of diabolical awesomeness out of *The Vampire Diaries* equation, Damon's decision to opt for "something poetic" as a punishment (as he said he would in "The Return") is fitting. He puts her in the same tomb he believed she was in since 1864. From Damon's perspective, death *would* be too kind for the wrongs she's committed against him and his brother. Now that Katherine has been captured and her werewolf boyfriend killed, what will Damon turn his attention to? Protecting Elena?

It is awesome to see this seemingly omnipotent character tricked and disempowered. But though Katherine didn't plan on being entombed, her goals for the masquerade ball have still been met: moonstone retrieved, Tyler made a werewolf. As it turns out, Katherine really did have a Plan C. Sarah. Though we didn't get to know Sarah or Aimee beyond their shared love for drinking and dancing around the Lockwood mansion, their deaths were not without impact. Katherine's admirable precision in first paralyzing and then killing Aimee in plain view on the dance floor, just to make a point, goes down in *Vampire Diaries*' history as one of the best death scenes — an unexpected and horrifyingly casual public execution with Stefan left standing there, holding the girl's lifeless body. The expectation was building that Matt Donovan would die at his best friend's hand; Sarah dying instead was an effective twist and one that Matt's many fans appreciated. Katherine is willing to use and dispose of people as she requires — she compelled Matt to act in total opposition to his character, killed Aimee and (indirectly) Sarah, and played god in Tyler's life. She has proven to be as formidable a villain as she promised to be when she chopped off John Gilbert's fingers in "Founder's Day."

Family and legacy are central concerns of *The Vampire Diaries*, and Tyler always seemed to get the short end of the stick in both areas, despite the power and prestige his family has in Mystic Falls. In "Masquerade," Tyler and his mother have their first heartfelt conversation in which they acknowledge that

while Richard Lockwood could be an obstinate jerk, they both loved him. Carol wants her son to know that he's not alone, but like so many other characters on this show, he is isolated by the secrets he must keep, Mason's secret and, after Sarah's death, his own. This scene of fond and honest remembrance of Richard Lockwood makes Matt's later attack on his memory resonate. A friend is trusted to honor secrets, not to violate that trust by mocking the most painful truths. Matt picks a fight with Tyler by targeting the source of Tyler's pain and weakness in the way only a best friend could know how to do. This scene, like many others on *TVD*, echoes an earlier incident: last season at a swank Lockwood mansion party, a similarly off-kilter Tyler beat up Matt after making out with his mother ("Under Control"). It was painful to watch Matt torment Tyler by desecrating his father's study and reminding him of what a "dick" Mayor Lockwood could be to his son. In an act so unlike him it's frightening, Matt reminds Tyler that his father let him down and damaged him, much like Matt's mom did to him.

It's been a long slow build for Tyler Lockwood — and for Michael Trevino — but he's finally there: the curse has been activated and Tyler has wicked wolf eyes. *The Vampire Diaries* has showed us how new vampires must find their way or be helped by another (or they end up dead) but Tyler's alone and in uncharted territory. Will he head down to the Lockwood dungeon on the next full moon and lock himself up like his uncle did? Will he become an ally to the vampires — assuming he finds out they exist — or let the natural animosity between them continue? Crucial to that last question is Caroline. She's there in the study not only to save Matt, but she's there for Tyler. Again we see the characters connect in unexpected ways as "Masquerade" pairs these two. She knows more about what he's about to face than he does since she's just gone through her own transition from clueless human to supernatural killing machine. Their scene together is a standout in the episode. A vampire and a werewolf may be unlikely friends but *The Vampire Diaries* is all about turning expectations upside down.

Caroline's arc in "Masquerade" is about turning her own expectations of herself upside down. In a charming Caroline way, she tells Stefan and Damon about her encounter with Katherine at the Grill. She's uncertain, "quasi-stalking" Matt, afraid of Katherine, and literally shaking. Her attempt to trick Katherine in the women's room fails. Threatened and scared, Caroline suggests that they just hand over the moonstone to her. But in working with her friends and successfully pulling off her part of the plan, Caroline gains resolve. She surprises herself when she finally tricks Katherine into the room. As it turns out, Caroline's good in a crisis. She shows it in the way she handled Mason in the forest, the deputies in the cellar, and Stefan in the well. She figures out quickly what's going on in the study, knocks Matt out to stop him, and deals with her and Tyler's mothers, covering up what really happened to Sarah. Though Tyler feels responsible for Sarah's death, Caroline knows that Sarah and Matt were under compulsion. Not only is Caroline

Tiya Sircar as Aimee Bradley and Maiara Walsh as Sarah

Originally from Texas, Tiya Sircar has been gracing television screens on shows like *The Suite Life on Deck*, *House*, *Numb3rs*, *Greek*, and *NCIS* as well as movies like *17 Again*, *The Lost Medallion*, and *Friends with Benefits*. She describes her *Vampire Diaries* character Aimee Bradley as "really friendly" and a "party girl." Tiya admitted that, after flying into Atlanta from L.A. to work on the show, "It's a little bit daunting when you first show up to set and there are the most beautiful men you've ever seen all around." But the cast and crew were very welcoming and Tiya's experience shooting the show was "so much fun that it hardly feels like work for me." After Aimee came to a bad end on the dance floor, Tiya landed a role in *Georgetown*, a TV pilot executive-produced by *Gossip Girl* creators Josh Schwartz and Stephanie Savage.

In the role of Aimee's BFF Sarah is Maiara Walsh, an actress who grew up in Brazil and speaks fluent Portuguese. Best known for her role as Ana Solis on *Desperate Housewives*, Maiara has also appeared on *Unfabulous*, *Cory in the House*, *The Secret Life of the American Teenager*, and *Mean Girls 2*. In her spare time, Maiara spends her time working with nonprofits and charitable organizations in an effort to "create positive change no matter where we are or what our circumstances may be."

---

more confident and capable than she once thought herself to be, but she's proving to be empathetic and resourceful too.

Jeremy also seems to have hit his stride, and the masquerade acts like a debut for him, his bid to be recognized as someone who makes his own decisions (whether or not his big sis approves). Jeremy has a driver's license, isn't a kid anymore, and can wear the hell out of a suit. He's accepted his family legacy, but he's found his own way to be a Gilbert, a way that he believes in.

Just as Caroline and Tyler are a new interesting pairing, Bonnie and Jeremy spending time together reveals their common ground and how desperately they both need someone — who isn't Elena or a vampire — who gets what they're going through. Both have lost loved ones and have felt isolated from those closest to them. Bonnie and Jeremy both instinctively want to fight the good fight; they just can't stay out of it. It'll be interesting to watch their dynamic develop, whether or not this episode's flirtation turns to romance.

Jeremy's interest in Bonnie's witchcraft also gives her an opportunity to open up. While he somewhat childishly thinks it's "cool" and considers the everyday, self-serving applications of a little hocus pocus, Bonnie sees her power as a burden she was born with, something that all but guarantees her a bad end. The first Bonnie-heavy episode in a long time, "Masquerade" proves that she is invaluable in the plan against Katherine. It is Bonnie who casts the spell on the room, who figures out why Elena's injuries are appearing out of thin air, and who, incredibly, uses Katherine's own witch to defeat her. In successfully forging an alliance with Lucy, Bonnie realizes that though she'll never have Grams back, she's not alone. There are other witches in her family who can provide direction and guidance. Lucy's loyalty to her family (and to the larger family of witches) overrides her connection to Katherine: she finds a way to technically pay her debt, simultaneously betraying Katherine. A witch controlled by vampires, like Emily Bennett was, Lucy doesn't think of herself as one of the "good ones" — like Bonnie and Grams who were independent. In the world of *TVD*, it seems that witches are often pulled reluctantly into vampire problems, usually in payment of a debt, or through some other involuntary bond. Though Lucy doesn't stick around, what she says to Bonnie seems like it will have a lasting effect on her: right in the middle of the fight is where she *should* be. Bonnie tells Jeremy she hates being torn between the desire to protect people and the desire to stay out of vampire problems, but Lucy's comment resonates with her and may help her come to terms with the role she plays in the Salvatore brothers' master plans. Because she will undoubtedly be called on again. While there were many charades on both sides of the fight in "Masquerade" it was ultimately the witches who held the true power and it will be their strength that decides which side will see victory.

COMPELLING MOMENT: Elena reacting to the stake in Katherine's back; the brothers try to kill Katherine and end up nearly killing the doppelgänger they love.

CIRCLE OF KNOWLEDGE:
- Katherine wears her daylight necklace on her wrist as a bracelet.
- Katherine spied on Stefan as he and Lexi attended a Bon Jovi concert; the band played Chicago's Rosemont Horizon (now the Allstate Arena) four times in the spring of 1987 on its Slippery When Wet tour. In "Fool Me Once," Anna says she saw Katherine in Chicago in 1983; perhaps Katherine spent most of the '80s in Chi Town.

The Vampire Diaries: Original Television Soundtrack — Song by Scene

- "RUNNING UP THAT HILL" — PLACEBO
  Uncle Zach asks Stefan why he came back to Mystic Falls ("Pilot").
- "CURRENCY OF LOVE" — SILVERSUN PICKUPS
  The Lockwood boys show off their arm wrestling skills at the carnival ("Brave New World").
- "HAMMOCK" — HOWLS
  Damon goads Mason with a punny game of Pictionary ("Memory Lane").
- "SLEEP ALONE (909s in the Dark Times Mix)" — BAT FOR LASHES
  Vicki and Jeremy make out at the Halloween party as Elena searches for them ("Haunted").
- "BLOODSTREAM (Vampire Diaries Remix)" — STATELESS
  Damon kisses Katherine on the Gilbert front porch, thinking she's Elena ("Founder's Day").
- "WE RADIATE" — GOLDFRAPP
  Elena and Caroline listen to the radio in the car on the way to Stefan's ("Memory Lane").
- "OBSESSION" — SKY FERREIRA
  Tyler, Jeremy, Aimee, and Sarah party at the Lockwood mansion ("Kill or Be Killed").
- "HEAD OVER HEELS" — DIGITAL DAGGERS
  Katherine and Stefan dance at the ball ("Masquerade").
- "DOWN" — JASON WALKER
  Elena breaks down after telling Stefan she can't be with him ("Lost Girls").
- "BEAUTY OF THE DARK" — MADS LANGER
  Damon attacks Vicki in the Mystic Falls cemetery as the song plays over the end-of-episode montage ("You're Undead to Me").
- "CUT" — PLUMB
  Stefan and Elena have sex for the first time ("The Turning Point").
- "ALL YOU WANTED" — SOUNDS UNDER RADIO FT. ALISON SUDOL
  Elena gets a call from Jeremy who tells her Vicki's body has been discovered ("Let the Right One In").
- "THE FELLOWSHIP" — SMASHING PUMPKINS
  In flashback, Mason Lockwood accidentally kills a man in a Florida parking lot ("Kill or Be Killed").
- "ON MELANCHOLY HILL (Feed Me Remix)" — GORILLAZ
  Matt, Tyler, Aimee, and Sarah do shots in Mayor Lockwood's study ("Masquerade").

- Caroline's control over her bloodlust is getting stronger and stronger: in "Plan B" she turns away when Elena slices her hand open, but in this episode she doesn't react to Matt's blood or Tyler's.

- The only upside to Elena getting kidnapped: if she had gone to the doctor for her injuries, alarm bells would start ringing at Mystic Falls General. First, John Gilbert shows up with severed fingers and a stab wound, then Jenna with another stab wound, then Elena with mysteriously acquired injuries.
- Poor Carol Lockwood. After having a girl die at her party, she's going to discover that completely trashed room that Katherine and the boys tussled in. But here's guessing she won't be deterred from hosting countless events in the future.

THE RULES: Lucy and Bonnie can sense each other, similar to how a witch can sense someone is a vampire by touching them. Bonnie is able to do a healing spell on Elena, something she was not capable of in "The Return" when Caroline was in critical condition. (Perhaps she's been studying up, to ensure that vampire blood isn't the only option for her friends when they inevitably get hurt.) The spell binding the vampires in the room at the Lockwoods' is similar to the tomb spell. As we learned last season, one witch can't override another witch's spell; Bonnie can't undo the spell that was binding Katherine and Elena just like Lucy couldn't undo the spell trapping Katherine in the room.

THE DIABOLICAL PLAN: Katherine is after the moonstone, which Lucy thinks she wants in order to break the Sun and Moon Curse herself. To ensure her safety while she gets it, Katherine has Lucy cast a spell, so that any injury Katherine sustains is also inflicted on Elena. Displaying his excellent detective skills and his predilection for pointing, Stefan puts together a few more pieces of the Katherine puzzle. Back in 1864, Katherine faked her death to escape whoever was after her; she gave the moonstone to George Lockwood in exchange for him arranging her release from the church before it burned. Katherine blames Damon's 145-year quest to get her out of the tomb she wasn't in for potentially exposing her to those who want her dead . . . again. The moonstone wasn't hers to give away, and now it seems whomever she took it from wants it back — and maybe wants her dead too. Compared to that (though it involves misdirection, binding spells, and an arsenal of weaponry), the master plan of Stefan and company is pretty simple: kill Katherine.

BITE MARKS: Lucy gets thrown against the wall for sneaking up on Katherine. Katherine kills Aimee by snapping her spine then her neck. Katherine slams Caroline into the wall, chokes her, and drags her along by the hair. The Salvatore brothers fight Katherine, and her wounds are also experienced by Elena, who is staked in the back, slashed on the arm, and gets a nice slice on her hand courtesy of Katherine. Under compulsion, Matt fights with Tyler. Caroline knocks Matt out. Sarah stabs Tyler with a letter opener, and he accidentally kills her. Elena is set upon by a kidnapper in the parking lot.

PREVIOUSLY ON THE VAMPIRE DIARIES: Jeremy was just as fascinated by Anna's vampire abilities ("Blood Brothers") as he is with Bonnie's witchcraft.

MEANWHILE IN FELL'S CHURCH: In *Dark Reunion*, Tyler Smallwood is indirectly responsible for killing a girl he goes to school with, which activates his hereditary werewolf virus.

OFF CAMERA: This is Charles Beeson's first time directing an episode of *The Vampire Diaries*; he is a regular for *The Mentalist*, *Supernatural*, and *Fringe* and his extensive list of directorial credits extends back to a handful of 1992 episodes of the British soap *East Enders*. The performers at the masquerade ball are part of Atlanta's Imperial Opa Circus, which combines a love of fire-eating with charitable work and fundraising. On October 22, Julie Plec tweeted, "Bonnie's on a very specific journey and we'll start to understand more of her pain soon."

FOGGY MOMENTS: Katherine says "hot" three too many times in this episode. . . . If Katherine compelled Matt to fight Tyler until Tyler kills him, will Matt try to fight Tyler again when he comes to? Or was there an (unseen) escape clause that if Tyler kills someone else, Matt can lay off? In "Fool Me Once," Grams opened the door to the tomb, and then Bonnie insisted they temporarily take down the seal so Stefan could get out. Grams and Bonnie tried to put the seal back up but were unsuccessful. The rest of the vampires leave the tomb because the seal is gone. How did the tomb seal get back up? Did Bonnie do it?

MUSIC: Cruel Black Dove's cover of the Psychedelic Furs' "Love My Way" kicks off the masquerade ball. Sarah, Aimee, Tyler, and Matt party in the study to "On Melancholy Hill (Feed Me Remix)" by Gorillaz, a song that appears on the first *TVD* soundtrack. Stefan agrees to dance with Katherine to another cover of an '80s song, Digital Daggers' version of Tears for Fears' "Head Over Heels" (also on the soundtrack). Damon talks Stefan back into carrying out the plan while Morning Parade's "Under the Stars" plays. Caroline and Matt exchange a longing look across the party to "People Change" by Joel & Luke. Bonnie searches for Lucy to "Fire in Your New Shoes" by Kaskade featuring Dragonette. Elena tells Stefan that she's not ready to get back together to Tawgs Salter's "Brave."

QUESTIONS:

- When Lucy asks Katherine if she's going to break the curse, does she mean the werewolf-tied-to-the-moon curse? Why would she want that? Is a werewolf the only thing deadly enough to take out whoever's on Katherine's tail? Who is Katherine running from?
- How and when did Katherine save Lucy's life?
- Why did the brothers leave the moonstone with Katherine in the tomb? Is the tomb the safest place for it? Will the moonstone soon be used as a bargaining chip once again, forcing that tomb door open and allowing Katherine to get some fresh air and fresh blood?
- If Katherine was telling the truth when she told Damon that Elena has to be protected, she was playing a pretty dangerous game with the spell tying them together. What if Bonnie hadn't figure out what was happening to Elena so quickly? They could have both been killed. Does Katherine only care about Elena surviving as long as she is living too?
- Was Lucy the witch who made Isobel's daylight jewelry?
- As far as we've learned so far, Emily Bennett stayed loyal to Katherine and helped to keep her from death with the tomb spell and crystal. What did Damon mean when he said to Katherine that she should have learned her lesson "messing with a Bennett witch"?

Damon: So noble, Stefan.
Stefan: I can't think of a better reason to die.

2.08 *Rose*

Original air date: November 4, 2010
Written by: Brian Young
Directed by: Liz Friedlander
Guest cast: Russell Comegys (Man)

Elena's kidnappers teach her some vampire history. Tyler tries to get the truth out of Caroline. Bonnie gets a significant nosebleed. Elijah makes a first impression not soon forgotten.

Elena is one of the only characters on *The Vampire Diaries* who doesn't suffer from being alone — she's got more love and attention than a girl can handle, friends and family who are unfailingly loyal, and more than one handsome vampire who can't think of a better reason to die than in saving her life. Her story arc in "Rose" — alone in a strange place with kidnappers, the discovery of new information about her identity, a homecoming with friends and family — is one that's echoed in less literal ways across the rest of the characters as they struggle with isolation and fear and find the key to overcoming it in companionship and family.

Back when Bonnie was first realizing she was an actual, factual witch, her Grams told her of witchcraft, "It's real and it's serious. You must understand it before you use it" ("Haunted"). Grams died before she could properly teach Bonnie about her power, and now Bonnie feels isolated and distanced from her friends. But what began in "Masquerade," with Bonnie reaching out to Lucy, develops more fully in "Rose." Bonnie's finally getting the kind of well-rounded characterization that will make her more than a tertiary character, a deus ex machina. In an interesting addition to the witchcraft lore, Bonnie reveals to Jeremy that there are limits to her powers. When she pushes too hard, she suffers physical consequences: a bloody nose, lost consciousness, and who knows what else if she keeps pushing. She opens up to Jeremy about her "weakness." Of course, he understands how alone she feels. Since the beginning of the show, Jeremy has struggled to find meaningful relationships, and those that he does find tend to end badly. The flicker of romance that began in the previous episode continues as Jeremy takes an interest in Bonnie — he pulls the telltale stare-at-her-sleeping move, a sure sign of a crush — and Bonnie is responding to his companionship and understanding. It certainly wouldn't be the first time that an older girl fell for Jeremy: Vicki had a couple of years on him, Anna a couple hundred. Jeremy is paying attention to Bonnie in a way that the other characters aren't. He sees the effect that witchcraft has on her, and he won't accept her insistence that "it's nothing." His persistence results in Bonnie's confession, a secret that now ties them together. Stuck at the Gilbert house with no way to help the Salvatores rescue Elena, Bonnie and Jeremy both realize that with all that has happened they don't know that Elena *will* be okay. But Bonnie realizes that they have the power to do what friends and family are always able to do for a loved one in need. They send a message that, besides being cool and witchy, takes away Elena's isolation and gives her hope and strength.

Despite a very stern command from Damon that Caroline stay away from Tyler Lockwood, she finds it impossible. Tyler is all alone with his secret and sees Caroline as the only person who can help him. The Tyler-Caroline scenes in this episode hit that great *TVD* mix of humor and intensity. Seeing Tyler accidentally rip the lock off his school locker or Caroline burst into giggles after Tyler's super-serious "I know what you are" speech gave this episode its moments of levity, while the makeshift memorial in front of Sarah's locker and the missing person notices for Aimee Bradley were reminders of the "collateral damage" and darkness that exist in Mystic Falls. Caroline meets Tyler's persistence and violent outbursts with a display of her own power, while her strong feelings of sympathy for the guy push her to take the great risk (to herself and the Salvatore brothers) of revealing her secret to Tyler. Every storyline in this episode touched on feelings of isolation and connection with others; Caroline and Tyler were no exception. He opens up in a way we've never seen before. Compare Tyler admitting his fear to Caroline here to his reactions last season when Jeremy tried to talk to him about Vicki or his father. Tyler feels guilty for killing Sarah, even though he didn't mean to, even though Caroline reassures him that it wasn't his fault. Hopefully Caroline can be there for Tyler as he struggles with his new supernatural identity, the way Stefan was there for her. Just as the new revelations about witchcraft in "Rose" created surprising new depth in Bonnie's character, the mythology serves to build the characters up rather than overshadow them: the werewolf and the vampire find common ground despite being natural enemies.

While last season focused closely on Mystic Falls, season 2 is opening up the story to the world that lies beyond its confines, and "Rose" is an exciting (though rather exposition-filled) episode for those into the lore of the *vampyre*. Rose and Trevor are old vampires compared to the Salvatore brothers but nothing compared to the Originals — the vampires' Founding Family. The calm, suit-wearing, head-removing, stakes-won't-kill-him Elijah brings an air of the Old World to what he calls the "armpit of civilization." Possessing an "old school" code of honor and a propensity for extreme violence dealt swiftly and with absolute composure, Elijah is remarkably unemotional (at least on the surface) and unlike any character seen on *The Vampire Diaries* before. Despite the general free-for-all we've witnessed so far, it seems there are laws or a code of behavior that governs the vampires, and that is taken very seriously by Elijah. A promise must be honored, loyalty is respected, forgiveness may be granted without a pardon. Rose fails to realize that Elijah did not promise to spare Trevor's life: part of what makes Elijah fearful is his capacity to be simultaneously a man of honor, of ultra-violence, and of cunning.

There's been danger, mortal peril, and high stakes but the introduction of these three new characters and the mythology they bring with them immediately ups the intensity of the story. Never mind the epic decapitation, the cavalier way they treat Elena, the heart of the show, demonstrates just how different things are outside of Mystic Falls. These vampires neither know nor love nor even respect Elena; they're not tied to her as a person in any way — she's simply the doppelgänger and Rose doesn't hesitate to smack Elena into silence when she refuses to do as she's told. Elijah discards Elena's precious vervain necklace and compels her. Meanwhile, Elena realizes that some of the strongest vampires she's ever met are frankly terrified of an Original. By the end of the episode, we see Elijah as a deadly force who's not so dead and who now knows there's a Petrova doppelgänger to hunt down as well as the location of both the moonstone and Katherine.

The previous Petrova doppelgänger may be a habitual liar but it turns out she wasn't lying when she told Damon that Elena was in danger. Getting kidnapped in the Lockwood driveway seems like small potatoes next to being the key to undoing the whole mysterious curse. That Katherine is not the original but a doppelgänger herself was a genius twist that opens the door for another doppelgänger in the future as well as for the unknown Original Petrova — of whom both Katherine and Elena are copies — who could appear in a future flashback or who could be a vampire herself and among the Originals. This new revelation about the doppelgänger mythology builds Katherine's origin story and completely alters the relationship between Katherine and Elena. They are doubles more than just physically. Elena is now in the very same life-threatening danger that Katherine found herself in 500 years ago; her number-one enemy just became the person who can understand her situation and advise her best.

It would seem that the bond that can develop between two vampires over hundreds of years is almost incomprehensible from a mortal viewpoint. Rose and Trevor have been together, and on the run, for 500 years (and who knows how long before that). Their loyalty to one another came with life-or-death consequences. While it wasn't explicitly stated, they seem not to be related by blood but they were nonetheless family, forever, because of the special strength of their bond. What gives them strength, and the courage to meet with Elijah, is their friendship and loyalty to one another. A silent observer of their familial tie, Elena responds to and understands that rela-tionship — it was fitting that she returned home to both Jeremy and Bonnie — and she opts to let Rose go free, the woman who had her kidnapped and was willing to give her over to her "worst nightmare." It's the kind of shady moral ground that we're often standing on in *The Vampire Diaries*: protect-ing your loved ones at any cost often has deadly consequences for someone else's loved ones. The lengths to which someone will go for those they love is a familiar theme on this show. Bonnie willingly suffers the physical effects of witchcraft to help save Elena; Stefan and Damon both would die trying to save her; Rose stood by Trevor no matter what; and he risked his life, and ultimately lost it, for Katherine. Rose spent 500 years on the lam with her best friend. Trevor's death leaves her completely alone and, now that she's been absolved of her crime by Elijah, purposeless. Without a companion, Rose offers to help the Salvatore brothers protect Elena from Klaus and from the legions of vampires eager to give him what he wants. Will her mention of Lexi — the best friend that Stefan lost — be enough to make him trust that she's also "one of the good ones"?

Rose and Trevor were tired of literally being on the run from the Originals. In this episode, Stefan and then Damon decide to stop running from the things they don't want to admit, and they give a pair of memorable speeches, one from each brother. Just as Tyler pushes Caroline and Jeremy pushes Bonnie to admit to the secrets they're holding, Stefan tries to get his brother to talk to him about the "elephant" between them: Damon's love for Elena. Unwilling to open up — at least not to his brother — Damon redirects the conversation to focus on the thing Stefan's not so proud of: his past violence and buried aggression. The brother-bonding conversations culminate in a moment in the Salvatore library with a simple and heartfelt apology in which Stefan acknowledges what he did that got Damon into this immortal vampire mess in the first place. He admits why he did it: he didn't want to live without his brother by his side. The Salvatore brothers' relationship has evolved since last season, and their time together in "Rose" shows that despite the complications and challenges they face, they're family — forever — tied by their shared history, their loyalty to each other, and their brotherly love.

Stefan admits that he acted selfishly in making Damon turn — like Tyler, Bonnie, Rose, and Jeremy in this episode, Stefan didn't want to be alone. And in light of that admission, Damon decides to echo his brother's speech. Before returning Elena's necklace, the necklace that serves as a symbol of her relationship with Stefan, Damon allows himself a selfish moment — the catharsis of actually admitting his love to Elena — and then he acts nobly. He puts his own feelings second and admits that he doesn't deserve her love the way his brother does. In his act of selflessness, he demonstrates the emotional lengths to which he would go for her (far more difficult for him than staking an Original). Though Elena doesn't know it, Damon becomes more deserving of her love — and ours. It was a mere seven episodes ago (much less than a month in *Vampire Diaries* time) that Damon stood in that same room and killed Jeremy, and here he makes a personal sacrifice in order to better protect Elena from being sacrificed. In the car on their way to save Elena, Stefan tells his brother that he gave up his bloodthirsty ways when he found something else to live for and, in Elena, he's found someone he's willing to die for. But for Damon, his love for Elena and his willingness to die for her goes unrequited. Though she is grateful to him, ultimately Damon is all alone.

COMPELLING MOMENT: This episode's is literally a moment of compulsion — Damon making Elena forget his declaration of love.

CIRCLE OF KNOWLEDGE:
- No Jenna, Matt, or Alaric this episode.
- Trevor's car has North Carolina plates.

- As nice as it was to see the halls of Mystic Falls High again, the stunning and creepy derelict plantation estate where Rose and Trevor are camped out is perhaps the coolest location ever on *The Vampire Diaries*.
- Rose's favorite fictional vampire is Alice Cullen. Or at least that's what her haircut suggests.
- Tyler's slam dunk seemed like a nod to 1985's *Teen Wolf*, whose teenage werewolf (Michael J. Fox) was an ace on the basketball court.
- Elijah's name means "Yahweh is God" or "strength of God." Elijah was a prophet in the Hebrew Bible's Books of Kings who challenged the reigning king to recognize the true god, worked miracles of judgment and healing, and was the key to Jezebel's downfall.
- Bonnie uses some of Elena's hair in her spell to contact her. It is commonly thought in witchcraft that hair (as well as nails and blood) contains the magical essence of a person; hair is also connected to psychic protection. The hair of an intended target is often taken in advance in order to cast or break spells on the target whenever desired.
- What Bonnie explains to Jeremy about pushing too hard and receiving "blowback" from using magic is an idea analogous to the Wiccan Threefold Law of Return, where an action is answered but magnified three times. Also called the Rule of Three, it is a disincentive to use dark magic, as the evil would return upon the witch in three times the magnitude. That law, like the one in *The Vampire Diaries*, controls the balance between a witch, her power, and the magical universe.

THE RULES: This week on *The Vampire Diaries*, we learned another way to kill a vampire: chop off his head. Very efficient. Just like the other supernatural creatures on *TVD*, witches have rules that bind them. There is a price to pay for doing witchcraft; if Bonnie does too much, she will be physically incapacitated. Bonnie performs two spells that she hasn't done before. The first is a tracking spell involving Jeremy's blood (though he's not biologically her brother, Jeremy is Elena's first cousin), candles, and a map. The second is a "send a message to your bestie in danger" spell (probably not what it's called in the grimoire . . .). Expanding on the established idea that vampires grow stronger with age, the Originals cannot be killed as easily as your garden-variety vamp, with a wooden stake (or coat rack) through the heart.

Lauren Cohan as Rose

Born in 1982 in Philadelphia, Lauren Cohan grew up in New Jersey before moving to the U.K. She studied drama and English literature at King Alfred's College at the University of Winchester, where she cofounded a theater company. With it, she toured before moving to London "to try and get one of our plays shown," explains Lauren. "And at that time, I went to meet with an agent, so did one of the other guys in the group and we both were successful in getting films in a few weeks. So we were like, 'We'll do [the play] in the spring, or in the summer,' but then things just kind of got off the ground with films and TV stuff. I really miss doing stage though, I really do." Lauren split her time between London and Los Angeles as she built her acting résumé with projects like *Casanova* (opposite Heath Ledger), *Van Wilder 2*, *Valentine*, *Float*, *Life*, *CSI: NY*, *Cold Case*, *Death Race 2*, and *Young Alexander the Great*. The role of Bela Talbot in season 3 of *Supernatural* was her first recurring character on a TV show, and Lauren wondered, when she landed the part of Rose, if supernatural shows on The CW would become her thing. But a role on *Chuck* (playing Vivian) mixed it up for the actress. The CW wasn't ready to let Lauren go, though: the network cast her in a pilot called *Heavenly* in which she plays a lawyer who works alongside an "ex-angel."

Says Lauren of *The Vampire Diaries*, "For me [growing up], it was *My So-Called Life* and *Dawson's Creek* and they were my kind of emotional, and it made sense for what I was going through. This generation does that with vampires and action. Paul, Nina, and Ian are just gorgeous and really good. It was fun to watch the scenes I wasn't filming." Lauren chopped off her hair for the role and found playing an "unglamorous" role a refreshing change: "It gave me a chance to explore things I hadn't gotten to before . . . It liberates me. Rose wasn't about being glamorous, she was about genuine friendship."

THE DIABOLICAL PLAN: Rose and Trevor hoped to make a bargain with Elijah: they hand off the doppelgänger and news of Katherine being alive in return for Elijah's pardon. Elena's very existence as a Petrova doppelgänger means that any vampire who knows about her will try to take her to Klaus, an Original more fearful than Elijah.

HISTORY LESSON: The Originals are the founding family of the vampires, the very first and most powerful. An Aztec shaman placed the curse on vampires and werewolves 600 years ago (or so goes the legend from "Bad Moon Rising"). According to Rose, the first Petrova doppelgänger (Katherine) appeared on the scene 500 years ago; and Elena, another doppelgänger, popped up in present day.

BITE MARKS: The man who was compelled to kidnap Elena is killed by Trevor. Rose hits Elena to shut her up. Bonnie slices Jeremy's hand for the spell. Bonnie suffers as a result of her spells, a nosebleed and a blackout. Caroline twists Tyler's arm and throws him to the ground. Tyler kicks a garbage can real hard. At the Forbes house, Tyler attacks Caroline and she retaliates. Elijah decapitates Trevor. Damon and Stefan attack Elijah, Elena vervain-bombs him, Elijah overpowers Stefan (after Stefan goes to town on him with a stake gun), and finally Damon stakes him through the heart with a coat rack. But Elijah cannot be beaten. . . .

PREVIOUSLY ON THE VAMPIRE DIARIES: This is Elena's second kidnapping, the first was by Anna ("Children of the Damned," "Fool Me Once"); in both instances she wakes up in the lair of her captors. Grams used a locator spell to find Elena and Bonnie in "Fool Me Once," like Bonnie does to find Elena. Damon and Elena went on a rescue operation to save Stefan in "Let the Right One In," and they took Damon's sweet car; it's back as Damon and Stefan save Elena. In "Under Control," Tyler tells Kelly Donovan that he has no one to talk to, and he says it again to Caroline in this episode. After the fight with Elijah, Stefan steps in front of Damon to embrace Elena. The moment plays like the reverse of Katherine's dream for Stefan in "Memory Lane" where Damon stepped in front of him as he approached Elena at the Grill. At the end of "Isobel," Isobel confessed to Alaric that she still loved him and regretted her decision to become a vampire, then erased his memory and returned his protective jewelry and vervain; here Damon makes a confession to Elena before compelling her to forget and returning her vervain necklace.

MEANWHILE IN FELL'S CHURCH: In *Dark Reunion*, Bonnie uses blood and hair in a spell to contact Stefan and ask him to return to Fell's Church; in this episode, Bonnie uses blood to find Elena and hair to send a message to her. There is a physical side effect to doing magic in the book series too; Bonnie scares Matt and Meredith by passing out after doing the summoning spell in *Dark Reunion*. Also in *Dark Reunion*, the concept of the Originals, or Old Ones, is introduced when Tyler Smallwood explains that Klaus is one, a vampire who has been around since ancient times. Like Elijah in this episode, Tyler says of the Originals, "You could stick a stake in his heart and it wouldn't do anything." The Originals are cloaked in mystery, the "ones who hadn't been made. They were where the line of continuity [from each vampire to his or her maker] stopped. No one knew how they'd gotten to be vampires themselves. But their Powers were legendary."

OFF CAMERA: Liz Friedlander, who directed this episode, also directed last season's "Unpleasantville" and "Blood Brothers." In addition to working on *90210, Pretty Little Liars, One Tree Hill,* and directing the dance movie *Take the Lead* (2006), Liz was at the helm of the pilot episode of *Secret Circle,* a project adapted from the L.J. Smith book series of the same name for The CW. The moment of relief for Bonnie when Elena returns home safe and the girls hug in the hallway was a standout scene for Kat Graham: "That scene didn't have any words for me but just having that kind of bond with Nina, [it's] probably one of my favorite moments just because it's so real for me. That was probably one of my favorite moments that I've shot."

FOGGY MOMENTS: Jeremy tells Stefan that Jenna's "cool" about his relationship with Elena, but that Elena sleeping over at Stefan's is pushing their luck. In "Plan B," Jenna told Stefan she overheard them in Elena's room (*awkward*). In "You're Undead to Me," Jenna knows that 15-year-old Jeremy has a girl, Vicki, in his room and is fine with it. But in "Children of the Damned" Jenna tells Stefan to keep Elena's bedroom door open so there's no funny business. What exactly are Jenna's rules when it comes to frisky teenagers?

MUSIC: Caroline relates the Tyler situation to Damon while Dragonette's "We Rule the World" plays. (Dragonette was also featured in "The Night of the Comet," and on Kaskade's song in the previous episode.) Tyler approaches Caroline to the very appropriately selected "Wolf Like Me" by TV On the Radio. In Damon's car, the Editors' "Blood" is on the radio (in "Lost Girls," another Editors song played over a Damon-Stefan scene). After having a song in "Brave New World," Andrew Belle is back with "In My Veins," which plays as Jeremy takes care of Bonnie post-blackout. Stefan tells Damon about his human blood consumption to "Love Song" by Cruel Black Dove (who had a song in "Masquerade" as well). Elena arrives home to a relieved Bonnie and Jeremy to The Afters' "Ocean Wide." Damon returns Elena's necklace to her, confesses his love, and then compels her to forget it all to "I Was Wrong" by Sleeperstar.

QUESTIONS:

- A question with a sure-to-be-interesting answer: if an Original cannot be killed with a regular stake through the heart, what does it take to kill one?
- How did Rose and Trevor find out that Katherine was in Mystic Falls, or even that there was another Petrova doppelgänger?
- Elijah was certain (until he gave Elena's neck a good sniffing) that the Petrova line had ended with Katherine. Why did he consider that a fact?
- What was Trevor's relationship to the Originals before he betrayed them? Why did he owe them his loyalty?
- Rose asks Elijah if he has the "authority" to grant a pardon and he says he does. What is the power structure amongst the oldest of the old?
- Why are the Originals chasing down the doppelgänger *for* Klaus — is there something preventing him from doing it himself?

❀

> *Katherine: I was looking out for myself, Elena. I will always look out for myself. If you're smart, you'll do the same.*

2.09 *Katerina*

Original air date: November 11, 2010
Written by: Andrew Chambliss
Directed by: J. Miller Tobin
Guest cast: Sandra Lafferty (Old Farm Woman), Trevor Peterson (Slater), Oleg Sapoundjieva (Father Petrova), Sia Sapoundjieva (Mother Petrova)

Bribed with a little blood, Katherine answers Elena's questions about Klaus and the curse. Damon and Rose go on their own fact-finding mission, while Bonnie flirts with the new man-witch in town.

Legends, rumor, centuries-old secrets, and lies — in "Katerina," the characters try to distinguish fact from fiction. Damon can't yet tell if Rose is trustworthy; Elena turns to a known liar for the truth; Caroline attempts to dupe Stefan into staying away from Elena, who doesn't want him to know she's turned to Katherine for help anyway; there's more to the Martin family

of warlocks' relocation to Mystic Falls than Bonnie or the rest of them know; Stefan vows to keep from Damon Caroline's little slip to Tyler that she's a vampire; and Slater is lying like a rug, thanks to Elijah's compulsion. It's in this atmosphere of duplicity that loyalty and friendship stand out, among humans and the supernatural, despite the mountain of evidence that suggests "caring gets you dead."

When Damon scoffs at Slater's choice to be the perpetual college student, Slater counters with an important question: how *should* he spend his eternity? It's this question that each vampire faces — will they go it alone, prioritizing their own survival, needs, and wants over everyone else's or will they choose to honor the bonds of family and love? Will they turn off their emotions or embrace them? Trevor embraced his — he metaphorically lost his head in his love for Katerina and, knowing the risk, helped her escape from Klaus. He also knew the bond he shared with Rose was unbreakable: she would help him help Katerina, no matter the cost. While Rose and Trevor's friendship lasted for over five centuries, Rose is just starting to build trust with Damon. She helped by taking him to Richmond, she shows insight into his feelings for Elena, and their impulsive fireside romp suggests the potential for something more. Just as Rose compares her new friend to her dearly departed Trevor, Stefan tells Caroline that she reminds him of Lexi, his recently murdered best friend ("162 Candles"). Stefan has helped Caroline find her way as a newbie vampire, encouraging her to be an "emotions on" kind of vamp and a loyal and loving friend. In "Katerina," Caroline is in an uncomfortable predicament, thanks to her two new friendships, with Stefan and with Tyler. She is forced to lie to them both — to protect Tyler and to honor her promise to Elena — but she still manages to be earnest and open with them. Though it's not often recognized, Caroline possesses integrity, regretting her deceptions but doing what she feels is necessary.

With its heartrending opening sequence, "Katerina" announces that our understanding of the character of Katherine Pierce, which has been growing since we first met her in "Lost Girls," has been built on a mere fragment of her story. Katherine's narrative, told to her doppelgänger who now faces the same decisions Katerina did over five centuries ago, is of a girl becoming a ruthless survivor. In the tomb, Katherine is cool and detached as she tells the tale of her past "shame" to Elena, but the raw portrait of the teenage Katerina, who begs to hold her baby just once before she's taken from her, reveals a different side of the character. Disowned by her family and banished from her country, Katerina Petrova adapted quickly to a foreign land and language. The traditional concepts associated with motherhood, the selflessness inherent in considering a child's needs before one's own, are in opposition to the Katherine we now see entombed. The fact that Katerina became someone who would betray those who love her without hesitation is less surprising now that we know how savagely all love was taken from her — her family didn't consider their bond with her to be unconditional. Then to be further punished by Klaus, slated for sacrifice, hunted, and her family murdered in punishment for her escape. Katerina has imitated the actions perpetrated against her, threatening Elena's loved ones because she knows that horror personally. Love has never been a permanent bond in Katherine's life, and she doesn't hesitate to take advantage of those who love her or are of use to her; she scoffs at the idea of loyalty and selflessness.

This glimpse of human Katerina raises the question of who she would have been if born in a different time or place or under different circumstances — and the answer may be, simply: Elena. Just like Elena, Katherine cared deeply for her family; she lost everyone — her daughter, her parents, every other Petrova. Could she allow herself to truly love anyone again, knowing what their fate would be, given Klaus's taste for vengeance? Unlike Trevor and Rose, or Stefan and Damon, Katherine made the decision to survive alone, but it appears that she isn't completely heartless. With Katherine's sorrow over her parents' portrait, what Rose says to Damon rings true: that while the way to survive is to not care about anyone, once a vampire is a couple hundred or so years old there isn't actually a switch to flip to stop feeling. Beyond the explicit doubling of the Original Petrova in Katherine and Elena, there's also a second split within Katherine herself — between the ruthless vampire Katherine and the human Katerina once was. In her effort to survive at any cost, Katherine plays different roles, shifting her identity to suit her purpose, so that it's nearly impossible to see where the "real" Katherine begins and the performance ends.

Seeing Elena's persistence to get what she wants, Katherine tells her she has the "Petrova fire." The empty reassurances of the Salvatore brothers are not enough: Elena needs to know the truth and she employs Katherine-like tactics to get it. Though she's a lot less threatening than Katherine was, Elena does force Caroline to help her (with some mild emotional blackmail), making her open the tomb door and distract Stefan. Elena also keeps Stefan in the dark because she knows he'll object to her seeking out Katherine. And Katherine has the same fire in her. In 1492, she refused to let someone else decide her fate, and she did whatever she could to escape it — taking advantage of Trevor and Rose, killing herself, using the human woman as a shield and a source of blood, and spending 500 years running from Klaus. "Better you die than I" is Katherine's motto, and it's that fierce sense of self-preservation that's earned her the nickname "psychotic bitch." It's strange to consider, after over a season of characters insisting that Elena is *not* Katherine, that the doppelgängers are family: Katherine's parents are Elena's "true ancestors," as Katherine says, and Katherine is both Elena's oldest living relative, a grandmother generations removed, and her identical twin.

Katherine's "origin story," which Elena believes to be true, shows Elena the fate she faces: will she make the same choice Katherine did and value her own survival over others'? Like her boyfriend, "the protector," Elena has always tried to protect her friends and family as best she could, often endangering herself. But how can she do that in this situation? If she turns herself over to Klaus and helps him to extinguish the curse, Tyler and Caroline (or another werewolf-vampire pair) must also die, and who knows what kind of chaos would result from the vampire free-for-all once the Sun and the Moon Curse is broken. If Elena decides to run or take refuge in immortality, her friends and family would suffer the same fate Katherine's did.

At the beginning of the episode, Damon says that Elena is "in denial"; more precisely it seems that she very deliberately turned off her emotions, refusing to be ruled by them, in order to find out more about Klaus, the sacrifice, and being a doppelgänger. Elena always needs to *know* (remember her impatience at being out of the loop in "Plan B"?) and in "Katerina" she goes straight to the source. She doesn't want to be coddled by Stefan or Damon — her chilly reply to Stefan's offer to take her to school ("I know where it is") serves as a hilarious example of that. But hearing that she is "doomed" from Katherine, the person who best knows the battle that lies ahead of her, and learning that her very existence endangers everyone around her brings Elena to a breaking point by the end of the episode. Stefan pushes her to turn that metaphorical emotion switch back on and open up to him. And in the final moments of the episode, Nina Dobrev brings her two very different characters to similar emotional places, as both Elena, in Stefan's arms, and Katherine, alone in the tomb, rue the danger they put their loved ones in as the doppelgänger.

That moment of honest emotion from Katherine is rare: she shut off her emotions in order to survive, but, just as Damon only plays at being emotionless, there is no true escape from the heightened emotional state of a vampire. There is only denial. Though Katherine and Elena lament their fate at the end of "Katerina," the Petrova fire suggests they will both refuse to give in to hopelessness. Contrast their can-do attitude with Rose who is more often seen crying than not. While Rose did just lose her sole companion of half a millennium, her multiple breakdowns are strikingly unlike the keep-fighting spirit of the Mystic Falls gang. In a somewhat clunky way, her character is used as a mouthpiece to impress upon the audience how fearsome Klaus truly is. More effective than Rose's tears is Katerina's first-hand experience with Klaus's insatiable need for vengeance. Will history repeat itself with Elena?

COMPELLING MOMENT: *Bulgaria, 1490.* Perhaps the series' most compelling opening sequence managed to answer one of *TVD*'s longstanding mysteries while delivering heartbreaking background on Katherine. The briefly glimpsed relationship between Katerina and her mother is particularly moving.

CIRCLE OF KNOWLEDGE:
- No Matt, Tyler, Jenna, or Alaric in this episode.

- This is the first episode where the "Previously on *The Vampire Diaries*" recap doesn't begin with the clip of shirtless Stefan and his voiceover ("For over a century . . ."). Instead it's straight to Alaric explaining the Sun and Moon Curse.
- Both Katherine and Isobel were teen mothers whose daughters were raised by someone else. Good thing vampires can't procreate or Elena might follow in the family tradition.
- Elena keeps her plan to speak to Katherine a secret from Stefan. This is the second time in three days that the couple has kept secrets: Stefan hid the kill-Katherine plot from Elena in "Masquerade."
- Mother Petrova was right: taking the baby away from Katerina turned out to be better for the child. She survived Klaus's vengeance.
- Damon tells Slater that Elijah is "beyond dead," and though he intends a different meaning, Elijah is in fact beyond dead because he is an immortal.
- Slater told Rose about the tomb under the church, not about the existence of a new doppelgänger. Presumably Rose and Trevor came to Mystic Falls in pursuit of Katherine but found something even better with Elena, a still-human doppelgänger.
- Like vampires growing stronger with age, the Code of Friendship dictates that the older friendship (like Caroline's with Elena) wins out over the newer one (Caroline's with Stefan) when it comes to keeping or spilling secrets.
- No one on *The Vampire Diaries* is completely evil: Elijah may take your head off for betraying him but he's a generous supporter of the arts. That was a hundred dollar bill he dropped in the guitar case.
- Elijah's coin toss is a variation on lithoboly, or a mysterious hail of stones. Victims of curses, demonic possession, or spells have reported hails of stones that come from nowhere and rain down on them. From Rose, Slater, and Damon's perspective, the window shatters inexplicably but they know it's caused by a malevolent supernatural force.
- When Katherine gave werewolf George Lockwood the moonstone in 1864 in exchange for faking her death, she was betraying her "species" as well as the future doppelgänger (she alone knew that one was still a possibility).
- In the final flashback scene, Katerina is able to enter her family home without an invitation because her entire family has been killed.
- According to *The Encyclopedia of Witches, Witchcraft and Wicca*, "blood sacrifice releases a flash of power which the magician uses for a spell or

conjuration. . . . The letting of blood, and the fear and death throes of the victim, add to the frenzy of the magician." The "highest sacrifice" is that of human life (an act the Aztecs engaged in infamously). In a sacrifice, the blood or life force is released and unleashes power; so powerful is blood in witchcraft that just a few drops are enough for spells and potions, as seen in Bonnie's spell to find Elena in "Rose."

• In an episode where both Damon and Elena seek information about the Originals, Klaus, and the curse, it would seem that too much knowledge is a dangerous thing: vampire history expert Slater is killed by Elijah.

THE RULES: When Bonnie touches Luka, she senses that he isn't a regular human, an ability akin to the one that allows her to identify vampires by touch and to sense family, like when she touched Lucy in "Masquerade." It's the UV rays in sunlight that vampires are susceptible to, which are also what cause humans to sunburn. Rose says that a vampire's ability to turn off his or her emotions doesn't really exist, and that after a few hundred years, vampires just fake it. (Which makes a lot of sense, since none of our vamps have been particularly convincing when they're supposed to be devoid of emotion.) Elijah is a "special vampire": he has the ability to compel another vampire. Caroline says Tyler also has the urge to kill people (not just vampires), which is interesting since werewolves don't use humans for sustenance the way vampires do.

THE DIABOLICAL PLAN: Katherine reveals what's driven all of her diabolical plans for the past 518 years and it's not exactly a surprise: self-preservation. Stefan was right to believe there was more to Katherine's return to Mystic Falls than her affection for him — she came to gather the pieces that are necessary to break the curse so she could negotiate a truce with Klaus. If one half of the Sun and Moon Curse is broken, the other half is permanent, which explains why a vampire who already has the ability to walk in the sun would care about it. If the werewolves break the moon curse and can shift at will, they are a mighty force against the vampires, the bulk of whom would be confined indoors all day. Breaking the curse is a complicated business: a vampire, a werewolf, and the Petrova doppelgänger must all be killed, plus a witch must break the spell bound in the moonstone. Vampires are easy to come by, witches a little trickier, and werewolves a rarity. But a Petrova doppelgänger is so rare that an Original must wait hundreds of years for her appearance.

If Klaus really does want to break the Sun and Moon Curse, it seems a little counterproductive for him to have Katerina's entire family slaughtered: without a Petrova bloodline, there is no chance for another Petrova doppelgänger. Or does the doppelgänger have to descend directly, i.e. from Katerina herself? If Slater is right and Klaus's real desire is to prevent the werewolves from breaking it first, then by killing off the Petrovas, Klaus believed he had prevented that from happening. Both Slater (compelled by Elijah) and Katherine suggest that if the moonstone is destroyed, the curse cannot be broken. Is that the answer to their predicament?

HISTORY LESSON: In 1490, Bulgaria had been under Ottoman rule for just shy of a century, and it remained a part of the empire until 1878. England was enjoying a reprieve from the War of the Roses under the rule of the miserly Henry VII (1485–1509). The Baroque period, which stretches from the 16th to 18th centuries, was marked by a dynamic and exuberant quality in art and architecture and, surely, in the behavior of its sexual deviants.

BITE MARKS: Damon shoves Rose and she returns the favor. Elijah smashes the glass wall of the café by throwing coins at it, injuring innocent bystanders and giving Rose and Slater rather severe sunburns. Under compulsion, Slater stakes himself in the heart. In the flashback, Katerina stabs herself in the gut and, after Rose feeds her blood to heal her, hangs herself. Rose slams Trevor against the wall. Katerina uses the old farm woman as a shield when Rose attempts to stake her, and then Katerina feeds on her, completing her change. Klaus has Katerina's entire family killed.

PREVIOUSLY ON THE VAMPIRE DIARIES: In "Bloodlines," Damon considers the possibility that Katherine had a baby before she was turned, but dismisses it immediately as a ludicrous idea; neither Damon nor Stefan knew about her daughter. In "Isobel," Damon explains to Alaric the emotion switch a vampire can "turn off," which Rose debunks as myth, something vampires who are well into their afterlives just fake. In the flashback in "Memory Lane," Damon asks Katherine, "Is my love not enough for you?"; that exchange is mirrored in Trevor and Katherine's in the 1492 flashback. Trevor and Rose's plan for Elena was similar to Katherine's: use Elena to barter for a pardon from Klaus. But Katherine is being more thorough about it, rounding up *all* the necessary pieces Klaus will need to break the curse, not just the doppelgänger. The woman whose house was used as a hideout for Rose and Trevor is the 1490s edition of Miss Gibbons, who owned the house where the tomb vampires took up residence in "A Few Good Men."

MEANWHILE IN FELL'S CHURCH: Katherine's backstory in the book series is also tied to Klaus: when human, Katherine was ill and dying, and he turned her (*The Awakening*). After she faked her death, she returned to Klaus, and he taught her to be a killer and draw Power from taking life (*The Fury*).

OFF CAMERA: Fluent in Bulgarian, Nina Dobrev made sure the opening scene's dialogue was accurate with help from her mother: "I think the writers had used an internet translator and it was so funny. All those online translators are never right. So we did it." Nina worked "really, really hard" on this episode and particularly enjoyed the opportunity to "play the innocence of pre-vampire Katherine." Of "Katerina," Julie Plec said, "We are incredibly proud of this episode, mostly because the work Nina Dobrev does is unbelievable. She plays Katherine as a human in Bulgaria with a Bulgarian accent, she plays human Katherine pretending to be English in the English countryside, she plays Katherine as a vampire in present day, she plays Elena. And a good portion of the episode is Elena and Katherine having a conversation, so she's essentially acting opposite nothing, a stand-in or air. This is her episode to shine."

Trent Ford resurrects Trevor for the flashback scenes. Trent, who grew up moving around the States and U.K. with an American father and British mother, has appeared in *Gosford Park*, *How to Deal*, *The West Wing*, *Smallville*, *The Class*, and in a Calvin Klein campaign with Scarlett Johansson. Trevor Peterson plays the ill-fated Slater; the actor has also appeared in episodes of *CSI: Miami*, *We Are with the Band*, *10 Dates from Hell*, and the movie *Prom*.

The coffee shop scenes were filmed at Noon Midtown café and bar (1050 Crescent Avenue, Atlanta), which closed in January 2011.

Standing in for the Petrova book is a tome with Latin text, which seems to be about religious martyrs, a fitting prop for *The Vampire Diaries* wherein characters are often putting themselves in peril for each other or for the greater good.

FOGGY MOMENTS: In the flashback, Elijah seems a little too easily duped by Trevor as they search for Katerina in the woods; Elijah says he can smell her blood — wouldn't he trust his Original-vampire senses over those of a younger vampire like Trevor? Katerina got herself strung up on that beam and dead rather swiftly. Perhaps the rapid-fire noose-making skill is something that's been lost over the generations, like the ability to whittle. How did the Aztec shaman get his hands on Petrova blood to bind the Sun and the Moon Curse? Traveling from Bulgaria to Mexico wasn't so easily done in the 1400s.

MUSIC: Jeremy flirts with Bonnie outside school to Atomic Tom's "You Always Get What You Want." David Gray's "A Moment Changes Everything" is playing at the coffee shop where Rose takes Damon to meet Slater. Caroline distracts Stefan at the Grill while Pete Yorn's "Precious Stone" plays; a Pete Yorn song was also included in the Lexi episode, "162 Candles." Slater talks college degrees and Klaus to Matt Duncan's "Puritan Heart." "Light Love" by Free Energy is playing at the Grill when Luka interrupts Jeremy and Bonnie's game of pool; a Free Energy song also played at the Grill during the bachelor auction in "A Few Good Men." Luka reveals to Bonnie that he and his father are "warlocks" to "Trap of Mirrors" by The Pass (who also had a song in "Kill or Be Killed"). Rose and Damon toast to friendship with Ben Harper's "Amen Omen" providing the soundtrack.

QUESTIONS:
- Rose describes Elijah as a "foot soldier" to Klaus, the Easter bunny in comparison to the legendary vampire. What makes Klaus the leader of the Originals — his age, his taste for vengeance, his determination to get whatever he wants?
- Has Katherine ever told anyone her life story before, or was Elena the first to hear it?
- Katherine says she was "taken with" Klaus at first: how strong were her feelings for him?
- Does Luka know his father is working with Elijah?
- If the doppelgänger was "created" as a way for the spell to be undone, does that mean Elena isn't actually human but in some way a supernatural creature herself?
- Katherine says she has no reason to lie. Is that a lie?
- If Katherine had known that her loved ones were in danger from Klaus (as Elena knows), would she have made the choice that she did?

❀

Caroline: There's a reason it's called a curse, Tyler.

2.10 *The Sacrifice*

Original air date: December 2, 2010
Written by: Caroline Dries
Directed by: Ralph Hemecker
Guest cast: Bree Condon (Alice), Trevor Peterson (Slater), James Harvey Ward (Cody Webber)

The brothers Salvatore, Bonnie, and Jeremy attempt to get the moonstone, but Elena has her own plan afoot: to turn herself over to Klaus.

Ever since Mystic Falls was founded back in the 1860s, the townspeople have lived by one credo above all others: protect the ones you love. In "The Sacrifice," the characters recklessly endanger themselves in the name of saving each other. Faced with no good options, their master plans tend to be barely thought-out and impetuous but reveal the selfless instincts these characters possess. Ironically the plans in "The Sacrifice," hatched with the best of intentions, all require either the full-on deception of those being protected or at least going against their wishes.

With the knowledge of what fate awaits Elena as the latest Petrova doppelgänger, her would-be saviors, Stefan, Damon, and Bonnie, have decided on a solution: retrieve the moonstone and destroy it. As in "Plan B" and "Masquerade," Elena is left out of the plan-making process, but when she finds out, she quickly sees the fatal flaw in their idea — even if they succeed, surely Klaus will seek vengeance on them. But the risk is acceptable to the boys and Bonnie, who proceed without Elena's consent. They don't even consider Elena's idea of a solution: she can surrender, sacrifice herself, and save her loved ones from the fate that befell Katherine's family. Katherine's primary motivation, as she said in "Katerina," is self-preservation, ahead of anyone and everything else. When Klaus was on her tail, she saw a way out: cease to be human (i.e., any use to Klaus) and become a vampire. Driven by the exact opposite sentiment, Elena puts self-preservation last.

And she's not alone; her friends prove just as willing to risk life and limb to save one another.

Elena is fascinating in "The Sacrifice": she uses Katherine-esque techniques with ease — going behind the Salvatores' backs, calling in the debt Rose owes her for sparing her, bargaining with Rose and Alice (with empty promises of a daylight ring and becoming a vampire, respectively), and outright lying. Elena's sympathy for Alice (an anti-Elena if ever we saw one) disappears the moment Rose tells her that Alice was self-interested and not really in love with Slater. Elena doesn't hesitate to use Alice and trick her into getting what she needs — information and a contact. With the stakes so high, she doesn't seem to even consider the idea that what she's doing is morally questionable; there's a greater good to serve, and Elena doesn't lose focus. Besides providing the hilarious Alaric and the Chunky Monkey ice cream moment that will live in *TVD* fans' hearts forever, the episode's opening sequence serves to remind us just what it is that Elena is so resolved to protect. The happiness, normalcy, the humanness that Jenna is experiencing is what Elena wants for everyone she cares about. And the intercut scenes that follow it — the Salvatore brothers visiting each doppelgänger — reinforce the idea that Elena and Katherine may have different motivations and endgames, but they are fueled by the very same Petrova fire.

Daniel Gillies as Elijah

Born in Winnipeg, Manitoba, on March 14, 1976, and raised in New Zealand, Daniel Gillies' first acting role was about as far removed from Elijah as could be: in a Hamilton Boys' High School production, he played Peter Rabbit's mother. By his early 20s, Daniel was a successful working actor on New Zealand's hit TV show *Street Legal* and performed in local theater productions. But he needed a change: "I had everything I wanted, but my heart was slowly breaking. I felt like I was falling into complacency, so I sold everything and left." He moved to Australia and then to Canada where he continued his acting work, but made his next (and so far permanent) home Los Angeles. There he landed some high-profile parts — in *Spider-Man 2* as Mary Jane's fiancé and in *Bride & Prejudice* as Wickham — and met his future wife, fellow actor Rachael Leigh Cook. Daniel continued to find work in film; among other projects, in 2006 he starred opposite Ian Somerhalder in *The Sensation of Sight* and the next year in *Captivity* with Elisha Cuthbert.

Around that time, he directed his first film, *Wait for Me*, in Panama with "just two guys, a camera and a couple microphones." His decision to make his own projects came from a desire to keep working on interesting projects. "I just never wanted to be one of those actors who is waiting around for a job, waiting for the phone to ring," explained Gillies. "I turned 29 and I made that decision. . . . I've been writing every day ever since. If you want to make any film, you *can* make it. I really believe that. And I don't think that people are talking about very interesting things in film at the moment." His next project was *Broken Kingdom* (thebrokenkingdom.com), which he wrote, directed, and starred in. The film (executive produced by Ryan Gosling) is about *los desechables* ("the disposable ones"), street children and prostitutes in Colombia, and the plot follows an eccentric writer (played by Gillies) and three other interconnected stories.

When he wasn't making films in Colombia whilst sporting an impressively full beard, Gillies was picking up television roles; an episode each of *True Blood* and *NCIS* preceded his stint on *The Vampire Diaries*. Of that mysterious accent and cadence he's given Elijah, Gillies explained to EW.com, "I know that this guy's been living in the States for a couple hundred years, but he's probably somebody who travels to Europe frequently, probably speaks 10 or 12 languages, including some extinct languages. I wanted him to sound a little bit like Kelsey Grammer [laughs], if that makes any sense. I wanted him to sound like old money from the United States, because I also thought that it lent a weight and, dare I say, dignity to his character, without being too foppish or overly gentrified." Clearly reveling in the role, Gillies jokes about Elijah, "He's always killing. Every week, I read [the script], and I think, 'Oh my god, I'm Jaws.'" Though there's been precious little information provided about Elijah's backstory, Daniel has a few theories about what gets Elijah going. As he told TVFanatic.com, "I think he derives something sexual from the terror he instills from just being around people. If he's charming somebody, and somebody else is frightened, that's a particular turn-on for him."

There are a lot of "idiot plans" in "The Sacrifice" and what undermines Elena, Jeremy, Bonnie, Damon, and Stefan as they each decide to put their own best interests aside in the hopes of saving their endangered loved one, is that they overestimate their own strengths while underestimating their enemy's. The unlearned lesson comes from Luka, as he explains to Bonnie about the blowback she's been getting from performing magic: trying to do too much on your own will harm you. His solution is to draw strength from what's around you — and that's what's lacking in everyone's "selfless" plans.

Bonnie and Elena try to draw strength by using others — Bonnie by drawing on Luka's power without his consent; Elena by lying and manipulating Rose and Alice. Though they both fail, neither girl is particularly regretful, nor do they consider the moral questions the way they usually do. They both overestimate their ability to get away with their plans: Bonnie doesn't anticipate Jonas interfering to save his son (though it's unclear if the spell would have worked anyway, since Luka passes out) and Elena is surprised that Rose is just as capable of deceiving her as the other way around. Like Stefan dashing into the tomb to save Jeremy, Bonnie and Elena feel like they have no choice but to act alone. In their minds, only an act of self-sacrifice will solve the problem.

Jeremy shares that instinct: after unsuccessfully trying to convince Bonnie to be cautious about overexerting herself with magic, he puts into motion the plan that Damon rejected out of hand because it came from a "kid." Like the rest of the half-baked ideas in "The Sacrifice," Jeremy's plan is *almost* a good one, but he underestimates his opponent in Katherine. What Jeremy does prove is how far he's willing to go to protect Bonnie and his sister. He reaches out to Bonnie romantically, tired of being off-limits because he's Elena's little brother, but Bonnie is still closed to that possibility. She's been alone for a great deal of her journey as a witch, and while she seems to appreciate having Jeremy to confide in, he doesn't fit the bill of a companion who can help her navigate the world of the supernatural. Grams was Bonnie's guide and instructor but after she died in "Fool Me Once," Bonnie was left alone. With Luka, she's once again able to learn the fundamentals of witchcraft. While the two have chemistry and seem to like-like each other, their relationship lacks openness on both sides. Luka has been instructed by his father, and presumably Elijah, to "bond" with Bonnie, while Bonnie takes advantage of Luka, abusing the bond he shared with her via his talisman.

On the flipside is Caroline's relationship with Tyler. Despite Tyler's resistance to involving her in something as intimate as his first transformation, Caroline refuses to let Tyler go it alone. Besides her convincing argument for her usefulness, in which she rhymes off her extensive résumé, Caroline's just been through a parallel experience in becoming a vampire. Without her, Tyler would be as alone as Mason was in the video. Caroline's already proven she's capable of self-sacrifice (by breaking up with Matt to keep him safe) and is once again putting her own best interests aside to help another: hanging out with a werewolf, the mortal enemy of the vampire, is a potentially fatal pastime. Tyler also demonstrates surprising insight concerning her relationship with Matt, seeing the less-obvious reason why she had to break up with him: it's not fair to either of them if Caroline has to lie about who she is. Tyler and Caroline's connection is building, shaped by a mutual understanding of what it is to become a supernatural creature, and by their ability to talk honestly about all that entails, something neither can share with Matt (not so long as he's in the dark about the secrets of Mystic Falls). But even as Tyler and Caroline connect — with her revealing to him that she killed a man on her first night as a vampire, a secret not easily said out loud — Caroline is keeping crucial information from Tyler: she fibs about never having been in the Lockwood cellar before. Like Bonnie and like Elena, Caroline's at the center of her own developing love triangle with Tyler and Matt. From Matt's perspective things already look sketchy at best. He sees his best friend with his ex-girlfriend, and he believes they have good reason to pull away from him after his behavior at the Lockwood party. He lives as an orphan, his sister is dead, and he's distanced from his only friends. If ever there was a tragic figure, it's Matt Donovan.

The episode ends with Stefan in a situation not entirely unlike Matt's — his girl with his brother. Trapped in the tomb, Stefan asks Damon to promise to protect Elena, a promise that doesn't really need to be made since Damon's already proven that he's just as ready to die protecting Elena as Stefan is. Though Damon calls his brother a martyr, the label could be applied to all of the characters who demonstrate courage and a commitment to follow through on their plans despite knowing that the likely outcome of it is harm or death. Bonnie risks enormous damage if she uses the spell, Jeremy takes on Katherine alone to prevent Bonnie from hurting herself, Stefan rescues Jeremy from Katherine at his own peril, Damon acts as a bodyguard to protect Elena, despite the threat posed by Elijah, and Elena plans to walk into the lion's den to prevent Klaus from hurting anyone she cares about.

Elena's desire to surrender to Klaus is just as fierce as Damon's is to save her from her kamikaze mission, and so their showdown turns on who can physically overpower the other. Clearly, Damon has no trouble restraining her at Slater's or at the tomb when she's ready to run in after Stefan. Elena's plan may be flawed (at least two other people will be killed in the sacrifice) but she has a point: why is it so hard for Damon to understand that she would want to save those she cares about when that's exactly what drives the Salvatores' actions, as well as Bonnie's and Jeremy's? Each of these characters has just as much reason and right to play the martyr as do the brothers whose last name means "savior." As "The Sacrifice" ends, with Damon as Elena's de facto prison guard, she is as trapped as Katherine is in that tomb — each doppelgänger has one Salvatore brother who can't leave her side.

Is Katherine right: did Stefan make a big mistake in asking Damon to swear to protect Elena? Damon and Elena have always been ferocious in the way they interact and this episode gives us some electric moments between them. And Stefan and Katherine similarly spark thanks to their emotionally fraught history, her flirtatiousness, and his combativeness. An intrigue-filled setup for the next episode, one that also promises the terror of Tyler's first transformation.

COMPELLING MOMENT: Tyler watching Mason go through his torturous first transformation. It's a terrifying preview of what's to come and heartbreaking to see its effect on Tyler.

CIRCLE OF KNOWLEDGE:
- The opening scene's home invasion, with Jonas creepily sneaking around Elena's room stealing her personal items is the perfect introduction to this episode's recurring theme of actions perpetrated on people without their consent.
- Absent since "Under Control," Elena's diary is now on the bed next to her during the opening sequence. Also, Mason's journal is introduced, as well as his video log of his transformation.
- Elena rather pointedly includes Damon as someone she cares about, even though less than a month ago, she told him he'd lost her friendship forever ("Bad Moon Rising").
- Witchcraft, the actual cause of global warming . . . ? Witches have long been credited with the ability to whip up the elements. Natural disasters were blamed on witchcraft and thought to be "maleficia," or punishment, brought upon the world.
- It's been a while since *The Vampire Diaries* acknowledged that other vampire franchise: vampire almanac Slater's password is "Kristen Stewart"; the actress plays Bella Swan in the Twilight Saga movies. Poor Slater didn't live to see *Breaking Dawn* part one or two.
- Once again, the mortals prove to be clever. Elena gets what she needs from Rose and Alice, and Jeremy has the wherewithal to toss that moonstone out of the tomb as Katherine lunges in for a bite. You go, Gilberts.

THE RULES: The Martins show us variations on a few of the spells and principles of witchcraft that we've seen before. Luka tells Bonnie she can draw power from nature, the elements, and other witches, and demonstrates by summoning the wind; Jonas uses talismans stolen from Elena's room to perform a "shadow spell," which allows Elijah to find Elena (and Elena to see his reflection in the window's glass). All three witches perform spells using a personal artifact, which can be used to find someone, to connect to another's power, or to hurt someone (in the case of Bonnie's spell with Katherine's portrait). From Mason's journal, Caroline and Tyler learn just how painful the first transformation is, but that the process gradually speeds up. Mason ingests watered-down wolfsbane to weaken himself, which we can safely assume is what he had with him in the Lockwood cellar in "Bad Moon Rising."

THE DIABOLICAL PLAN: Katherine offers the moonstone and a promise to leave town in exchange for freedom from the tomb, but Damon and Stefan don't trust her. The brothers' plan is to get the moonstone from Katherine and destroy it so the curse cannot be broken, which they believe will save Elena from harm. The moonstone is theirs by the episode's end, but the cost is Stefan trapped in the tomb with Katherine. Elena tries to turn herself over to Klaus in an attempt to prevent any of her friends from being killed along with her in the sacrifice. Elijah kills Cody and his two vampire buddies to ensure that news of the doppelgänger's existence doesn't spread. But Rose knows. Does that put a target on her back?

HISTORY LESSON: The portrait of Katherine that Bonnie uses in her spell is likely a daguerreotype, the first photographic process invented in the 1830s, which imprinted a one-of-a-kind image on a silver-plated sheet of copper.

BITE MARKS: Jeremy stakes Katherine and disables her with Bonnie's magic portrait ash. Katherine bites him. And then bites him again. Damon grabs Elena's arm and blocks her punch. To take down the tomb seal, Bonnie drains power from Luka, weakening him and causing him to have a nose-bleed and pass out. Katherine elbows Jeremy in the head to shut him up. Stefan throws Jeremy out of the tomb and pins Katherine against the wall. Elijah snaps the neck of one vampire and rips the hearts out of the other two with impressive precision.

PREVIOUSLY ON THE VAMPIRE DIARIES: In "Bloodlines," Bonnie used a talisman, Elena's necklace, in an attempt to do a locator spell. Matt's apology to Tyler echoes Tyler's attempted apology to Matt in "Isobel" following their blowout in "Under Control." Stefan darted into the tomb to save Elena from Anna in "Fool Me Once," knowing that he'd be trapped once he was inside; here he goes in to save Jeremy from Katherine. Elena hates sitting around helplessly: in "Let the Right One In," she insisted on being involved in the rescue op and got out of Damon's car against instructions. Also in "Let the Right One In," Elena witnessed Damon trick Alaric into helping by lying to him (he falsely suggests that Pearl could help find Isobel); here she uses the same kind of trick with Rose and Alice. This is not the first time Caroline's helped Tyler: she intervened when Mayor Lockwood was being rough with Tyler at the Grill in "Founder's Day." Bonnie and Grams combined their powers to take down the tomb seal in "Fool Me Once," like Bonnie tries to do with Luka. In "Haunted," Damon blocks Elena when she goes to hit him in the parking lot after Vicki's death, just as he blocks her attack at Slater's.

MEANWHILE IN FELL'S CHURCH: Tyler and Caroline are also allies in *The Struggle* — except they are working together to ruin Elena and Stefan (in between make-out sessions in the photography class dark room). In this episode Damon holds an orange while he talks to Elena and Stefan in the Gilbert kitchen, bringing to mind a classic Damon moment from *Dark Reunion*: "Damon was lounging near the window, peeling an orange, not even dressed yet."

OFF CAMERA: Though Ralph Hemecker directed the episode, the video of Mason's transformation was directed by Marcos Siega. Candice Accola and Michael Trevino were watching a blank screen when they filmed their reactions to Mason's video: the actual footage was put in during postproduction. When asked why Caroline helps Tyler, Candice Accola said simply, "She recognizes that Tyler needs a Stefan." The moment where Jeremy leans in to kiss Bonnie wasn't scripted. "It was only one take that happened," explained Steven R. McQueen, "and we were just kind of very close to each other and it was just a moment I felt would have been a cool beat. So I went for it, and they ended up choosing that take, which was cool for me as an actor because we always experiment with different things, and to see it work out like that was really cool."

FOGGY MOMENTS: Neither Stefan nor Damon notice with their superior vampire senses that Bonnie has blood dripping out of her nose after she performs the spell on Katherine's portrait. Is Jeremy not ingesting vervain or can Kat drink his blood because of her vervain tolerance? Does it seem sketchy that Bonnie didn't mention to the Salvatores or Jeremy that the Martins are witches? A new supernatural element in Mystic Falls seems like something worth bringing up. When did the tomb get a skylight?

MUSIC: *The Vampire Diaries'* own Katerina Graham covers "Only Happy When It Rains" by Garbage, which plays as Matt apologizes to Tyler for his behavior at the masquerade ball. Caroline explains to Tyler why she cares about him to Joel & Luke's "Love's to Blame"; a Joel & Luke song also played during a Caroline moment in "Masquerade." Bonnie and Jeremy talk at the Gilbert house to "No Way Out" by Rie Sinclair (a track cowritten and coproduced by Michael Suby, composer of *The Vampire Diaries* score).

QUESTIONS:
- Was Katherine lying about wanting out of the tomb in "Katerina," or is she lying now?
- Since they clearly know where Elena lives, why did Elijah have Jonas do the shadow spell? More complicated than a simple locator spell, it "tracks" Elena. Does that mean there's a longer-lasting connection established between Elena and Elijah?
- Just what is the deal with Elijah? Does he want Elena kept safe so he can turn her over to Klaus in one piece, or does he have his own Klaus-free agenda? How did he learn to kill vampires with such finesse? Will he let Damon and Bonnie try to remove the spell from the moonstone, or does he want it in good working order?
- Dr. Martin asked Luka to bond with Bonnie, and Luka followed orders: how much does he know about what's going on? Does he know who Elijah is and/or what his father is up to?

❀

Elijah: Thank you for having the good sense to be frightened.

2.11 *By the Light of the Moon*

Original air date: December 9, 2010
Written by: Mike Daniels
Directed by: Elizabeth Allen

Tyler undergoes his unforgettably torturous first transformation.

In changing from man to wolf, Tyler loses all control of his body, overtaken by a force greater than him, more powerful and undeniable. In less literal and visceral ways, the rest of the Mystic Falls crew loses their self-determination or will in "By the Light of the Moon," subjected to the control of various outside forces, whether they're aware of it or not. Bonnie thinks she's being resourceful, but her course of action was set in play by Luka, his father, and Elijah when Elijah had Slater call Rose about the moonstone in "Katerina." By extension, the Salvatore brothers, so focused on deactivating the moonstone, are actually just pawns, playing into whatever Elijah's endgame is. Trapped in the tomb with his delightfully evil ex, Stefan suffers mind games and the manipulation of his subconscious, as Katherine creates a realistic and sexy tomb romp for them. And Elena is literally trapped inside her house by her best friend's spell: Bonnie and Damon are able to control her, refusing to let her do what she most wants: turn herself over to Klaus for sacrifice. Like teenagers everywhere, Elena just wants to make her own decisions instead of having the terms of her life dictated to her — of course, most 17-year-old girls aren't facing ritual sacrifice at the hands of the oldest, most vengeful vampire in the history of time.

In "The Sacrifice," Elena proved herself capable of, and talented at, manipulating people in order to get what she wants. Rose and Alice were strangers to her, but Damon, Bonnie, and Jeremy anticipate that Elena will be willing to use those same tactics against them to get her way. By taking the moonstone and trying to get out of the Gilbert house, Elena is once again presented as the inverse of Katherine, who back in 1492 stole the moonstone and escaped; their actions are the same but their purpose opposite. Katherine avoided the sacrifice rather than running headlong into it. Elena's plan to martyr herself is thwarted by the genius idea to bind her in her house, the lighthearted (at least for Jeremy and Damon) equivalent of locking up someone who's a suicide risk. Though they mean the best for her, Elena's friends have taken away her freedom and her right to self-determination, placing her in the role of a helpless damsel, something Elena hates.

In her present predicament, there's no way Elena would refuse Elijah's deal: it solves her unsolvable situation. Elijah will limit the damage Klaus can do, and her friends and family will be protected by witches. After shocking her with a trademark *Vampire Diaries* hiding-behind-the-door scare, Elijah offers Elena his hand as he introduces himself, and their handshake acts as both a sign of civility on his part and a symbol that their "peaceful agreement" will soon be in play. He tells Elena what she most wants to hear — he doesn't intend to harm her family — and convinces her that he is capable of protecting them if she promises to cooperate with him. Their deal, like any other, is only as good as each side's commitment to it. Elijah carries out the first part of it (freeing Stefan from the tomb), but whether he is as honorable as he seems to be, or if Elena will prove worthy of *his* trust, remains to be seen.

Elena has the good sense to question whether or not Elijah is being honest with her; Bonnie, on the other hand, blindly trusts Luka, thinking she's being cautious enough by not revealing what spell the moonstone is tied to. Luka easily manipulates her with talk of loyalty and the familial bonds that exist between all witches, but he also seems to genuinely like Bonnie and believe in what he's saying. Is there a code of loyalty among witches? In "Masquerade," Lucy's attitude toward Katherine's caper changed drastically when she learned there was another witch involved, and she seemed unwilling to fight Bonnie, now matter how distant a blood relative she is. Given this, it looks as if the Martins are abusing witch loyalty, as they force Bonnie to help them (by getting the moonstone from her without her knowledge) while allowing her to believe she is the one receiving aid from them. The tension between Luka and his father, which we saw a glimmer of in "The Sacrifice," is amped up in "By the Light of the Moon": Luka deliberately places the moonstone on the table instead of in his father's hand. He obeyed his father's instructions, but he clearly doesn't like betraying Bonnie; he doesn't seem to think their actions are right. In this father/son dynamic, we see an echo of several other intergenerational relationships on *The Vampire Diaries*. The older generation — like Giuseppe Salvatore, Uncle John Gilbert, and even Grams Bennett — tend to make decisions that the younger generation isn't comfortable with, despite the mollifying argument that it's for the greater good. Does Jonas believe the ends justify the means?

With Stefan in the tomb, Damon acts as the de facto leader of the group and does a not-bad job of it. All his bases are covered: "Vampire Barbie" is on wolf patrol; Jeremy is babysitting Elena, who can't leave her house anyway; Bonnie is on Project Moonstone; and Alaric and Damon are working the Mason-Jules situation. But as Damon's plan plays out, everyone (with the exception of Caroline) fails in their duties. Elijah finds a way into the Gilbert house, Elena makes a deal with their supposed enemy, Bonnie unwittingly gives up the moonstone, and Jules is wise to Damon and Alaric's trickery. Despite the plans going awry, leadership is an interesting new position for Damon, and it shows how much more trusted he is now. He and Bonnie are working together and — incredibly — agreeing on what to do (both of them think that trapping Elena in her house is "for the best"). Bonnie's reluctance to work with vampires has clearly been sidelined or overcome; Damon and Jeremy — the guy whose neck Damon snapped just a short while ago — are sharing a chuckle over Elena's frustration; and Alaric, who's always had a love-hate relationship with Damon, plays along at the Grill and later talks a "marked" Damon into heading home. With the common goal of protecting Elena from death, the differences that once divided our protagonists have been set aside.

In a rare moment when she's not crying, Rose makes a clear distinction between sex and love: she's happy to sleep with Damon but there's no danger of her falling in love with him. In an interesting commentary on Damon, Rose says, "I don't love men who love other women. I think more of myself than that." Who she loves is a matter of choice, not an uncontrollable feeling that overtakes her, and she believes she deserves love in return. Consider the glimpse of still-human Damon in "Memory Lane," compelled by Katherine to leave her bedroom after his painfully vulnerable question ("Is my love not enough for you?"). Damon has played second fiddle to his younger brother twice in his century and a half, and despite the persona he has forged as a cocksure vampire lothario, what he wants more than anything is to "love and be loved in return" (to quote *Moulin Rouge*).

Katherine insists that she does love Stefan, and if that's true, then Rose's words also apply to her. Stefan's heart belongs to Katherine's doppelgänger. Trapped in the tomb together, their manipulations of each other came across, in the end, as ineffectual — even if Katherine's control of Stefan's dream was certainly more entertaining than Stefan's blatant attempt at emotional black-mail. Katherine is aware of the wrongs she's committed. She just believes that her survival was worth the cost to others. That attitude is what makes her roll her eyes when Stefan expresses no concern about himself, only about Elena. As Stefan did with Damon early last season, he attempts to draw out the goodness in Katherine, asking her to prove herself to him, and she points him in the direction of Isobel. When Stefan leaves Katherine in the tomb, his goodbye has a sense of finality to it. Whatever twists and turns and heart-breaks and hookups the future holds for the doppelgängers and the Salvatore

brothers, it's clear from Stefan and Elena's joyful reunion in her bedroom — after being apart since their forced breakup in "Plan B" — that their love is strong and requited. Has Stefan ever looked so happy?

While Bonnie, Jeremy, and Damon talk of Elena playing the martyr, unbeknownst to any of them, Caroline is putting herself in grave danger in her choice to help Tyler navigate his first excruciating transformation: one bite and she's dead, a tiny detail she didn't share with her lycanthrope pal. She refuses to leave Tyler's side until the very last possible moment — only to feel terrible about leaving him at all. Her tearful apologies outside the door while he screams in the final throes of his transformation were heartbreaking. Though Tyler says there's nothing she can do for him as he writhes in agony, Caroline standing by him when she really should run is the most and the best thing a friend can do. Though it was horrifying to watch Tyler go through the transformation — those cracking noises, that arm bending unnaturally, the dry-heaving after he drank wolfsbane — the connection between Caroline and Tyler made this supernatural experience very human. The emphasis was on the characters rather than on a special-effects display. Those wolf-transformation shots were incredibly creepy and well executed, but what mattered most was how Tyler and Caroline were reacting to a situation well beyond their control. It was a wonderful paradox: Tyler becoming a dangerously powerful creature, driven and deadly, in front of Caroline's eyes, while revealing to her his most vulnerable and terrified self. Michael Trevino has brought Tyler a long way from last season, and in "By the Light of the Moon" he gave us a visceral, brutal, and honest performance of Tyler in appalling pain and heartrending sobs. Tyler and Caroline were without a doubt the heart of this episode.

This werewolf-heavy episode culminates in the inevitable bite, but instead of Tyler chomping on Caroline, Jules nicks Rose — and though the bite doesn't instantly kill her, there's clearly some truth to that legend of the fatal werewolf bite. The true danger inherent in Caroline and Tyler's newfound closeness will be revealed in the fate that awaits Rose, and in the threat that Jules poses them. Caroline proves to be the best friend Tyler could hope for on the most difficult day of his life, but she also lies to him about his uncle, suggesting that Mason might just be on a surfing trip when she very well knows he's been murdered. That kind of dark secret, kept by a self-proclaimed "terrible liar," has a way of coming back with a bite.

COMPELLING MOMENT: Caroline holding Tyler while he shuddered in excruciating pain, in particular their final exchange: "You're okay." "No, I'm not."

CIRCLE OF KNOWLEDGE:

- In addition to Tyler's transformation taking place "by the light of the moon," the moon's power fuels the Martin witches when they remove the tomb seal. The magical power of the moon is said to be greatest at midnight on the night of a full moon.
- This episode was the mid-season finale, the last episode before a seven-week winter hiatus.
- Both Bonnie and Damon say it's "for the best" that they've bound Elena inside her house; the last time someone told Elena something was "for the best," she snapped back. In "Kill or Be Killed" when Caroline said her breakup with Stefan might be for the best, she said, "It's not 'for the best,' Caroline; none of this is 'for the best.'"
- Funny that Elijah is posing as an author writing a book about small town Virginia when he called Mystic Falls and surrounding areas the "armpit of civilization" in "Rose."
- After a season and a half of characters pretty much always leaving the Grill without paying, Alaric finally slaps down some cash. Way to be, Mr. Saltzman.
- Tyler tells Caroline that he doesn't think his pants will stay on through the transformation, not like the Incredible Hulk's do. The Marvel Comics superhero, who debuted in 1962, is scientist Bruce Banner's alter-ego. Though much larger than Banner, Hulk always manages to retain trousers when he completes his change from mild-mannered human to raging humanoid monster. In *The Wolf Man*, not only does Larry Talbot keep his pants on through the transformation, but once he's in wolf-man form he has a jacket on that he wasn't wearing pre-transformation. Refreshingly, David Kessler in *An American Werewolf in London* wakes up stark naked after his night as a wolf-man . . . as does Tyler.
- In Elena's room is a poster for *Brigadoon*, a strange choice for the average teenage girl's bedroom. The musical, first staged on Broadway in 1947 and turned into an Oscar-nominated film in 1954, tells the story of two American hunters lost in the Scottish highlands who stumble upon a mysterious village, Brigadoon, which has been protected by a magical spell from

Bryton James as Luka Martin

Though it's his first time playing a character with supernatural powers, Bryton James (sometimes credited as Bryton McClure or simply Bryton) has been on television since he was two years old. Born in Lakewood, California, on August 17, 1986, to a stay-at-home mom and musician father, Bryton grew up in a household filled with music. He was an outgoing child, so his parents were encouraged to get him in front of TV cameras, and little Bryton landed his first audition, a commercial for Disney Mattel. Just a year later, at three years old, Bryton was a regular on sitcom *Family Matters* as Richie Crawford, a role he played for nearly nine years. Just a few years into his career, Bryton became involved with charitable causes, working with Heal the World and D.A.R.E. among other anti-drug campaigns, and his own foundation against drunk driving. Explained the actor, "It's always been important for me and my family to use being on television, being someone who's recognizable, to share messages with other kids about safe ways to live your life."

As *Family Matters* came to an end, Bryton's career took a turn: he landed a recording contract at age 13 with Universal Germany and sold over 9 million copies in Europe, where he toured. In 2004, Bryton returned to acting with a role on CBS's long-running soap opera *The Young and the Restless*. His work on the show as Devon Hamilton has since earned the actor a Daytime Emmy (as well as three more nominations) and an NAACP Image Award (as a youngster Bryton presented this same award to Michael Jackson). Bryton continues in his role on *Y&R* and he does voice work on animated series like Nickelodeon's *Zevo-3*. Somehow, the busy actor manages to find time to cast a few spells in Mystic Falls: "I'm truly lucky and blessed to have had the life that I've had."

(See page 252 for an interview with Bryton.)

the corrupting influences of the outside world. Just once a century the town comes alive for a day (it's 1754 in Brigadoon) and it's idyllic for all except the one man who thinks it's a curse to be trapped inside the town's borders. Tommy, one of the hunters (played by Gene Kelly in the film), falls for local beauty Fiona (Cyd Charisse) and is forced to choose between living only one day a century inside the fairy tale and returning to the empty hustle of New York City. A place that exists just out of reach of the mortal realm, Brigadoon is a place of innocence now lost to the modern world. The story of true love being found across centuries is something Elena can relate to.

• In season 1, Damon was the mastermind who came into town with a diabolical plan; in the first half of season 2, that role was played by Katherine. But in this episode the mantle has been officially passed on to the one and only Elijah.

THE RULES: No question about it: werewolves got the fuzzy end of the lollipop with sickening pain, breaking bones, and hours and hours of it. Ingesting wolfsbane weakens a werewolf, and drinking enough of it prevented wolf-Tyler from escaping. Apparently a werewolf is strong enough to destroy a rig set up to withstand 5,000 pounds. A werewolf's transformation normally happens at the moon's apex, though a first transformation can happen earlier. Generally, a werewolf stays in wolf form for a few hours, give or take. A werewolf can "sniff out" a vampire, and Jules can also tell that Tyler is a werewolf, presumably also by scent. Jonas and Luka lift the tomb spell "before [they] lose the full moon," suggesting that they draw on the power of that celestial event to fuel their magic. A werewolf bite isn't lethal to a vampire . . . at least not immediately; the wound does creepily fester and bubble, which would dampen one's desire to get frisky with a "special friend."

THE DIABOLICAL PLAN: Trapped in her house to prevent her from wantonly handing herself (and the moonstone) over to Klaus, Elena manages to make a deal with Elijah when he comes to her: he'll protect her loved ones in exchange for her agreement to help him lure Klaus out. Using Luka to fake out Bonnie, Elijah is also now in possession of the moonstone. Why is Jules looking for Mason, and what's her interest in Tyler?

BITE MARKS: Jules, in wolf form, bites Rose. Damon stabs wolf-Jules with a decorative sword.

PREVIOUSLY ON THE VAMPIRE DIARIES: In "There Goes the Neighborhood," Elena expressly states that she doesn't want a chaperone, bodyguard, or babysitter even though she's in constant danger; being a prisoner in her own house must be her worst nightmare. Damon uses the same strategy — poisonous herb in a drink — to out Jules at the Grill that Mason used on Damon in "Kill or Be Killed." After Sarah dies and Tyler's curse is activated in "Masquerade," Caroline repeats his name, asking him what's happening, and he tells her to get away but she stays, witnessing his first moments as a werewolf; that scene was a preview of their relationship in this episode. In "The Turning Point," Alaric interrupts as Mayor Lockwood tries to make Tyler and Jeremy fight, and the Mayor says to Alaric, "You just marked yourself," like Jules does in this episode to Damon. Luka uses Bonnie for a supernatural scheme just like Ben McKittrick used her for

Transforming Tyler

When it came to bringing about the change from man to wolf on *The Vampire Diaries*, executive producer Kevin Williamson knew what he wanted to see and what he didn't. "I remember seeing *American Werewolf in London* as a kid for the first time," said Williamson in an interview with the *New York Post*'s PopWrap blog. "I really responded to the idea that a werewolf transformation is so painful. When David Naughton [who plays werewolf David Kessler] fell apart in the living room and just started ripping his clothes off, it was such a wow moment. That showed how horrible it is. This is a curse and I want people to know it's a curse." Trying to achieve werewolf transformation effects that look good is "the hardest thing" he's ever done. Williamson wanted to steer clear of the cheesiness, something many critics felt took away from the watchability of Wes Craven's *Cursed*, the 2005 film Williamson wrote that featured less-than-awesome (to be kind) computer-generated werewolves. For *TVD*, Williamson's approach was more cautious: "Every time you do a big special effect, it can look phony. And our schedule doesn't allow months and months for special effects, so we tried to limit it; be selective about the shots we chose and be classy about it."

Before it was Michael Trevino's turn to show just how much of a curse it is being a werewolf, it was Taylor Kinney's, both in "Bad Moon Rising" and in the video Mason makes of his first transformation seen in "The Sacrifice." Trevino watched while Taylor Kinney filmed that sequence, saying the actor set the tone for werewolves on *The Vampire Diaries* with his performance. Season 1's co-executive producer Marcos Siega directed that video, as well as Tyler's transformation scenes; the rest of "By the Light of the Moon" was directed by Elizabeth Allen. For Michael Trevino, it was important to have someone he knew well guiding him through what was the biggest challenge of his acting career: "To have that relationship where you totally, 100 percent trust that person — that was Marcos." In preparation, Tyler watched videos of women in labor and of wolves feeding, and he trained for the filming process as if it were a marathon: he had to make sure he had the emotional and physical stamina to go through the scenes over and over again, take after take. The scene was shot over two 14-hour days, and Trevino spent almost all of it in real metal chains, an experience he understated as being "rough." Candice Accola was by his side the entire time and empathized with her fellow actor, who had to be emotionally raw and next to naked for such an extended period of time. "It's a very vulnerable thing for anybody and especially at the workplace," explained Candice. "You have to remember that it's not just us two in the room; there's probably like 50 to 100 people on set on any given day. To be crying and screaming and hurting — it was hard to watch, but in a great way. Because everyone was just so respectful and aware that he was working so hard to create a great moment for the fans."

Anna's ("Unpleasantville," "Children of the Damned"). The man witch dupes Bonnie with a visually impressive but ultimately empty magic trick, which she herself successfully pulled off in "Isobel" when she pretended to deactivate the Gilbert device. Elijah says to Elena, "We're negotiating now?" echoing their first encounter in "Rose" when she tried to negotiate using her knowledge of the moonstone.

MEANWHILE IN FELL'S CHURCH: In *Dark Reunion*, Tyler transforms into a werewolf under a full moon, but the creature he becomes is much more of a man-wolf hybrid, still able to speak. The change from teenage boy to monster happens in an instant, not over bone-crushing hours. Damon says to Elena in *The Struggle*, "You do have some sense. You're right to be afraid of me; I'm the most dangerous thing you're ever likely to encounter in your life," which is comparable to Elijah's comment to Katherine at the tomb door.

OFF CAMERA: This episode's promo featured footage of Katherine and Stefan making out in the tomb, causing the fandom to explode online with speculation (and more than a little shipper outrage); the creators of the show have no control over which clips are selected. Kat Graham describes Bonnie as a "very compassionate character for being so young. And [always] look-ing out for her friends and being loyal. I've really enjoyed it. I'm so proud of the character she is. But she's also capable of really being a bitch. Which I love, and I'm not against it at all. People are like, 'Bonnie was such a bitch to that person,' and I'm like, 'Good, she needed to be.' I stick up for her and I'm all about the balance of that kind of strength, so I'm happy about that." Matt Davis likes playing Alaric Saltzman "because of his relationships. I love working with Ian and his character and our banter, and I love that [Alaric's] not a supernatural figure. He's just a man and he's a teacher and he's been thrust into this supernatural circumstance. And I like the elements of action behind him. He makes his own weapons, and he's his own investigator and he's sort of paired up with Stefan and Damon. And Damon in particular, who's the bad guy you love to — he's not really the bad guy, he's just sort of amoral [laughs]. He's constantly challenging Alaric in that aspect. But for those reasons, I enjoy playing Alaric. And his name."

FOGGY MOMENTS: Bonnie isn't at *all* suspicious when Luka immediately forgives her for nearly killing him? It was a little disappointing to see Bonnie so easily duped.

MUSIC: Jenna explains her new historical society duties to Alaric at the Grill to Ra Ra Riot's "Shadowcasting." Caroline and Tyler arrive in the woods to "This Time Next Year" by Goldhawks. The Drums' "Let's Go Surfing" is playing as Jules arrives at the Grill. Alaric approaches her to Agent Ribbons' "I'm Alright." Superchunk's "Everything at Once" plays as Damon runs down the lodging options in Mystic Falls. Jules ends the ruse to "Quarry Hymns" by Land of Talk. Caroline finds Tyler curled up on the floor to Howie Day's "Longest Night," which continues as Stefan and Elena get back together. (Day's first song on *TVD* was in "You're Undead to Me.")

QUESTIONS:
- Why was Jules in Mason's apartment? Who did Jules call after leaving the Lockwood estate? Is Jules a friend of Mason's or is she part of some secret werewolf society, analogous to the Founder's Council or the vampires' Originals?
- Assuming that Elijah told Elena the truth, did he do something to get kicked out of Klaus's inner circle? Why does he want to kill Klaus?
- Why is Jonas Martin working for (or with) Elijah? Is he in his debt, or is he on his side? Is Jonas simply interested in building his grimoire library, or is he collecting the books in search of a particular spell?
- When Katherine controls Stefan's dreams, is she controlling his reactions too? Or is Stefan acting on his own subconscious desires?
- How much human consciousness does a werewolf have when in wolf form?
- If Elijah plans on killing Klaus after drawing him out of hiding "when the time is right," why does he care if Katherine is in the tomb where Klaus can find her? Is she part of his plan in some way yet to be revealed, or just an added incentive for Klaus to come to Mystic Falls?
- Katherine tells Stefan that Isobel found her, but in "Isobel," Elena is told the opposite: that Katherine found Isobel. Did one of them lie or is this just an inconsistency?

Damon: I feel, Elena. And it sucks.

2.12 *The Descent*

Original air date: January 27, 2011
Written by: Elizabeth Craft and Sarah Fain
Directed by: Marcos Siega
Guest cast: George Bryant (Maintenance Worker), Anna Enger (Dana), Jason Ferguson (Eddie), Ahna O'Reilly (Jessica), Ryan Proffitt (Park Ranger Martinson), Allee Sutton Hethcoat (Jill)

Damon and Elena take care of Rose as her werewolf bite slowly and painfully kills her.

Loss of bodily control was explored in Tyler's werewolf transformation in "By the Light of the Moon," which though impossibly painful was only temporary. Here, Rose loses both mind and body to the ravages of the werewolf bite. The violence of illness is alien to vampires — they don't get so much as a cold — and so Rose's death becomes an incredibly human experience for a supernatural creature who's missed being human for five centuries.

Traditionally on *The Vampire Diaries*, death is swift. To use a Carolineism, when it's curtains for vampires, werewolves, witches, and humans it happens suddenly, often instantaneously. But in "The Descent," Rose's deterioration lasts a day, giving her a chance to let go of her fear of death and to reflect on how she's lived her life and the choices she's made. Though Damon describes her as "maudlin" in how she evaluates her life, Rose is right to say that she is without a home, friends, or a purpose. In all the ways that matter to *her*, after living for 560 years, she doesn't matter anymore — everything has changed and everyone she knew is gone. Her isolation is in large part a result of one choice: to spend her life on the run from Klaus, driven by fear, unwilling to build a life for herself, with no true companion other than Trevor. Damon asks Elena to play nursemaid to Rose: not that after vomiting blood, clean sheets aren't important, but Elena's true purpose is to ensure that Rose has company. When Rose is scared, Elena can give her the comfort of her presence and reassure her that she isn't alone. Rose reminds Elena that to be loved the way she is, by the Salvatore brothers as well as by her friends and family, is not something that's guaranteed in life, and it's something worth fighting for. Rose sees fear as a major motivation in Elena's deal with Elijah and calls her willingness to die "giving up." But the scary-as-heck scenes of Elena evading Crazy Rose's attack show that Elena's sense of self-preservation is still alive and kicking. Is Elena motivated by selflessness or fear? Is she going to surrender without a fight?

The romantic exchange between Elena and Stefan in his room at the beginning of the episode is cut short by him "ruining the moment" with talk of the doom and gloom that faces them. There's no separating the sweet, peaceful, or pleasant from the darkness that faces each couple on *The Vampire Diaries*. Most significantly, in the kindest act Damon's ever committed, he creates the perfect ending for Rose, and then he has to kill his friend. Caroline can't avoid her problems. Though time seems to stand still for a moment as she and Matt kiss, she immediately pushes him away; she can't tell Matt she loves him without tears in her eyes. And Caroline loses herself only for a second when Tyler kisses her before pushing him away too. She doesn't want to betray Matt, but it's undeniable that there's something between her and Tyler. It's a tricky situation to navigate, especially since Matt and Tyler are best friends. Her secrets and the danger in Caroline's mixed feelings for her suitors make for great television. Their love triangle is believable, complicated, and compelling because the set-up has been handled with so much heart and with delicacy, especially in this episode where Caroline's locking lips with both. It's a reminder that *TVD* writers take good care of their characters, building their relationships carefully.

Until Jules's werewolf pals roll into Mystic Falls, her impact on Tyler lies mainly in how the information she gives him will affect his relationship with Caroline. His friendship, and budding romance, with Caroline is built on shared secrets and on trust. If Tyler believes that Caroline is deceiving him (which she is, although altruistically), everything that binds them together could unravel in an instant — especially with Jules's accusation that it was Caroline and her vampire pals who murdered Mason. Jules paints Caroline in a way that brings to mind the actual dynamic that existed between vampire Katherine and werewolf Mason. If Tyler's faith in Caroline is destroyed, the raging side of his personality, now equipped with werewolf strength, may be unleashed. Many of Caroline's relationships are marred by her inability to tell the whole truth — never mind her vamp-hunting mother, she can only be partially honest with Tyler or with Matt, and that limitation threatens to destroy what she has with them. Like Tyler, Matt trusts Caroline but he

senses that there's something she isn't telling him, the *something* that's keeping them apart. (Besides Dana. Not now, Dana!)

In an exchange that echoes Damon's compassionate response to Rose's illness and death, Caroline tells Tyler why she put herself at risk to help him: she didn't want him to be alone. Even her nickname ("Care") speaks to her personality now. Despite being a vampire, Caroline's humanity is strong and this is what drives her to overcome the numerous boundaries (and obstacles) that once existed between her and Tyler.

While that's entirely in keeping with who Caroline is and wants to be, Damon is ill at ease playing the "nice guy." He denies to Stefan and Elena that Rose's life matters to him, but his words don't match his actions. Damon takes care of her, he tries to get a cure out of Jules, he comforts and reassures Rose, and, in the end, he does the kindest possible thing. In a dream he's controlling, he brings her to her favorite time and place — back when she mattered and had a home — he takes away her pain, and he ends her life. Beautifully filmed and acted, the scene shows both vampires at their most human. Damon may have been right when he quipped earlier to Elena that "death happens," but his implication, that its commonness makes any one person's death ordinary, is wrong, and he knows it. Though Damon refuses to acknowledge that he has feelings, he does. Rose's death and Elena's insistence that he should emote drives Damon to a breaking point. Like his breakdown in "The Return" — when the pain of rejection from both Katherine and Elena drove him to get drunk and attack Jeremy — Damon is overwhelmed with feeling again: guilt for Rose dying in his stead, frustration at his relationship with Elena being so close and yet so far from what he wants it to be, and anger at not being human but desperately missing it.

Since we first met Damon in the road waiting for victims in the opening scene of the pilot, he's slowly evolved (with stumbles along the way) from a ruthless monster to a humane vampire. After learning that Katherine had never been trapped in the tomb in "Fool Me Once," Damon has tried to find a new purpose — primarily to protect and love Elena as well as be a better brother to Stefan. But Rose's death makes him question the meaning of his existence. Now lying again in the road, lost in his struggle between monster and man, Damon laments that his efforts to be who Elena, and Stefan, wants him to be fall short again and again. Damon calls Jessica his "existential crisis": whether to kill or not to kill is the question central to his identity struggle. What is the point of trying to be human if he can never actually feel human again? Shouldn't he let his vampire instincts take over? So soon after

Michaela McManus as Jules

As a kid growing up in Rhode Island, Michaela McManus would often go to the theater with her four siblings to see their mother perform on stage, and it was there that she caught the acting bug. After high school, Michaela studied drama and fine arts at Fordham University, then went to NYU's graduate acting program. She left the East Coast behind for Los Angeles, where she landed her first major role in 2008 on The CW's *One Tree Hill*, playing Lindsey Strauss. She joined the long-running *Law & Order: Special Victims Unit* as A.D.A. Kim Greylek in its 2009–2010 season. Michaela also guest-starred on episodes of *CSI: New York* (2009), *Castle* (2009), and *Hawaii Five-O* (2011). She landed a lead role in a series picked up for the 2011–2012 season, ABC's *Awake* (an "*Inception*-flavored thriller").

Jules wasn't the first *Vampire Diaries* part Michaela auditioned for: she tried out for Rose but that part went to Lauren Cohan. But when she did land a gig on *TVD*, she was on a plane the very next day headed for Atlanta. Luckily, because her then-fiancé (now-husband) Mike Daniels is a writer for the show, she was already very familiar with the series. "It's kind of rare when that happens when you've actually seen every episode," explained Michaela, "so I was really lucky in that I knew the world and I was very familiar with the characters and the story so it was easy for me to jump right in."

As the werewolf who comes to town stirring up trouble and butting heads with Damon, Jules is not the most beloved of characters. But Michaela doesn't mind, as she told TheTVChick.com, "I'm definitely not a stranger to audience opposition. When I was working on *One Tree Hill*, there were a lot of people that were not big fans of my character. I came in and was sort of the cause of why this one relationship didn't work out [laughs]. And almost every job I've had there have been people who are not huge fans of the character. But I think it's all a matter of perspective. I think if you really put yourself in Jules's shoes, you can see where she comes from and what it's all about. I don't think she's doing this to make enemies. She comes from a very honest place."

Acting opposite Ian Somerhalder was a particular highlight for the actress: "In real life, he's such a charmer and so funny. When you're working with him, he's just completely unafraid to take risks. He changes things up; he's always in the moment. It's just a good time whenever I have a scene with him."

ensuring that Rose has the most humane death imaginable, Damon chooses to give in and kill again. It may not be his best option, but it's the easiest.

COMPELLING MOMENT: Damon biting into his existential crisis — a fascinating and dark turn for the character in a great Damon episode.

CIRCLE OF KNOWLEDGE:
• No Bonnie, Jeremy, or Jenna in this episode.

- *The Descent* is a 2005 horror movie that follows a group of women who explore caves and find they've accidentally stumbled into the subterranean dwelling of creatures hungry for their flesh. In addition to being absolutely terrifying, the film served as the visual inspiration for the tomb in "Fool Me Once" — so dark that the creepy creatures are barely glimpsed. Like Elena, the protagonist, Sarah, lost her family in a car accident, and she must fight to survive in a world where heartbreak and loss aren't the only horrors awaiting her.
- When Mason arrived in "The Return," Tyler called him the "black sheep"; here, Jules puts on a sheepskin jacket — two wolves in sheep's clothing.
- Akin to the old vampire trick of lying in the road to stop a passerby, werewolf Jules plays the victim with the park ranger, and then attacks, which foreshadows the old lie-in-the-road vampire trick at the end of the episode when Damon attacks Jessica.
- Unlike Stefan's room, Damon's room is sparse, devoid of mementos or memories.
- The copy of Margaret Mitchell's 1936 novel *Gone with the Wind* that Elena picks up in Damon's bedroom appears to be a first edition. For more on the epic romance, see page 218.
- At the barbecue, the school's marching band plays the same song they did in "Founder's Day."
- Though still very involved in school activities, Caroline isn't a cheerleader anymore; she's not in uniform at the boosters' barbecue. (And Bonnie seems to have quit the squad too.)
- Never offer a stranger help. At least not in Mystic Falls. That seems to be the moral of this episode: the park ranger, the kindly janitor, and the woman in her car all stop to help a stranger and end up dead.

THE RULES: A vampire bitten by a werewolf suffers from incredible pain, chills, delirium, and rabidity. At Jules's campground we see firsthand what Henry described in the "Memory Lane" flashback: werewolves are capable of tearing humans limb from limb.

THE DIABOLICAL PLAN: Elena knows that the moonstone was not destroyed and is in Elijah's possession. Jules has called in her wolf pack: what sort of troublemaking will they get up to? Uncle John is back, after being driven out of town by Stefan in "The Return." Looking forward to see how well he works with vampires to protect his estranged daughter from ritual sacrifice . . . and with no magical Gilbert ring to raise him should he die.

BITE MARKS: Jules wakes up to discover she's dismembered at least four campers. She beats a park ranger to death with one of their limbs. Rose attacks Elena, hallucinating that she's Katerina, and Elena cleverly evades her attack by exposing her to sunlight and digging her nails into her werewolf wound. Rose kills the maintenance man and the blond couple. Damon stakes Rose in the heart, euthanizing her. Damon feeds on and kills Jessica.

PREVIOUSLY ON THE VAMPIRE DIARIES: In "Haunted," Elena wore a nurse's costume for the second Halloween in a row; here she plays nurse to Rose. In "A Few Good Men," Isobel's phone number led fans to a voicemail message; the number Alaric texts to Stefan leads to a new message. Rose's murder of the handsome but banal couple in the school parking lot was reminiscent of Damon's early season 1 kills ("Pilot," "Night of the Comet"). After Rose apologizes for her killing spree, Damon replies, "It happens," which we've heard twice before from him: in "There Goes the Neighborhood" when Kelly Donovan tells him she slept with the manager of the Grill's boyfriend and in "Let the Right One In" after Alaric punches him in the face.

OFF CAMERA: The paintings in Damon's room are replicas of those stolen along with other pieces in a huge heist from Boston's Isabella Stewart Gardner Museum in 1990: the portrait of the man in the top hat is a copy of Edouard Manet's *Chez Tortoni* (1878–1880) and the painting over the fireplace is a copy of Rembrandt's *A Lady and Gentleman in Black* (1633). Damon's bed really is as big as it looks onscreen: it was custom made for the show to be larger than large. As Ian Somerhalder described it: "This thing, I'm not even kidding you, it's gigantic. You splice together two king-sized beds . . . Damon could fit an entire sorority on this bed, which I'm sure at some point he will."

One of Julie Plec's favorite season 2 scenes is Rose's death. As she said during an interview at Chicago's pop culture convention C2E2, "When I saw that episode for the first time all assembled, I sat there and I cried like a baby and I was sobbing. It was so embarrassing because I wrote some of this, and I'm crying. . . . Those are the moments that you just live for when something that was in your head [is] executed in that perfect, poetic way."

Kevin Williamson wrote Damon's "existential crisis" speech at the end of the episode, which Plec described to Zap2It as "brilliance in action. It changed everything. It really reinvigorated all of us for that character, because Damon is all about how deliciously bad he can be and how epically *good* he can be, and how the two are always at odds with each other."

FOGGY MOMENTS: Elena drinks some diluted vervain before handing over the glass to Stefan. Is Stefan no longer feeding from her? Or will he be getting a two-in-one effect — building strength from her blood and immunity to vervain? Did Rose hear Damon and Elena's conversation in the hallway about how likely it is that she'll die? Seemed like they were well within vampire-hearing range. Did Elena forget about the doors to the patio opposite the front door of the Salvatore house? Her instincts in that chase scene were totally clever, save for this horror-movie moment of "running up the stairs when she should be running out the door" (to quote *Scream*'s Ms. Sidney Prescott).

MUSIC: The Booster Club's barbecue kicks off with Anberlin's "Impossible." (Anberlin's cover of "Enjoy the Silence" in "Lost Girls" is one of the series' best music moments.) Alaric hangs out at the Grill to "The Last Time" by The Daylights. Stefan gets a text from Alaric with Isobel's phone number while Broken Bells' "The Mall & Misery" plays in the background. The barbecue continues and Caroline hauls a big bag of trash to Stars' "Take Me to the Riot." Liz and her deputies call Damon for help while Telekinesis's "Country Lane" plays. Tyler meets up with Jules at the Grill to "I Like It a Lot" by Death Ships. Damon's existential crisis speech is accompanied by TV On the Radio's "DLZ." (The band also had a song in "Rose.")

QUESTIONS:
- A point of curiosity: was Rose a blood-bag feeder before she started hanging out in Mystic Falls? She says she never liked taking human life, but (in "Rose") Trevor tore into the man he'd compelled to kidnap Elena. Did they have different philosophies or did Rose consider feeding on, compelling, and/or killing humans a sometimes-necessary evil?
- Elena isn't upset with Stefan for trying to find Isobel despite her earlier objections. Has Elena's resolve been shaken by Rose, on the one hand, telling her to fight in spite of her fear, and Damon, on the other, accusing her of giving up?

- Stefan goes off to find Isobel but returns with John. Where is Isobel?

❧

Caroline: You just stood there, when they were going to kill us, you just stood there. You didn't do anything.
Tyler: I didn't know what to do.
Caroline: You help your friend — that's what you do.

2.13 *Daddy Issues*

Original air date: February 3, 2011
Written by: Kevin Williamson and Julie Plec
Directed by: Joshua Butler
Guest cast: Stephen Amell (Brady)

Werewolves come to the heart of vampire country to claim Tyler while John's return stirs up family drama.

An episode like "Daddy Issues" takes viewers so far beyond the common perception of what a series like *The Vampire Diaries* can accomplish, and it serves as a good explanation of why the fandom reacts so strongly and emotionally to the show. Here, the writers explore core questions of who we are, who we want to be, and how we should behave with our family, friends, lovers, and enemies. In a single episode *TVD* tackles morality, the meaning of trust, family and friendship, and loyalty and duty, all of it through the characters' search for identity and their actions in the face of crises. *The Vampire Diaries* gives us all that, and a bubble bath, for those who feel like diving in.

In Mystic Falls, trust issues run more rampant than unwelcome werewolves, and the fallout for being untrustworthy ranges from being a pariah (John) to a brush with death (Caroline). With no consideration for how the news will affect Jenna, nor for how the truth will affect Elena's relationship with her, "Uncle Daddy John" reveals he's Elena's birth father. Jenna is flabbergasted that he and Elena were capable of keeping a secret of that magnitude. Alaric meanwhile has to keep up the pretense that he didn't already know (never mind that he is keeping *way* more head-spinning secrets still). Caroline, Stefan, and Elena keep the Tyler situation a secret from Damon, afraid of what he'll do if he knows. Bonnie feels betrayed by the Witches Martin, refusing to believe Jonas when he says Elijah will stay true to his word. No one trusts John, who returns to town demanding that Elena, Stefan, and Damon prove themselves trustworthy before he'll let them in on what he knows.

The episode begins with Caroline facing Tyler and ends with her unwittingly being outed as a liar to Matt. Elena is two for two in the "who can you trust" game: Elijah proves to be an Original who keeps his promise, and, judging by John's trip to the tomb to see Katherine, Elena's instinct not to believe in him is a reliable one. And then there's Tyler who doesn't know who to trust. Both Jules and Stefan make their cases — Jules offering a new life with other werewolves, Stefan offering the chance to stay in Mystic Falls and hold on to his old human life — and both argue that they mean only the best for him. But Tyler doesn't seem capable of making up his mind, not under such a barrage of information and with no time to consider it. He's left floundering between the werewolves he barely knows and his friends who've turned out to be vampires responsible for killing his uncle. Not an enviable position.

The werewolf code espoused by Jules and Brady is based on an old-school "pack mentality": protect your own above all others, be loyal to your kind, fulfill your duty, and know your enemy — in their case, every last vampire. When Brady looks at Caroline in the cage, he doesn't see a teenage girl crying in pain and for mercy; like Giuseppe Salvatore and John Gilbert before him, he sees a vampire — an evil creature that deserves no pity, no kindness, no existence at all. There doesn't seem to be any place in Jules and Brady's ethos for Tyler's complicated feelings for Caroline. In choosing Caroline as the vampire who is kidnapped and tortured by Brady and Jules, the writers make it particularly difficult to sympathize with their side. Candice Accola has won many devoted fans for Caroline, particularly in season 2, and to have her scream out in pain all but guarantees that viewers will see the error in the werewolves' vengeance. As Stefan says, the grudge between werewolves and vampires is an outdated concept, one that could be overcome by trust and friendship. Though neither Brady nor Jules seem willing to tell Tyler, it seems clear that Mason chose a different path than the one they present as the only natural one. He was in love with a vampire and tried to be peaceful with the Salvatore brothers (at least until Damon stabbed him in the gut). He followed his own rules rather than the pack's. But because of Mason's

The Forbes residence. The two Covington houses that serve as the Forbes and Gilbert homes are situated next door to each other.

guardedness and his untimely death Tyler is clueless about what kind of man his uncle really was.

It's telling that from the time Tyler arrives with Stefan at the werewolf RV headquarters to the end of the battle, the only thing he says is "What the hell's going on?" Stefan tells Jules that Tyler is free to make his own decisions, but ultimately it's Tyler's indecision that determines which side he's on. Caroline feels so hurt and betrayed by Tyler just standing by, dumbstruck, while Jules holds a gun to her head ready to kill her, that she tells him he's destroyed their friendship. She directs him to return to the pack, and he does. So often on *TVD*, characters' actions in a crisis help define who they are, and it is pretty tough to watch Tyler falter and fail to stand up for his friend, despite the danger he knows she put herself in to stand by

CANDICE
ACCOLA

his side through his transformation. With no ties left save for his mother, it will be interesting to see how Tyler's identity evolves: will he stay with the wolf pack or fight for Caroline's friendship and his life in Mystic Falls?

Tyler's a character still so early in his journey that he could believably go in any number of directions.

Like Tyler, Damon is in the midst of an identity crisis, going a little crazy as he tries to be both the man Elena wants him to be and the killer he feels he truly is. Elena doesn't know that he's killed again, so she wholeheartedly believes in Damon's ability to be "the better man." And while Damon is very aware of how Stefan and Elena perceive his journey from villain to potential hero, he doesn't trust himself to pull it off. Damon feels out of control, vacillating between being the "good guy" and the kind of guy who indulges in the tub with Andie. He seems to believe that to be the hero he has to destroy all that is bad within him. Stefan, on the other hand, knows that the darkness will always live inside him, but he just won't let it control him. In practice, being good means behaving better than we are, making the right choice over the easy or self-serving one. There was a time, not that long ago, when Damon wouldn't even consider staving off temptation by ignoring Andie at the Grill; he now knows that it's in her best interest (and "the best interest of women everywhere") if he does. Has Damon's love for Elena changed him, as Andie suggests, or will he always eventually give in to his bloodlust? Perhaps his double life — helpful Salvatore brother by day, lady killer by night — will blow up in his face, destroying the friendship he's rebuilt with Elena. Or maybe it's just the thing he needs in his life: a little balance. In the meantime, it's fascinating to watch Damon's dip into darkness, and it's refreshing to see such a traditionally vampiric moment: Andie realizing she's in the tub with a killer, Damon compelling her not to be afraid, and finally biting into her neck as a river of blood flows down her back.

After Jeremy tries to give his uncle's ring back, on the assumption that that's why he came back to Mystic Falls, John asks him what kind of man he would be if he took it back. It's clear from John's final conversation with Elena in this episode that the question is on his mind. He tries to convince Elena that he *is* a better man than he was when last she saw him, that he's seen the error of his past behavior, that he had lost his way after losing his brother. His character is wonderfully complicated: watching his family reject him again and again made him pitiable. But Jenna, Jeremy, Elena, and the brothers Salvatore each have good reason to be wary of him, and John definitely makes no effort to be loved, particularly in the way he interacts with Jenna. While John certainly lost his way, as he describes it, in his hateful actions of last season, his trip to the tomb to visit Katherine suggests his old habits die hard. Will he protect Elena and the Gilbert family as he has pledged to do? Can the weapon he gave Damon be trusted?

Elena suffers from the episode's titular daddy issues, and she refuses to let John get away with anything. Elena declares that she will never be John's daughter. In Elena's heart, her parents Grayson and Miranda will always be near perfect — they didn't survive long enough to have a relationship with her as an adult and they will remain in a frozen idealized state for her. John sullies the idea of "parent" for Elena, never mind his insistence that, as her biological father, he has some right to voice his opinion about her choices. Blood relation doesn't mean "family" to Elena, and she's fiercely protective of the memory of her parents in this episode with John, just as she was when she met her birth mother in "Isobel." In the same way, Elena will always be Jeremy's sister even though they are only cousins by blood. Luckily for Elena, she not only has Jenna and Jeremy but a wealth of support in her girlfriends, Damon (who immediately asks her if she's okay after hearing about the John debacle), and Stefan who always seems to show up right when a teary-eyed Elena needs a hug.

Though he's struggled in the past with the monster inside him (and as he's sure to face that demon again), Stefan has found a way to consistently be the "better man." He tries to act as peacemaker with Tyler and the were-wolves, he's there for Elena as she deals with her daddy issues, and he knows that no matter how strong and resilient Caroline is, she still needs the support of her friends after a harrowing and traumatic experience. Stefan gets that Caroline needs to slumber it with her best girlfriends, so he facilitates that. He knows that's what you do — you help your friend.

COMPELLING MOMENT: The Caroline-Bonnie-Elena hug.

CIRCLE OF KNOWLEDGE:
- "How is it even possible to keep a secret like that?" Oh Jenna, just you wait.
- Andie Star is a news broadcaster for WPKW9, the same local channel Logan Fell worked for before his untimely death(s).
- Interestingly Elena tells Damon to do whatever it takes to get Caroline back, except killing Tyler, which implies that she's fine with him killing

other werewolves. The moral ground that girl stands on gets shakier every episode.

- In the werewolf RV, there's a calendar marking the lunar cycle hanging by the door.
- Hats off to Ian Somerhalder for his perfect delivery of Damon's reply to Andie calling him "Mr. Tall Dark and Handsome": "I'm not that tall."

THE RULES: Jonas is capable of taking down specific individuals and leaving others safe from the brain-pain spell. John (via Isobel) says that the way to kill an Original is to stab him in the heart with a dagger coated in the ash of a white oak tree that dates back to the genesis of the Originals.

THE DIABOLICAL PLAN: Jules wants to take "the boy," Tyler, away from Mystic Falls to live with her and her werewolf pack; Brady wants revenge on the vampires who killed Mason. Brady and Jules are very interested when Tyler mentions the moonstone, so it appears they are aware of the Sun and the Moon Curse. John makes a big show of determining whether or not the Salvatore brothers and Elena can be trusted, but he's working in secret with Isobel to get Katherine out of the tomb. When Stefan thought Katherine was being helpful in telling him to seek out Isobel for information on Klaus, he was actually being used as an errand boy. Elijah proves to be a man of his word, sending Jonas to save the gang as he promised Elena he would.

BITE MARKS: Tyler shoves Caroline against her car. Stefan pins Tyler to the wall to prevent him from crying out. Jules sprays vervain mace in Caroline's face. Brady shoots Caroline in the head and, after she's imprisoned in the cage, shoots her again in the chest and shoulder and, just for kicks, sprays her with vervain from a water gun and shoots wooden splinters into her neck from a blow dart. In the fight with the werewolves, Damon rips out one's heart and nearly kills Brady, before Jules shoots Damon. Stefan snaps the neck of a werewolf, throws a stake into another's neck, and disables a third before being staked in the back. Jonas takes down the werewolves with the brain aneurysm spell, sparing Damon, Stefan, Caroline, and Tyler. Damon bites Andie in . . . the bubble bath.

MEANWHILE IN FELL'S CHURCH: The friendship between Elena, Meredith, and Bonnie is central to the book series, and the girls come to each other's sides when in pain. In *The Awakening*, Meredith and Bonnie comfort Elena in the cemetery: "If nowhere else, she belonged with the friends who cared about her." John tells Damon that the ash of the white oak tree on the dagger will kill an Original; in *Dark Reunion*, a stake made from white ash wood is the only weapon that can kill Klaus, an Original.

OFF CAMERA: Candice Accola had to show yet another side of Caroline in this episode and found the "surroundings and the environment helped out a lot. The cage was a real cage. I couldn't get out of it myself. It took a couple of crew members to help me out every single time. And I was an absolute mess. It was really long hours, so it made it easy to feel frustrated and tired, in the most positive way. And Stephen Amell, who played Brady, was really, really wonderful. You're always as good as the scene partner you're with, so he really helped out a lot as well." Toronto-born Stephen Amell has a long list of TV credits including Canadian shows *Rent-a-Goalie*, *Da Kink in My Hair*, and *Heartland* and stars in 2011's *Justice for Natalee Holloway*.

FOGGY MOMENTS: After Richard Lockwood died in "Founder's Day," Carol Lockwood was named interim mayor, but in this episode she's referred to as the mayor. Will there still be an election in Mystic Falls? Curious that neither Katherine nor John mention the last time they saw each other, when she left him for dead and missing most of his right hand.

MUSIC: At the Grill, while Jenna and Alaric have lunch, Adele's "Don't You Remember" plays. Damon talks to Uncle John about drinking vervain to "Only One" by Alex Band (who also had a song in "Bloodlines"). Andie Star approaches Damon to Hurts' "Stay." (Hurts' first time on *TVD* was in "The Return.") Elena and John face off outside the ladies' room to Natasha Bedingfield's "Strip Me." Stefan brings the girls over to Caroline's and Damon and Andie share a bath to "Losing Your Memory" by Ryan Star.

QUESTIONS:
- The werewolves were well prepared to take out vampires with wooden bullets, vervain-filled water guns, wooden blow darts, blow torches, and stakes. How do they know so much about vampires' weaknesses yet the

vampires were not even sure werewolves existed until recently? Does Katherine know about this pack of werewolves? Was she exaggerating the rarity of lycanthropes to Stefan in "Memory Lane"?

- John tells Damon that if Isobel accomplishes what she's trying to do, Klaus will never come to Mystic Falls. What is Isobel up to? What sort of unholy alliance do John, Isobel, and Katherine have, and what's their endgame?

❀

Luka: Elena has to die.

2.14 *Crying Wolf*

Original air date: February 10, 2011
Written by: Brian Young
Directed by: David Von Ancken
Guest cast: Stephen Amell (Brady), Erik Stocklin (Stevie)

Elena and Stefan head to the lakehouse, but the werewolves are on their tail and on the hunt for the moonstone.

No one believes a liar, even when they're telling the truth — that's the moral of the fable of the Boy Who Cried Wolf, and it's a lesson some of our Mystic Falls friends take to heart by the end of "Crying Wolf." Since the very first episode when Stefan struggled with hiding the truth from Elena and covering up his brother's bloody tracks, one of the main recurring conflicts on *The Vampire Diaries* has been deception and its consequences. In "Crying Wolf," there are bold-faced lies; lies of omission; altruistically motivated deceptions as well as the good old-fashioned self-serving kind; information gathered through trickery, coercion, witchcraft, and torture; and a dash of honesty thrown in for good measure. Matt calls Caroline and Tyler out for lying to him again and again. Alaric laments having to lie to Jenna all the time, and John plants the first seed of her suspicion, calling Alaric a liar and raising questions about the not-so-dead Isobel. Damon and Alaric don't trust the ash-and-dagger solution John has given them. Bonnie tricks Luka into sipping that roofied coffee. Damon makes Andie Star lie to herself about her feelings for him ("You're falling hard."). Tyler does some texting espionage after stealing Caroline's phone. Brady and Jules keep reminding Tyler that the vampires *lied* to him. And, in the end, Stefan points out (between groans of pain) that they've been lying to Tyler by leaving out rather pertinent details about that pesky Sun and Moon Curse. With the exception of Jenna and Matt, everyone in Mystic Falls is leading some kind of double life: some are hiding the truth for their own gain, others to protect their loved ones.

Elena asks Stefan to take her far, far away from Mystic Falls, in a blatant attempt to avoid John and escape the constant drama. At the lakehouse, she tries to play house with her boyfriend, having romantic moments, dinner and wine, but the heavy issues in her life won't take a vacation. Looking around her, she's confronted with the loss of her parents, the memories of her childhood, the not-yet-discussed problems inherent in a future with Stefan, and finally, a rampaging werewolf. Elena is also faced with the fact that her parents were keeping a world-changing secret from her and Jeremy their whole lives when she discovers that vampire-slayer closet hidden in the lakehouse. The dark truth in her life was also in her parents' lives. Nobody likes the puritanical John, but judging by that hidden cache of weapons, he may be more like Grayson and Miranda Gilbert than Elena would like to think.

The playful deception that starts Elena and Stefan's time at the lakehouse — she pretends only John can invite him into the house — foreshadows the revelation that she's been deceiving Stefan about her deal with Elijah. In "The Descent," she tells him that Elijah's promise is "to keep me and everyone else safe as long as I play by his rules"; it's no wonder Stefan inferred that Elena was safe from the sacrifice if Elijah upheld the deal. Just as Elena was justifiably upset with Stefan last season because he was keeping secrets, Stefan feels betrayed that she would keep this from him, carrying on like her death was not imminent.

What upsets Stefan in particular is that she asks about their future together (before shutting the conversation down): how could she if her plan is not to have one at all? The question of what their future would look like has never been a focus of their relationship (another example of how *TVD* is not "*Twilight* for TV"). Instead the writers have addressed the big issue through smaller moments: at the career fair in "The Turning Point" where Stefan explains he can never stay in one place for too many years, in "Bloodlines" when Elena discovers that the relationship Lexi had with a human lasted only because he became a vampire, in "Isobel" when Elena's vampire mother

calls her a liar for saying she's never considered turning, and in "Memory Lane" with Caroline (acting as a mouthpiece for Katherine) reminding Elena of the obstacles and the sacrifices the couple faces in any kind of long-term scenario. With Elena keeping the lid on that "box" closed indefinitely, Stefan and Elena have to instead deal with their honesty issues: they have kept plans from each other repeatedly this season, knowing the other would object.

Though Elijah is lying to the ladies of the Mystic Falls Historical Society by masquerading as a gentleman of letters, he otherwise appears to be one of the most honest characters on *TVD*: he keeps his word and chooses his words carefully. In "Rose," Elena witnessed the consequences of making a poorly worded deal with Elijah — Trevor lost his head. Elena was savvy enough to realize when she made her bargain that Elijah had made no guarantee to save her from Klaus, just to protect her loved ones. That choice, whether heroic or tragic in Stefan's eyes, has already saved her friends' lives — and Damon's life three times over.

Like the werewolves who blaze into Mystic Falls unaware of the powers resident there, Damon's cocky attitude gets him in hot water in "Crying Wolf." He scoffs at Elijah using the surname "Smith" and plans to waltz into the tea party uninvited and leave with the information he desires: Elijah's endgame. Instead he gets schooled by an Original in the importance of respecting one's elders and knowing one's place, a lesson Damon's unlikely to take to heart. On the same mission as Damon, Bonnie chooses a more accessible source of information, Luka, and she is willing to break any bond of loyalty she's supposed to have with another witch as payback for his moonstone trickery.

In a moment that flies by in this very full episode, Bonnie has to make a choice: whether or not to make Luka tell them how to kill Klaus. Luka pleads with her not to, saying he'll be killed for telling, and Jeremy briefly protests, perhaps feeling some kinship with him since Luka's also trying to save his sister. But without much consideration, Bonnie decides to press on: information that could potentially save Elena is worth the risk to the "traitor warlock." Has Bonnie given up her role as "morality police"? She's been working with Damon and Stefan since "Masquerade" and it seems she's willing to go to increasingly extreme lengths as the target on Elena's back comes into focus. Instead of judging Damon's actions, she's working on parallel missions with him, passing the information she learns straight to him. Caroline encourages Bonnie to be less judgey in her personal life as well, after seeing how into Bonnie Jeremy is. Following Caroline's advice, Bonnie decides to accept Jeremy for who he is now, instead of holding on to her past impressions; after a day of tricking one potential love interest, she's emotionally honest with her other. If that kiss leads to more, Jeremy and Bonnie have the potential to be the first couple in Mystic Falls that is completely honest with each other — no monstrously violent pasts, supernatural secrets, clandestine pacts, or hidden agendas.

Though John Gilbert goes about it in a weaselly, self-interested way, he's not wrong when he says that Alaric's relationship with Jenna is marred by incessant lies, and Alaric knows it. Alaric has lied about Isobel, about the existence of supernatural creatures right under Jenna's nose, and on a day-to-day basis about what he's up to when they're not together, a thousand little white lies creating a relationship weakened by deception. Like Caroline not telling Matt she didn't show up at the Grill because she'd just been tortured by a werewolf ("Daddy Issues"), Alaric doesn't tell Jenna he failed to meet her because he'd been lying on Damon's floor temporarily dead, killed by a werewolf. When will Jenna find out what's actually going on? Clearly, keeping her in the dark has not ensured her safety. She has already innocently invited more than one vampire into the Gilbert house, allowed Katherine to use her as a spy, and nearly killed herself under compulsion ("Plan B"). Is John doing the right thing by planting suspicion in Jenna's mind that all is not what is seems?

Though Tyler insists on being filled in about the curse at the beginning of the episode, he makes his choice without full knowledge of the implications and consequences of his actions. He agrees to deceive Caroline and kidnap Elena, swayed by Jules's promise that there's a way for him to be free of the werewolf curse, and even goes so far as to shoot Stefan in the leg before finally learning that the cost of his freedom from the curse is Elena's life. Once Tyler knows the whole truth, he asks Elena for forgiveness (which in true Elena fashion she grants instantly and with a hug). As he heads out of town with Jules, he makes her promise "no more lies," echoing Matt's earlier insistence that Caroline and Tyler stop lying. Depending on what Jules is like when she's *not* trying to kill our favorite characters, Tyler's departure could be a really good thing for him, a chance to figure out how to live with what he has become and come into his own away from the daily craziness. Before he leaves, Tyler makes amends with Matt, clearing up the weirdness between them in a speech that manages to explain everything without revealing his or Caroline's supernatural secrets. That's about as honest as it gets in Mystic Falls.

COMPELLING MOMENT: Elijah with the pencil in the study. Show a little respect, Damon.

CIRCLE OF KNOWLEDGE:
- Jules uses the same strategy to get Tyler's help that Katherine used to get Mason's: convince a suffering Lockwood man that if he gets the moonstone and breaks the curse, he won't ever have to turn into a werewolf again.
- Caroline warning Jeremy and Bonnie that her mom will be home in an hour or two is a funny reminder that these are teenagers, but instead of drinking or otherwise misbehaving, they're performing witchcraft in the living room.
- Luka says that Klaus has been using witches for centuries to find a doppelgänger-free way of breaking the curse; turns out Klaus believed he had foolishly ended the Petrova line when he killed Katerina's family in a fit of vengeance. His quest to subvert the rules of a spell is not dissimilar to Damon's last season, when he sought to open the tomb even after the crystal had been destroyed.

THE RULES: Bonnie's expanded her repertoire of spells: from Mason, she could only get scraps of information ("Plan B") using her innate psychic ability; with Luka, she puts him in a trance (drawing power from the circle of candles) and forces the truth out of him by overpowering his will. She also has a recipe for a fast-acting witch roofie. Werewolves are particularly vulnerable to having their hearts ripped out by vampires.

THE DIABOLICAL PLAN: The werewolves are determined to break the curse themselves, but their attempt to get the moonstone and the doppelgänger fails. John Gilbert wants his magic ring back and he's willing to blackmail Alaric to get it. Bonnie comes up with a plan to steal information straight from Luka, and she discovers why the Martins are involved with Elijah: Klaus has Luka's sister. The secret part of Elena's plan is revealed: she knew that her deal with Elijah didn't protect her, it only protected her loved ones.

BITE MARKS: At the Grill, Matt grabs Tyler by the shirt and then Tyler knocks into Caroline, knocking her bag to the ground. Bonnie roofies Luka and then makes him answer her questions against his will in what looks to be a painful process. Damon gets in Elijah's face and is rewarded with a pencil in the neck. Stevie stakes Alaric, killing him, then jumps on Damon's back and empties a frighteningly large needle filled with vervain into his neck. Stevie then uses a torture collar with wooden nails on Damon's neck. Brady shoots Stefan in the chest with a wooden bullet; Tyler shoots him in the leg. Elena stabs Brady in the gut and stakes him in the back. Stefan rips Brady's heart out. Elijah pulls out the hearts of three werewolves and snaps Stevie's neck with a hard elbow to the head.

PREVIOUSLY ON THE VAMPIRE DIARIES: John Gilbert mentioned to Jeremy that there is more than just the one original Johnathan Gilbert journal in "Miss Mystic Falls." As Damon mentions whilst being tortured, he tortured Mason for information about the moonstone in that very chair ("Plan B").

MEANWHILE IN FELL'S CHURCH: Damon uses Smith as a fake last name in *The Struggle*, like Elijah does in this episode. In *Dark Reunion*, Tyler fears he will be killed if he reveals too much information about an Original, but the gang coerces him to anyway, like Bonnie does with Luka in "Crying Wolf."

OFF CAMERA: After this episode aired, Daniel Gillies (Elijah) tweeted, "Truthfully, the moment took me. I simply thought Damon looked like an excellent pencil-case."

FOGGY MOMENTS: The shots of the text messages between Elena and "Caroline" don't match ("with" is spelled out, then it's just "w"; lakehouse is one word, then two). Do werewolves' powers get stronger the longer they're around, like a vampire's do? Relatively new werewolf Mason showed some superior fighting skills and strength ("Brave New World"), but Jules and company have super-speed and agility that goes beyond that. Is that because they've lived many moons? Not that it's the first time there have been inconsistencies in supernatural ability, but Damon doesn't realize there's an intruder already in the hallway of his house until Alaric and Stevie crash into something, but Caroline, a much younger vamp, can sense that someone (Tyler) is lurking outside her house? Not that it seems unlikely that Elijah is somehow all-knowing, but how did Elijah know that Damon was mere seconds away from death, and, in the previous episode, how did Jonas know that the gang was in serious trouble? Did Stefan drop Brady's heart before he hugged Elena?

MUSIC: Bonnie tells Caroline her plan while Free Energy's "All I Know" plays at the Grill; another song by Free Energy played in "A Few Good Men." Matt calls Caroline out on her lies to "All Die Young" by Smith Westerns. Ladyhawke's "Manipulating Woman" is the appropriately titled song playing as Bonnie gives Luka the witch-roofie iced coffee. Elena looks around her parents' old room to Kyler England's "You Wait for Rain." The scenes of Tyler leaving Mystic Falls are set to "Family Tree" by Matthew West.

QUESTIONS:
- Luka reveals that Elijah's plan is to kill Klaus when he is weakened after Elena is sacrificed. Why would *Klaus* be weakened and vulnerable after the doppelgänger sacrifice? Isn't a witch performing the ritual? And are the doppelgänger, vampire, and werewolf all sacrificed at the same moment? This is one complicated curse.
- Where will Jules take Tyler?
- Is Stefan right: is Elena's choice more tragic than heroic?

❧

Stefan: Elena, you've agreed to sacrifice yourself to Klaus. To say that we have a difference of opinion is the understatement of the century.
Elena: You would know.

2.15 *The Dinner Party*

Original air date: February 17, 2011
Written by: Andrew Chambliss
Directed by: Marcos Siega
Guest cast: Carissa Capobianco (1864 Girl #2), Kelly Finley (Honoria Fell), Valee Gallant (1864 Girl #1), Arielle Kebbel (Lexi), Joe Knezenich (Johnathan Gilbert), Daniel Thomas May (Thomas Fell)

Still at the lakehouse, Elena hears about Stefan's dark past; back in Mystic Falls, Damon hosts a dinner party.

With the werewolf chapter over, the Salvatore brothers shift their focus to Elijah — the charming, well-mannered, dashing, badass, smoking-hot

Original who plans to use the doppelgänger to lure Klaus to Mystic Falls and then kill him. It's a strange situation when the enemy of our heroes comes across as a gentleman with admirable "old school" values of honor, truth, and keeping one's word. Elijah may be capable of tearing out the hearts of two attackers at once without mussing his hair, but that incredible capacity for violence aside, Damon, Katherine, John, and even Stefan, Bonnie, and Alaric look like sneaks and liars by comparison. As Andie Star says to Jenna, "Trust is key," and on *The Vampire Diaries* trusting anyone is a dangerous game.

Katherine uses the oldest trick in the book, reverse psychology, on Damon to get what she wants — herself out of the tomb. She doesn't care that Damon would die if he killed Elijah with the dagger. It's an interesting commentary on their feelings for each other: he's willing to abandon in a tomb for eternity the woman he once loved so much he died for her, and she's willing to have him suffer his final death in order to gain her liberty. With Katherine, the viewer is usually just as in the dark about her true motivations as the Salvatore brothers are; we never know for certain if there's a grain of truth among her lies. But here we already know she's in cahoots with John who's helping her to escape the tomb. Knowing that, Damon comes across as *incredibly* gullible as he tries to trick her into giving him the information he wants, thinking he's in control when she's once again manipulating him. Her choice of wording, telling Damon, "killing Elijah would be a suicide mission," is classic Katherine cleverness. There's a hidden meaning to her words that even the audience isn't privy to until the lore surrounding the dagger is revealed. Never mind that it's of the utmost importance for her to get out that tomb (she's already desiccated by the time Damon feeds her some blood), for Katherine, every conversation is an opportunity for play, for toying with her opponent like a cat with a mouse. She fools Damon into behaving just as she needs him to, and it's entertaining to watch — as was Damon's stunned reaction to her nonchalant emergence from his shower, stark naked. Whatever her reason for staying in Mystic Falls instead of running as Damon had predicted she would, now that Katherine's out of that tomb, we're sure to be in for more doppelgänger hijinks and high-stakes trickery.

John returned to Mystic Falls demanding that Elena, Stefan, and Damon prove themselves trustworthy before he would be forthcoming with them about what he knows. In "The Dinner Party" John's plan to kill two birds with one stone — or two vampires with one dagger — almost works

Stefan's Diaries

In August 2010, HarperTeen announced a new Vampire Diaries trilogy of books to be released over the coming year: Stefan's Diaries would reveal "the truth about what really happened between Stefan, Damon, and Katherine — and how the Vampire Diaries love triangle began." The covers of the three novels (*Origins*, *Bloodlust*, and *The Craving*) feature both L.J. Smith's name ("Based on the novels by") and Kevin Williamson and Julie Plec ("and the TV series developed by"), but are written by a fourth party hired by Alloy Entertainment and HarperTeen. Rather than following the story established in the TV series, the Stefan's Diaries novels present a third alt-Vampire Diaries world that exists outside of both book and TV series canons. Certainly closest to the television series, key moments seen in flashback scenes in "Lost Girls" and "Blood Brothers" are replicated (with details oddly and inexplicably changed) in *Origins*, which covers Katherine's arrival in Mystic Falls and the Salvatore brothers becoming vampires. Book 2, *Bloodlust*, takes the brothers to New Orleans where Stefan meets Lexi (a plot line that contradicts the flashback seen in "The Dinner Party") and Damon turns evil. The setting shifts once again for *The Craving*: Stefan arrives in New York City, thinking he's thrown off his brother but there's Damon hamming it up with Manhattan's high society. *The Craving* introduces the threat of Klaus, who targets the brothers via a strangely beastly creature named Lucius; this plot contradicts what's established in season 2 regarding the brothers' knowledge of the Originals and Klaus (i.e., not much of anything). Enjoyable enough reads for a *TVD* fan, but erroneously described as a "prequel" to the TV show. The series will continue with three more volumes, *The Ripper*, *The Asylum*, and *The Compelled*.

as Damon is mere moments away from plunging the dagger into Elijah and unwittingly killing himself in the process. (Ironically it's the original John Gilbert that foils his plans via his fastidious journal-keeping.) It's no surprise that John wants Damon dead (he did leave him in a burning building to die alongside the tomb vampires in "Founder's Day"), but his determination to get his ring from Alaric at any cost plays out as more than a little dastardly. He behaves with no regard for how his actions will affect Jenna, a woman who is not only the guardian of his daughter and nephew but (sorry to remind you) someone he used to have an intimate relationship with. John has sabotaged Jenna's relationship with Alaric by raising questions about Isobel and her death, giving Jenna doubts about Alaric's trustworthiness, and he now blackmails Alaric into handing over the ring by threatening to drag Jenna into the dangerous world of vampires. While John's motives are decidedly selfish, can we really say he's wrong about it being time for Jenna to know what is going on in Mystic Falls? Is Alaric's instinct to protect her by keeping her in the dark misguided? Jenna makes guileless mistakes — inviting vampires into the house and falling prey to compulsion, for example — simply because she's clueless about the consequences of seemingly normal acts.

Trust is clearly so important to Jenna; her tearful reaction to learning that Alaric is not being honest with her serves as a preview to how she'll react should she ever learn that it's not just Alaric who's keeping secrets from her but everyone she knows — from Elena and Jeremy to Carol Lockwood and Sheriff Forbes. Even Andie Star knows more than Jenna does. Andie's relationship with Damon is a twisted perversion of a healthy one, with Andie feeling lucky for having a boyfriend so open and honest with her when the sad reality is that she's being fed on, compelled to fall for him and not to fear him, and told what to say and what not to say. As Alaric says at the Grill, it's too weird seeing them act like a cutesy, happy couple.

Alaric used to be in the position that Jenna is now in. In his marriage to Isobel, as seen in flashbacks in "A Few Good Men," he knew something was wrong, but he had no idea that his wife's secret would destroy the life they shared. Alaric hates lying to Jenna, because he knows firsthand what it feels like to be the one lied to. But his need to protect her from the big, bad supernatural world has now cost him her trust and his incredibly handy Gilbert ring of resurrection. Whether or not he's right to keep the truth from her, by handing over that ring to John, Alaric has proven that he values Jenna's wellbeing over his own safety and that he "more than likes" her.

In "The Dinner Party," Alaric plays the part not only of the liar, but of the lied-to. Damon boldfaced lies to Alaric about there being no sneak attacks planned at his friendly soiree; he intends to do the exact opposite: surprise Elijah with a dagger through the heart. After Alaric's stunning surprise killing of Elijah, he demands that Damon stop lying to him. As Damon's friend ("and you don't have any friends"), Alaric deserves not to be played like an adversary or a clueless human but to be in the know about the plots afoot.

The Mystic Falls gang seems to be realizing that there's an advantage in being honest, forthcoming, and truthful with each other. Elena makes a similar demand of the Salvatore brothers that Alaric makes of Damon. They pledge to be honest with her and to let her call the shots from now on, a commitment that comes on the heels of some major secret-keeping on both

sides. Stefan and Damon kept the existence of the Original-killing dagger and their plot to murder Elijah from Elena, and Elena kept mum about the fact she would die in the bargain she made with Elijah. Stefan and Elena's romantic getaway last episode was a total bust, and at the beginning of "The Dinner Party" the couple is at odds with one another in a way we haven't seen before. The distance between them is both literal — Stefan outside on the dock while Elena's inside the lakehouse — and emotional, their complex "difference of opinion" exacerbated by Elena's choice of reading material. Johnathan Gilbert's journals remind Elena that Stefan wasn't always the man she fell in love with. He was once a monster. The flashback scenes reveal the dark days of Stefan, when he was a "ripper," murdering at will, without care, and recklessly. The opening dinner party at the Fells', which Stefan interrupts, as well as Stefan's little party where his guests served as his supper were clever counterpoints to Damon's present-day supper. Elena tells Stefan that these stories of his past make him sound like Damon, but Stefan considers his past behavior worse than Damon's. It must be hugely difficult for Elena to reconcile that monstrousness with the Stefan she knows and loves. Though the couple has trust issues at the moment (even as they pledge to stop keeping enormous secrets from each other), the amount of trust that Elena puts in Stefan every minute they are together is enormous. The monster he once was still lives inside him (as she saw in "Miss Mystic Falls") and she trusts in his ability to keep it at bay. For the first time, Elena learns *how* Stefan was able to shed his identity as a "ripper" and build one closer to who he once was as a human. His dear and departed best friend Lexi sorted him out, putting Stefan on the path he's now on, a vampire who feels every moment of *How I Met Your Mother* (to paraphrase Damon). She convinced Stefan that a vampire's intense capacity for love makes opening himself up to the pain a vampire feels worthwhile, that fighting to re-embrace his humanity is a "good part" — the most important part — of being a vampire. Stefan had given up, but Lexi made him fight.

And in "The Dinner Party" he convinces Elena to do the same. Elena has made her priorities clear — she will put her loved ones' lives ahead of her own — but Stefan convinces her that there's still room to fight for her own survival. And in the end she does. Elena channels that Petrova fire and manages to outwit Elijah, convincing him that she's ready to pull a Katherine and give up her human life. By actually plunging that knife into herself, she puts Elijah in a position of weakness and is able to take him out with the concealed dagger. She doesn't even consider the option of taking the renegotiated deal. That entire sequence — from Elijah's arrival to Damon's final quip — was a classic *Vampire Diaries* twist, as well as an important turning point in the season and for our heroine. Elena has more than proven herself capable of doing things her own way from here on.

COMPELLING MOMENT: Elena's first kill is an Original.

CIRCLE OF KNOWLEDGE:
- No Matt, Tyler, or Caroline in this episode.
- When Jenna says that men are very territorial, Elijah responds with some amusement, "Yes, they are," not "we are," perhaps considering himself so removed from mortal men as to not be one of them.
- Damon better hand over his Scout's badge: he swears by "Scout's honor" to Alaric, but then goes against his word, breaking a most solemn oath according to Baden-Powell's Scout's Law.

- Lexi calls Stefan a "ripper." The term is used for vicious murderers who mutilate their victims (most famously Jack the Ripper, the London serial killer of the 1880s) and, in pop culture, as a shorthand to indicate darkness, violence, and depravity. On *Buffy the Vampire Slayer*, watcher Rupert Giles's dark past behavior — practicing black magic and raising demons — earned him the nickname "Ripper."
- Perhaps because he's feeling so relaxed and well fed, Damon tosses out a few more references than usual this episode: *Guess Who's Coming to Dinner* is a 1967 film about the prejudice faced by an interracial couple; *The Lion, The Witch, and The Wardrobe* is the first novel in the Chronicles of Narnia by C.S. Lewis, published in 1950.
- The text we can see on the page of the Gilbert journal with the drawing of the dagger is made up of snippets from Bram Stoker's *Dracula* (1897). Either that journal, from the later years of Johnathan Gilbert's life, contains Gilbert's favorite random quotations of the quintessential vampire story, or *TVD*'s prop department was having a little fun.
- The best part about killing an Original is that they never *really* die. There will always be the possibility of more Elijah in the future. When will he rise again?
- Alaric asks where John disappeared to: he was likely popping by the tomb to let Katherine know she was free from Elijah's compulsion and now at liberty.

THE RULES: If an Original dies, those under his compulsion are freed from it. According to the Gilbert journal, the alchemic bond between the dagger forged by witches and the ash of the ancient white oak tree is capable of killing an Original — as long as the dagger's left in place in the vampire's heart. The Original resurrects once the dagger is removed. If a vampire uses the weapon, that vampire dies too, a punishment for going against one's own kind.

THE DIABOLICAL PLAN: Elijah is searching for the spot where a whole lot of witches were killed in the late 1700s, for what precise reason he won't say. That revelation (that he needs to find the site of the witch massacre) explains why, with the moonstone and the doppelgänger in hand, he hadn't already lured Klaus to Mystic Falls. Katherine's plot to get out of the tomb by provoking Damon to kill Elijah is a success, as is John's ploy to get the Gilbert ring from Alaric.

Dawn Olivieri as Andie Star, Action News

Born February 8, 1981, in Florida, Dawn Olivieri has a slew of TV credits including *Veronica Mars*, *How I Met Your Mother*, *Knight Rider*, *Entourage*, *Cold Case*, *Rules of Engagement*, *Californication*, *True Blood*, and the SyFy Channel movie *Hydra*. In season 4 of *Heroes* she played Lydia, which made her most well known for her parts on genre shows. She first met Ian Somerhalder, her future onscreen beau and a friend of her real-life boyfriend, in Vancouver while filming *Stargate: Atlantis* in 2008. In 2011, she filmed a pilot for Showtime, *House of Lies*, playing the ex-wife of Don Cheadle's character.

Of her *Vampire Diaries* character, Dawn told *EW*, "It's almost like Andie's split in half, because she's got this one part of herself that's just being created with Damon, and then her real self is locked away and is not getting a chance to partake in the reality that's happening." She didn't want Andie to be a boring drone but she had to balance the character with the compulsion. She explained the difficulty and how she addressed it to the *New York Post*'s PopWrap blog, "I decided that she doesn't have any fear when she's compelled, so it's been fun trying to figure out how you act when nothing frightens you. All I can refer to is how I would act, and I'd be funny — I have a good time, I'm laid-back, I'm making jokes. If life doesn't scare you, you're going about it in a way that's super fun."

Filming the bathtub scene was memorable for the actress. It was filmed on Ian's birthday: "We're in the bathtub, full of bubbles, blood everywhere, and here's this cake coming. He blows all the candles out, and then he takes this huge bite of the cake. No hands, nothing. He just digs his face into the cake and takes a huge bite. It was so cute."

HISTORY LESSON: Mystic Falls was not founded by the "much-lauded" founding families, but by people who migrated from Salem, Massachusetts, around the time of the witch trials of the 1690s. (Bonnie's ancestors were among them, as Grams mentioned back in "Haunted.") Over a hundred year period, they built a settlement; an outbreak of anti-witch hysteria led the neighboring town to round them up and burn them at the stake in a field. Elijah expresses interest in surveying the land owned by freed slaves, saying the descendants of the slaves are the true keepers of American history. Though the Civil War has been the historical backdrop for *The Vampire Diaries* since the pilot, the ravages of the war are shown for the first time in the flashback with Lexi and Stefan in the camp of wounded and dying Confederate soldiers. The founding families erroneously laid claim to Mystic Falls' origin, and the journals of Johnathan Gilbert hid much information from those same families, which raises the idea that there may be a true and untold history of the town that differs from commonly held conceptions. (This subject also came up in season 1 with the falsification of records concerning the Battle of Willow Creek by Giuseppe Salvatore and Johnathan Gilbert).

BITE MARKS: In flashback, Stefan kills Thomas and Honoria Fell and Johnathan Gilbert (who comes back to life). He also feeds on three women, killing one, and on injured soldiers; he tells Elena that he has killed many more than that. Off screen, Damon had a little Andie blood for breakfast. In flashback, Lexi tackles Stefan after he stalks her. Alaric grabs John's shirt, and John brushes him away. Alaric stabs Elijah with the dagger, killing him. Using magic, Jonas throws Jeremy against the wall and steals Bonnie's powers from her in what looks to be a painful process. Elena stabs herself in the gut with a knife and then stabs Elijah in the heart with the dagger.

PREVIOUSLY ON THE VAMPIRE DIARIES: Honoria Fell was mentioned in "Family Ties." In "You're Undead to Me," Stefan tells Elena that he did a lot of things he's not proud of, some of which are shown in this episode's flashbacks. In "A Few Good Men," Damon partied with sorority girls and fed on them, only to be interrupted by his brother; in the flashback, it's revealed that Stefan was the first Salvatore brother to throw such a party. Lexi's introduction in this episode echoes hers in "162 Candles": she stalked Stefan in his house and then tackled him to the ground. In "Katerina," Elijah threw coins at a glass wall smashing it; here he takes down the lakehouse's door with thrown pebbles. In "Blood Brothers," Alaric asks Damon not to kill anybody on their expedition, but Alaric ends up being the one who kills Henry, just as he's the one to kill Elijah at the dinner party. Elena deliberately echoes her predecessor's actions by stabbing herself in the gut just as Katerina did in 1492 ("Katerina"). In "Blood Brothers," Elena convinced Stefan not to give up, but to go on fighting, as he does for her in "The Dinner Party." Elena stood before Elijah offering to go with him in "Rose," but then vervain-bombed him, much as she pulls a surprise attack on him at the lakehouse.

MEANWHILE IN FELL'S CHURCH: A founding family member in both the books and TV series, Honoria Fell, who is murdered by Stefan in this episode's flashback, was a witch and protector of Fell's Church who comes to the gang's aid in *The Fury*. In *Dark Reunion*, Stefan convinces Matt that no matter how daunting the evil they face, they have to fight, even if they know they're going to lose, just as he convinces Elena to do in this episode.

OFF CAMERA: Many viewers found it unbelievable that Elena wouldn't have read the crucial detail about keeping the dagger in place, and in hindsight the writers agreed it was a weak plotting moment. At the C2E2 convention, Julie Plec explained, "It's very funny, because that episode was the very last [script] that we had to deliver . . . before Christmas break. We'd been writing for, like, nine months straight and we were exhausted and our brains were dead. And what we wrote made perfect sense at the time. It wasn't until we saw the cut of it; it took that long for us to watch and be like, 'There had to be a better way to execute that in which Elena just doesn't turn the page . . .' Those are the things, as writers, Kevin and I make fun of ourselves all the time. . . . But we get a good laugh out of it anyway, and people seem to make a good joke of it as well."

For Paul Wesley, playing Stefan as a "ripper" is "so much easier" than his usual good-guy persona: "It's just really easy to be devious and cunning. It's innately difficult to just be a really decent character who just has a good soul. Someone who chooses to be pacifist or isn't as showy, I think there's a silent power in that. It's definitely not something that you want to undermine or underestimate."

FOGGY MOMENTS: According to these journals, Johnathan Gilbert knew that witches and magic existed, but in season 1 he believed he had actually invented the vampire compass himself. Did he only learn of magic after the purge? Why did Emily create two Gilbert rings? Is there another 1860s Gilbert not yet mentioned? How did Johnathan Gilbert find out all this very useful information about the Originals? How does one conduct research into the most mysterious of all vampires?

MUSIC: Foster the People's "Pumped Up Kicks" plays at the Grill when Jeremy approaches Bonnie. Alaric chats with Damon and Andie to Pet Lions' "When I Grow Old." The XX's "Islands" is on in the background as the gang eats dinner. "Lemonworld" by The National plays as they reassemble for dessert. With an opening line that couldn't be more appropriate, The Airborne Toxic Event's "Happiness Is Overrated" begins as Damon sees "Little Miss Katherine" in the shower.

QUESTIONS:

- Were Bonnie's ancestors among the witches rounded up and burned at the stake?
- Does Damon actually know where the witch massacre took place or was he just toying with Elijah? How is that land connected to Elijah's plans?
- How will Bonnie get her "witchy ju-ju" back? Will Jonas agree to work with the gang now that Elijah's been taken out? Or will he try to resurrect Elijah and proceed with Plan A?
- Does Stefan know that Damon asked Lexi to help Stefan before he left in 1864?
- Why did Katherine stay in Mystic Falls and not run for the Klaus-free hills? Is she banking on using the Salvatore brothers' intense desire to protect Elena as a kind of shield, going for a safety-in-numbers strategy over her usual solo act? Does her presence have anything to do with whatever she has brewing with Isobel and John?

❀

Katherine: I'm not a threat to you, Elena. If any of you are going to believe anything, believe that.

2.16 *The House Guest*

Original air date: February 24, 2011
Written by: Caroline Dries
Directed by: Michael Katleman
Guest cast: Brad Davis (Band Singer), Mia Kirshner (Isobel Flemming)

The Mystic Grill goes up in flames.

After Elena stumbled upon Jenna and Alaric getting all Chunky Monkey in "The Sacrifice," she assured her aunt that as long as Jenna was happy, she was happy, a sentiment she echoes here in "The House Guest," about Matt and Caroline, and Bonnie and Jeremy. When your daily existence includes deadly threats, Elena knows that you have to take the moments of joy where you can find them. Like Caroline sings in the lyrics of "Eternal Flame," no one in Mystic Falls wants to "lose this feeling"

but happiness and requited love are rare and fragile commodities for them. As the central figure in this group of characters, Elena finds herself responsible, in part, for others' happiness: Alaric's ability to be with the woman he loves depends on Elena's decision to open up to Jenna, Bonnie wants

Elena's permission before she and Jeremy get too smoochy, Elena's advice spurs Caroline to sing her heart out, and even Matt looks to Elena, who gives him a small approving nod, before climbing on stage for that big romantic moment.

Love and good intentions prove to be not enough to overcome the blowback from keeping secrets. Both Caroline's and Alaric's relationships are on the precipice of total disaster. In the previous episode, Alaric made a huge sacrifice in giving up his ring to keep John from telling Jenna the truth. Here he proves ever the gentleman by explaining to Elena that it's her choice to tell Jenna, not his. His respect for Elena's relationship with her aunt prevents him from being honest with the woman he loves. If only Jenna knew why he's holding back. And if only Alaric had chosen his words a little more carefully on the porch. Instead, Isobel appearing at the Gilbert front door very much alive, minutes after Alaric said she was dead, makes him look precisely like the picture John painted of him: a total liar.

In Elena's conversation with Alaric in his classroom, she wonders how she would tell someone something so life altering. Caroline doesn't even get the chance to try with Matt. Instead she's forced to show him her secret in the midst of a crisis. Elena tells Caroline and Bonnie that though they've tried to protect their loved ones from the truth, they've hurt them in the process. Caroline literally protects Matt, saving his life after Jonas attacks him with the broken beer bottle. She overcomes the huge temptation of his gushing neck wound, proving how strong and capable she's grown to be, and feeds him her blood, saving his life. Caroline's hand was forced with Matt: when he wakes up, she explains how she brought him back from the brink of death. The scenario she had imagined — her telling him the truth, him accepting it because he loves her — goes unrealized. His unexpected reaction — "oh my god, Vicki" — endangers her fervent hope that they'll hold on to the connection they shared on stage at the Grill. It's painful to watch as Caroline tries to bring Matt back to the place they were only hours earlier, together and in love, while Matt freaks out at the possibility that his girlfriend may have attacked, or even killed, his sister.

In the earlier conversation between Caroline and Jenna — a clever pairing that allowed them to say what they wished they could to Matt and Alaric respectively — Jenna says that when you love someone, you owe them the truth. Which is precisely what Elena, Alaric, Caroline, and company have *not* been doing, believing they were "doing the right thing" by keeping Jenna

Covington residents are now used to the sight of TVD fans taking photos outside the "Grill" (which is not actually a restaurant but home to offices).

and Matt (and many others last season) in the dark. Ignorance of Mystic Falls' supernatural secrets almost always results in someone getting physically hurt and relationships destroyed by lies. Jenna makes the argument that her journey over the past year proves she can handle whatever ugly truth Alaric is hiding from her, and the idea of being honest even when the truth might do damage is a theme that repeats across several storylines in "The House Guest." Damon demands the truth from Katherine, however painful. He asks if she knew he would die if he used the dagger, and Katherine tells him more than that — she admits that her deal with John Gilbert required her choosing which Salvatore brother could live, and she chose Stefan. The scenes between Damon and Katherine spark with their combative banter and physicality, but the real joy in these moments is in seeing how changed

Randy J. Goodwin as Dr. Jonas Martin

Born and raised in Omaha, Nebraska, in a family of five children, Randy J. Goodwin grew up performing — singing, dancing, and acting in local productions from the age of eight. A man of many talents, Randy studied architecture at the University of Nebraska, is a licensed cosmetologist, and was in the U.S. Air Force for three years. In 1994, he moved to L.A. where his acting career took off. He's since been in more than 30 films and network TV shows including *Fast Track*, *Abby*, *Girlfriends*, and *CSI*. The father of four girls and two boys, Randy is still connected to the community theater group, the GBT Academy of the Arts, where he used to perform as a child; he serves on its board of directors, headed by his mother Dr. Mary J. Clinkscale-Goodwin. In 2011, Randy acted in the first project all of his six children could safely watch — no one's burned alive or attacked by a doppelicious vampire in *Annie Kringle*, a Christmas special.

Damon's attitude and behavior toward Katherine is compared to in "The Return." Back then he was desperate for her love and attention, just as he had been in 1864, but now Damon ain't buying what Katherine's selling. He may be hurt by Katherine choosing Stefan over him, again, but it doesn't derail him. He calls her a liar, refuses to believe her cooperative and helpful act, and he keeps information from her. He goes so far as to stake her in the gut in payback; she'll heal quickly but his "tit for tat" point is clear. At the end of the episode, in a classic Damon-Katherine tussling moment, their roles are beautifully reversed: Damon rejects an awesomely and unapologetically minxy Katherine, kicking her out of his bed. The coldness and meanness he displays only makes her more interested in him. She's a girl who wants what she can't have and always gets what she wants.

As the unwelcome house guest, Katherine forces an uneasy alliance with the Salvatore brothers and Elena, making a solid argument for her usefulness in the opening scenes and proving it by the end of the episode by coming up with an elegant (if brutal) solution to the problem of Jonas. She's willing to use herself as bait in a scheme against the seemingly all-powerful witch. Just as Elena's shown a capacity for deception and manipulation, traits associated with Katherine, in "The House Guest" Katherine shows how reliable and useful she can be. When she is, for once, true to her word, Katherine is a powerful ally. Can they trust her to keep Elena safe from Klaus? Or will Katherine try to use her as leverage for a pardon, as she once planned to? Though Elena, Stefan, and Damon do trust her in the plan to take out Jonas, the boys carefully guard their secret about the witches' massacre site.

Katherine's isn't the only tenuous alliance made in this episode. Stefan, the perennial negotiator, arranges a peace talk with the Martins, looking to unite against Klaus. Though Jonas agrees to it, he has no intention of honoring the alliance, and that choice costs him his son's life and his own. Keeping true to his alliance with Elijah (and, really, can you blame him?), Jonas's plan is to resurrect Elijah and have him take out their "enemies" in a plan that Luka agrees to. Instead, their attack backfires in a horrifying moment, and Jonas watches his son die, unable to save him by human or magical means. Deciding to put his daughter's life and freedom ahead of the welfare of Elena, Bonnie, Matt, or any of the no-name patrons of the Grill, Jonas again chooses the "kill or be killed" way of thinking, refusing to heed Bonnie's pleas that they all work together. Katherine and company take a similar "it's us or them" stance when it comes to killing Papa Witch. She says to Bonnie he *had* to die, and Stefan seems to agree. Jeremy expresses disturbingly little regret for Luka's death. It's only Bonnie who expresses some reluctance at taking Jonas's life, but even she had just moments earlier expressed more concern over her powerlessness than over Luka's death. Though Jonas was unwilling to trust Stefan as a reliable ally, in his final act, he entrusts Bonnie with the information necessary to kill Klaus, returning her powers and telling her how to do it. That move is not only convenient it's unsurprising: a witch is more likely to trust another witch than a vampire.

Bonnie knows how to kill Klaus, Damon knows where the witches were slaughtered, Katherine has pledged to help, Isobel's on the Gilbert doorstep, and Matt's mind has just been blown. With only six episodes left in the second season, "The House Guest" very much feels like the setup for the final chapter.

COMPELLING MOMENT: Caroline and Matt's kiss — the most gleeful, romantic thing that's ever happened on *The Vampire Diaries*. And even in that happiest moment you just know everything's about to go up in flames. Perfection.

CIRCLE OF KNOWLEDGE:
- No Tyler in this episode.
- This was the last episode aired before a six-week break.

- There's a chess game set up in Stefan's room, visible in the scene where Katherine first tries to convince Stefan, Damon, and Elena that she will play on their side to defeat Klaus. Is she on their team or is she using them as pawns?
- Katherine likes a particular chair at the Salvatores: she's reading in the same spot in this episode as she was when reading Stefan's diary in "Memory Lane."
- Caroline wants to rewatch the tearjerking romance *The Notebook* (2004), which stars Ryan Gosling and Rachel McAdams as soul mates kept apart in their youth, by her meddlesome classist mother, but who grow old (and senile) together. A quintessentially Caroline choice.
- When a witch dies violently, mystical power inhabits the place of her or his death. Meaning Dr. Jonas Martin's legacy is turning Elena and Jer's bathroom into a mystical hot spot.

THE RULES: The body of an Original cannot be destroyed (according to Katherine and based on Damon's failed incineration attempt). The Witches Martin demonstrate a new kind of spell: a "crazy-ass psychic witch attack," as Damon calls it. With Jonas grounding him, Luka is able to locate someone (in this case, Elijah) and, though Luka's invisible, manipulate physical objects and be physically harmed. In addition to being able to take a witch's power from her, Jonas is able to return those powers, as well as perform some sort of psychic transmission of information that will be useful for the season finale.

THE DIABOLICAL PLAN: Damon goes into research mode, trying to discover from Johnathan Gilbert's journals the location of the witch massacre. Katherine tries to convince Elena, Stefan, and Damon that she is there to help, telling Damon that John made a deal with her that includes her staying in Mystic Falls and helping to kill Klaus in return for her freedom from the tomb. She also admits that she was the one who outed Emily Bennett as a witch to the Council back in the 1860s; Katherine likes her "loose ends" tied up (in this case, one of the only people who knew she wasn't in the tomb). Despite making a deal with Stefan and telling him why they were looking for the witch site, Jonas Martin planned to resurrect Elijah and continue with his original strategy to take out Klaus. In his final moments, he passes the torch on to Bonnie

BITE MARKS: Damon chokes Katherine and Stefan chokes Elena, thinking she's Katherine. Damon and Katherine slap each other's hands before he tackles her onto the piano bench. Luka stakes Katherine in the gut. Damon sets Luka on fire with the blowtorch, killing him. Jonas disables Stefan with the aneurysm spell. Damon stakes Katherine as she recovers on the couch. At the Grill, Jonas explodes the lights, smashes glasses, and sets the place on fire before turning his attack on Bonnie, who appears to pass out. Caroline lunges at Jonas, who retaliates with the aneurysm spell. When Matt comes to her defense, Jonas sticks a broken beer bottle in his neck. Caroline breaks all of our hearts when her voice cracks in anguish as she screams for Matt. Katherine bites Jonas, nearly killing him; when he comes to and grabs Bonnie, Stefan snaps his neck, killing him. Damon tosses Katherine out of his bed.

PREVIOUSLY ON THE VAMPIRE DIARIES: In "Under Control," Alaric asks Elena how she deals with lying to those she cares about during a conversation in his classroom, a topic they revisit in this episode now that the issue has come to a head with him and Jenna. The photo of Matt and Caroline on her device is from "Miss Mystic Falls." The writers reach back to the pilot episode when Matt remembers the moment Vicki wakes up in the hospital to say one word to her brother — vampire. He now realizes that Vicki wasn't "tripping out" but telling him what had attacked her. Isobel's arrival at the end of this episode echoes the end of "Blood Brothers" when she showed up at the Grill. Alaric saying her name was the last line of that episode, as it is in this episode when Elena says it.

MEANWHILE IN FELL'S CHURCH: Though it's not one iota as sexy as Damon kicking Katherine out of bed in "The House Guest," Damon very satisfyingly rejects Katherine in *The Fury*, telling her to "Go to hell" in a moment when he seems about to yield to her will.

OFF CAMERA: Michael Katleman directs this episode of *TVD*, his first for the show; Katleman has been directing network television since the early 1990s as well as producing. Candice Accola, who originally moved to California to pursue a music career, has recorded an album, and performed on Miley Cyrus's Best of Both Worlds tour, got to show off her pipes as Caroline took to the stage at the Grill. But the actress doesn't plan on reviving her singing career, as she told Zap2It.com: "I never want to get to a place again where music isn't fun, and for a while it wasn't fun anymore. It felt like a job. What I've found interesting about working in this medium of the entertainment industry, as an actor, is that even though it is my job, and I wake up and I get tired, it's still fun. Even on days that are really long, I go home and I'm like, 'That was still fun.' I don't feel like I'm compromising my artistic self by any means. If it happens, it happens, and it'll come from that fun organic place."

FOGGY MOMENTS: While the opening scene's Katherine-Elena confusion was delightful to watch (and Katherine's trickery foreshadowed the deadly prank they pulled on Jonas at the end), it seems a little unlikely that Damon wouldn't have told Stefan and Elena that Katherine's out of the tomb between the time she stepped out of his shower in "The Dinner Party" and the following morning. Not only is Elijah's body indestructible, so are his clothes! The fire goes out instead of continuing to incinerate his suit.

MUSIC: The girls decide to order in pizza while Angel Taylor's "Epiphany" plays. They arrive at the Grill while S.O.Stereo is on stage playing "I'll Take the Bullet." Candice Accola as Caroline joins S.O.Stereo to sing "Eternal Flame," The Bangles' 1989 ballad. Elena walks in on Matt and Caroline making out in the washroom while S.O.Stereo performs "Hello Miss Heels." In his bedroom, Jeremy expresses his worries to Bonnie to "Broken Strings" by James Morrison (featuring Nelly Furtado).

QUESTIONS:
- Jonas wears a wedding ring. Where is his wife? Is she alive? Is she also a witch?
- Was Katherine telling the truth about her deal with John Gilbert? That she had to pick between Stefan and Damon and agree to help with Klaus in order to get her freedom? Or did she make up that story to needle Damon?
- Jenna says that whatever secret Alaric is keeping from her, she can handle it. Is she ready for the truth? Or when she hears what's really happening in Mystic Falls, will she head straight for Señor Tequila?

"It's not going to get any easier,

is it?"

"*She loves you and she needs you. And, to be honest, she deserves someone like you.*"

— Tyler, "Crying Wolf"

- How helpful will Katherine be with the Klaus situation? Will she share the information she knows or will she guard her secrets as closely as Damon and Stefan guard theirs?
- Why is Isobel back?

❀

> *Matt: I feel like she died.*
> *Sheriff Forbes: She did.*

2.17 *Know Thy Enemy*

Original air date: April 7, 2011
Written by: Mike Daniels
Directed by: Wendey Stanzler
Guest cast: Mia Kirshner (Isobel Flemming), Michael Roark (Frank the Cowboy)

Katherine double-crosses Elena, a compelled Isobel double-crosses Katherine, and Klaus arrives in Mystic Falls . . . in Alaric's body.

So much of "Know Thy Enemy" is driven by what the characters feel *compelled* to do, whether it's literal compulsion (Isobel) or simply what they feel they "have to do." Their actions are for their own benefit (Katherine betraying the boys again), in the name of others (Alaric and Elena keeping the truth from Jenna, and Matt from Caroline), or because it's what they think they're fated to do (Bonnie). But these are betrayals, however motivated, and they're counterbalanced by moments of forced honesty. The trust issues that boiled over in "The House Guest" continue to have messy consequences.

When Isobel rolled into Mystic Falls last season, she was Katherine's messenger. Here, unbeknownst to John or Katherine, she's Klaus's, compelled to be his puppet, the same way she has compelled innumerable humans to do her bidding. Isobel has been leaking information: willfully from John to Katherine and unwittingly from both John and Katherine to Klaus. Though she has no choice but to do what Klaus has compelled her to do (deliver Alaric, Katherine, and the moonstone; abduct Elena and then kill

Isobel's choice of lodging — the swankiest uninhabited mansion in Mystic Falls.

herself), Isobel is compelled by her own conscience to atone for the wrongs she's committed against Alaric and Elena (though, tellingly, she makes no such attempt for a final moment with John). To Alaric, she reveals that she compelled him to move on from her; she's honest with him about how much he once meant to her and lets him hold on to that memory, instead of erasing it as she did in "Isobel." If Alaric can survive being physically possessed by an Original, perhaps with Isobel's final death, he will be able to have true closure on that relationship. But Isobel's self-described petty and jealous act of introducing herself to "Auntie Vanilla" has caused devastating harm to his and Elena's relationships with Jenna.

Elena couldn't slam the door on Isobel fast enough to prevent that damage from being done. Isobel chose her words carefully to ensure maximum damage, and with them, Jenna instantly realizes that she's the only one who didn't know Isobel was alive. Elena tells John this situation is his fault, but while John's being his usual weaselly self about it, it wasn't John planting seeds of doubt about Isobel's death that caused this conflict. The decision to keep the truth from Jenna was actually Elena's. Jenna's "rage and betrayal" at seeing Isobel alive stem from Elena and Alaric's inaction, not from John's bad behavior. If Elena and Alaric ever manage to tell Jenna the whole truth, will it only make Jenna *more* upset, to know that not only was she made a dupe, believing that Isobel was dead, but that secret is nothing in comparison to the very dangerous ones kept from her by everyone she loves? Sara Canning is a master of the instantaneous tear, and Jenna and Elena looking at each other — the cat out of the bag — is one of the season's most subtly heartbreaking moments.

Between Isobel's return and John's continued meddling, "Know Thy Enemy" forces Elena to deal with her birth parents in a way she's been avoiding, and by the end of the episode she's realized that the comforting binary of thinking of Grayson and Miranda as "good" and John and Isobel as "bad" is too simple to fit the reality of her situation. As with everything else on *The Vampire Diaries*, black and white blur into grey. Isobel not only creates a rift between Elena and her guardian and mother figure Jenna, she also interrupts Elena as she remembers Miranda, the woman she identifies as her real mother, in her acceptance speech for the memorial scholarship donation. (Nothing like a lifeless body tumbling down the stairs to ruin a historical society luncheon.) Isobel's speech at her own gravesite complicates Elena's feelings for her. Here is her birth mother, who in their previous encounter acted like her enemy as opposed to the person who should innately care the most for her welfare. For the first time, Elena sees the human part of Isobel: Isobel *did* want to know Elena, something that John echoes at the end of the episode when he explains how difficult it was for Isobel to give up Elena and how much she loved her daughter. Elena, a proven believer in the idea that humanity still lurks in the heart of every vampire, will never have the chance to try to draw out those loving qualities in Isobel; instead her last memory of her birth mother is watching her go up in flames.

Klaus must have known that the final part of his compulsion — Isobel killing herself — would happen in front of Elena. There was some debate after this episode initially aired as to whether Isobel's final act was one of free will or compulsion. But Julie Plec confirmed that by intentionally echoing an earlier moment they were signaling that Isobel was still under compulsion: in "A Few Good Men," the man under Isobel's compulsion makes sure

Elena understands that she's to stop looking for her, then says "I'm done now" and steps in front of oncoming traffic, killing himself. Here Isobel definitely seems relieved to hear that she is "done" — she won't live to betray her flesh and blood again. Nonetheless the phrasing and sequence of actions (not to mention what we know about Isobel's character and that innate Petrova fire) indicate that her suicide was Klaus's decision, not her own.

Though Elena was gleeful earlier that day when Alaric punched John in the face, she feels differently about him after witnessing both Isobel's betrayal and her display of humanity. John explains to Elena that he trusted Isobel because of her love for Elena and because of his love for her. John's methods may be disruptive, hurtful, and often immoral but his motivation has always been to protect his town, his family, his daughter — and Elena acknowledges the potential in him when she lets him stick around. It's strange that the tentative words "maybe I can learn not to hate you" are such a huge step forward in their relationship, but Elena and her only surviving parent have reached a turning point.

Just as John believed in Isobel because she was the first girl he ever loved and that trust turned out to be misplaced, Caroline has no hesitation in her trust in Matt. She believes what he tells her because she loves him and fervently wants their relationship to beat the vampire-human relationship odds. Candice Accola continues to shine in her ability to make us feel everything Caroline feels, and in this episode Zach Roerig takes Matt to new and dark places. There's a rage brewing in him when he confronts Sheriff Forbes about Vicki's death, and Matt can barely contain his conflicting emotions when he confronts Caroline at her house. Deeply hurt, scared, and betrayed, Matt also feels, once again, completely alone — no family, his friends are all liars, and Caroline is a monster. All Caroline wants to do is fix this mess, and when Matt insists on being compelled to forget, she complies in a scene that only grows in its emotional impact when the twist is revealed. Matt lied to Caroline to get information from her, he's full of vervain and in league with her mother, and her compulsion didn't work. One thing Matt doesn't like is a liar, and he's now become one. So far, Stefan's hope that Matt, like Elena, will come around and accept that Caroline as a vampire is unrealized. Between Jenna hightailing it out of the Gilbert house after learning that Isobel is alive and Matt and Liz grieving Caroline, Team Human has just upped Mystic Falls' tragedy quota.

Nothing like a little teamwork to help you cross off "harness ancient dead witch power" from the To Do list. With the information Jonas passed on to Bonnie, Damon's historical knowledge of Mystic Falls' killing spots,

The "witch house" (seen from the Covington public road that borders the property) was made to look decrepit by the TVD art department.

and the strength to withstand what seemed like a harrowing spell — those screams were not of this world, Bonnie Bennett! — the girl who was without power just one episode ago is now a super-witch. Though she rather cavalierly shows off her new abilities to Jeremy by raising a storm, Bonnie understands the witches' warning: there are fatal consequences to using the full power she now possesses. If she kills Klaus, it will take everything she's got and it will kill her — a price she's willing to pay. None of the characters mention the potential larger impact of letting Klaus (or any vampire) break the Sun and the Moon Curse, but if vampires could roam around day or night as their little hearts desire, there would likely be a corresponding increase in humans dying and being used as puppets and playthings. When Bonnie tells Jeremy that her resolve to kill Klaus isn't just for Elena's protection or for Jeremy's but for everyone's, we could take her to mean *everyone*.

Bonnie feels that this is what she was born to do — and while it's a noble idea, she wasn't actually *born* with super witch powers, she acquired them of her own free will. What she interprets as something she "has to do" isn't necessarily a calling or her fate; it's her choice. Bonnie already expressed the idea that, as a witch, she is guaranteed a bad end. When she and Jeremy were first connecting in "Masquerade," she told him that it "never ends well for people like me." But a refrain on *The Vampire Diaries* is that there is always a choice: as Bonnie says, the decision to take out Klaus will be hers and hers alone. Her resolve is what made her keep the severity of the witches' warning from Jeremy: since she has no intention of changing her mind, Bonnie felt that being honest with him was unnecessarily cruel to him or potentially harmful to her plan. Jeremy is also now faced with a choice: he can keep Bonnie's secret or, as the only person who knows that Bonnie's witchcraft has had any weakening effect on her in the past, he can tell the rest of the gang in an effort to save Bonnie from herself. He is motivated by the same instinct that made him try to prevent Bonnie from using her witchcraft in "The Sacrifice" and try to stop Elena from martyring herself in "By the Light of the Moon."

Jeremy's decision will be critical to the Salvatores' plan: Damon and Stefan realize, at the end of "Know Thy Enemy," that their one tactical advantage against Klaus is their secret weapon, Bonnie. The web of liars, information leaks, and self-serving alliance-makers has been revealed, and knowing what Klaus and Katherine each know will hopefully help Stefan, Damon, and Elena through the rest of the season.

In the opening scenes of "Know Thy Enemy" Katherine told Stefan to "be smart," and it seems like the brothers Salvatore are finally getting their strategy together. Keeping a mystical object in a soap dish may not be the best hiding spot, but they were clever enough to avoid telling Katherine about their progress with the witch-power plan. Stefan and Damon are attempting to know their enemy. They figure out why Klaus would let the doppelgänger roam free before the sacrifice — he's confident Elena won't follow in Katherine's footsteps by running or turning vampire. And he knows that she has two trusty bodyguards (although she *is* kidnapped on their watch, like, all the time). Using his confidence to their advantage, they borrow Isobel's clever safehouse idea. Katherine's idea of playing it smart involves ditching and picking up alliances depending on who she thinks will give her the best chance of survival. She tells the boys she's on "Team You" but she's always on "Team Me." That strategy fails when she trusts in Isobel — "two of the world's most selfish and uncaring vampires" were "genuinely friends," according to John — and Katherine fails to consider that Isobel could be under Klaus's compulsion.

Now Katherine knows what the rest of the gang doesn't: Klaus is in Mystic Falls in the guise of a handsome history teacher we all know and love. The super creepy blood transfusion set-up, the witch bowing before his

master, and the smirk on Matt Davis's face as he greets *Katerina* in Bulgarian was the perfect ending to the first episode in the hotly anticipated Klaus chapter. Possessing Alaric is a clever tactic: Klaus has the ability to get to know his enemies by walking among them, masquerading as a trusted member of their circle — a circle they mistakenly believe has just been whittled down to only those who can be trusted.

COMPELLING MOMENT: The unexpected and clever twist of Klaus's debut.

CIRCLE OF KNOWLEDGE:
- No Tyler in this episode.
- The phrase "know thy enemy" comes from the ancient Chinese text *The Art of War*. Our *TVD* heroes could do well to heed the wisdom of Sun Tzu: if you know your enemy and yourself, victory is all but assured; if you do not know your enemy or yourself, you endanger yourself.
- The philosophy of "kill or be killed" has seen a lot of play this season; Bonnie puts a twist on it: kill *and* be killed.
- Jenna mentions that she has a thesis to write; in season 1 she says she's a psychology major.
- Hilariously, Damon's closet is *full* of black leather jackets.
- Whether Katherine earnestly loves Stefan is up for debate, but she certainly loves to beat up on him. In flashbacks, she's bitten him. In "The Return" she throws him across the Gilbert living room and later stabs him in the gut. In "Memory Lane" she throws him across his own bedroom and across the basement cell, and then stakes him in the leg. In "Masquerade" she throws him across the room. And in "Know Thy Enemy" she vervains him and tosses him over the Lockwoods' shrubbery.
- The witches were burned in a field ("The Dinner Party"); the house that Damon takes Bonnie and Jeremy to must have been built on the site where the hundred witches were burned.
- Klaus says "*Zdravei*" to Katherine, which is Bulgarian for hello.

THE RULES: The spirits of the witches are able to mess with Damon when he enters their home — perhaps it's Emily who disables his ring, since it was she who originally spelled it — and they throw Jeremy away from Bonnie when he attempts to intervene. Bonnie demonstrates advanced storm raising with her newly harnessed powers. Despite taking small doses of vervain to build up his tolerance, Stefan is still susceptible to a full vial of it injected into his bloodstream. Demonstrating a Jonas-level of expertise,

Klaus's witch (Maddox) has no trouble taking down Katherine. And, of course, there's the kicker: with Maddox's spell and a transfusion of (what is presumably) Klaus's blood, Alaric is possessed by Klaus — a brilliant twist that builds on what the show has established about witchcraft, compulsion, possession, the power of the Originals, the mystical qualities of blood, and Klaus's reclusive character.

THE DIABOLICAL PLAN: "Know Thy Enemy" is the most twist- and turn-filled episode when it comes to secret plans and double-crosses. From John's perspective, Isobel has been working with him to protect Elena since last season's plot to kill all the tomb vampires. Their motivation then was to prevent those vampires from letting word get out that Katherine was alive, which in turn would cause Klaus to come to Mystic Falls and surely find Elena. Since John's return to town, he has been sharing all his information with Isobel while she sought out Klaus. Exactly what John thought Isobel would do when she found him is not made clear. Isobel, on the other hand, had very clear intentions: she planned on negotiating for Katherine's freedom by using the doppelgänger as a bargaining chip (which is what she means when she says to Elena that she betrayed her own flesh and blood). Katherine is happy to have more than one option: she has Isobel working the Klaus-negotiation angle, while she tests the waters with the Salvatore brothers. She'll take whichever plan she thinks will work. Klaus, however, has plans of his own: he compels Isobel to return to Mystic Falls, dupe Katherine into getting the moonstone, secure the doppelgänger, and help Klaus's witch get Alaric. Then he has Isobel kill herself. The Salvatore brothers believe that because neither Katherine nor Isobel knew that Bonnie got her original powers back, none of them, notably Klaus, know about Bonnie's newfound super witch power — she's the literal secret weapon, as Damon says. Matt and Liz work together to trick Caroline into telling Matt about the vampire situation in Mystic Falls; what Liz plans to do with that information remains to be seen.

BITE MARKS: Alaric punches John in the face. Katherine and Isobel greet each other like vampires — with chokeholds and a slam into the nearest wall. The witches' spirits trap Damon in a patch of sunlight and deactivate his ring, making him sizzle. Alaric is taken down with head pain by Klaus's witch. To create a distraction, Isobel bites into John then throws him down the stairs, killing him (temporarily). Stefan slams Katherine against Elena's car; she stabs him with a vervain dart and throws him in the bushes. The spirits throw Jeremy across the room, while Bonnie screams in pain as she receives the power of the witches. Matt grabs Sheriff Forbes, and she flips him onto the hood of her squad car. Under compulsion from Klaus, Isobel kills herself by removing her daylight necklace. Damon holds up John by his shirt, until Elena calls him off. Alaric is used in some sort of creepy possession blood transfusion ritual.

PREVIOUSLY ON THE VAMPIRE DIARIES: In "Under Control," Jeremy approached Sheriff Forbes at the Lockwood mansion to ask about the Vicki Donovan investigation, just as Matt does here. Jeremy later tells Elena, "The truth is the only thing that will let people move on." In "The Dinner Party," Damon takes the moonstone from Elijah's jacket pocket and calls it the "moonstone bar of soap," a clue to its later hiding spot. Frank the Cowboy makes a repeat appearance in this episode as Isobel's human boy toy, after debuting with Cherie in "Isobel." With Isobel dead and gone, he's free at last. Bonnie used the "find the book" spell (which she uses to find the right grimoire at the Martins' apartment) in "Isobel" to prove her magic skills to Damon, pulling his favorite book, *Call of the Wild*, from the shelves of the Salvatore library. Damon tells the Sheriff and Carol to trust him that John will come back to life, a reference to Damon's firsthand experience killing John and having him resurrect, at the Lockwood house in "Under Control." Isobel apologizes to Elena for being "such a disappointment," echoing the moment in "Isobel" when Elena thanks her for "being such a monumental disappointment. It keeps the memory of my real mother perfectly intact."

MEANWHILE IN FELL'S CHURCH: Bonnie is able to control the weather with her new powers; in the book series, vampires like Damon, Katherine, and Klaus can control the weather with their massive amounts of Power. In *The Struggle*, Katherine possesses Vickie Bennett (but she doesn't require a blood transfusion to do so). In *The Fury*, Bonnie is given a choice by the spirit of a dead witch; Honoria Fell tells her, "Your secret powers are a responsibility. They are also a gift, and one that can be taken away." Bonnie chooses to keep the powers and learn to "deal with them somehow." In order to battle Klaus in *Dark Reunion*, Bonnie calls on the hundreds of "unquiet spirits" in Fell's Church, whose violent deaths have left a mystical power on the field where they were killed. She is willing to do "whatever it takes" against the big bad in Fell's Church, no matter how perilous it gets.

OFF CAMERA: This is the first *Vampire Diaries* episode for director Wendey Stanzler who has an impressive list of credits including *Sex and the City*, *Desperate Housewives*, *Ugly Betty*, *90210*, *Dollhouse*, *Gossip Girl*, *The Middle*, *Parks and Recreation*, and *Pretty Little Liars*.

FOGGY MOMENTS: In "Daddy Issues," John said Isobel is working on a plan to keep Klaus from ever setting foot in Mystic Falls. What was it? Was that Isobel misdirecting John? Isobel bites into John to cause the distraction at the Lockwood house, but doesn't react as if his blood is poisonous to her. Is John not on vervain or has Isobel developed vervain immunity? The birth date on Isobel's tombstone (January 18, 1978) is different from the date listed on her driver's license (October 17, 1975), which was seen in "A Few Good Men."

MUSIC: At the Lockwood mansion, before the luncheon begins, the Piano Tribute Players' cover of Lifehouse's "Halfway Gone" is playing. As Matt and Liz talk in her police car, "Give Me Strength" by Snow Patrol plays, carrying into John's speech about Isobel.

QUESTIONS:
- How much did Caroline tell Matt? Does he know about doppelgängers and the Sun and Moon Curse?
- What will Sheriff Forbes do with the information Matt gives her?
- Will John keep his pledge to do as Elena asks him?
- What does Klaus want with Katherine?

❀

Damon (to Stefan): I don't mind being the bad guy. I'll make all the life-and-death decisions while you're busy worrying about collateral damage. I'll even let her hate me for it. But at the end of the day, I'll be the one to keep her alive.

2.18 *The Last Dance*

Original air date: April 14, 2011
Written by: Michael Narducci
Directed by: John Behring

Guest cast: Mark Buckland (Chad), Anna Enger (Dana), Terrence Gibney (Mr. Henry)

Klaus makes his Mystic Falls debut at the high school's 1960s Decade Dance with Bonnie on his hit list.

Mystic Falls loves to go all out for its many events but the only one from our gang who truly got into the spirit of the Decade Dance was Damon, dancing up a storm in his leather pants while the rest were as grim as if attending their own funerals — and with good reason. In "The Last Dance" it's hard to see which terrible choice is the "better way": as Klaus makes his presence known, the characters realize they are short on options.

With the deed to the Salvatore house now in Elena's name, the boys agreeing to follow her lead, and Bonnie armed with super witch power, Elena is in better and peppier spirits than we've seen her in ages, but once the-villain-so-awful-he-seemed-imaginary becomes a real, viable threat, she deflates, unable to even fake interest in what to wear to the dance. And in that moment she doesn't yet know that the things that were making her feel secure and protected are not surefire or free from complications: Klaus can get into the house as Alaric, Damon will ignore her wishes, and Bonnie will die if she kills Klaus.

Jeremy finds himself with a lose-lose proposition: he can either be loyal to his girlfriend and let her save his sister's life, or he can fulfill his obligation to tell Elena the truth and try to save Bonnie's life (thereby putting Elena's back on the line). Jeremy has lost his parents, Vicki, and Anna, and he doesn't want to lose Bonnie or Elena. Though Bonnie lies to him, saying she won't *necessarily* die, Jeremy remains unconvinced and can't hide from Elena that something is wrong. He finally comes clean with Stefan, expressing how trapped he feels in his no-win scenario. There's no clear answer to what Jeremy "should" have done in this situation: Damon describes him as squealing while Stefan is grateful to know.

Despite being just as freaked-out as Jeremy, Matt manages to pull off his deception with Caroline. While the rest of the students choose counterculture costumes, Caroline opts for Jackie and JFK for her and Matt. Though she picks up on Liz's and Matt's moments of awkwardness, she believes what they tell her: Matt's shy to kiss her in front of the Sheriff; he stares at her oddly because of how pretty she looks, and Liz is just overwhelmed with work stress. Matt gives Caroline what she wants from him

— romance — using physical affection and flattery to distract her from what's really going on. However, now that he knows the nature of the major secrets she's been keeping from him, he also realizes that when Caroline brushes off Elena's frantic search for Stefan as the "same old drama" there's something serious and probably dangerous afoot. Alone together with what they know, Matt and Liz seem to be just on the precipice of understanding that being a vampire (or a chronic liar) doesn't necessarily make you evil. The options available to them form another impossible choice: betray your loved ones or let monsters run your hometown.

As the students think about their costumes for the Decade Dance, "AlariKlaus" picks out his wardrobe from Alaric's closet, preparing for his part as the "haggard history teacher" with forced help from his prisoner, Katherine, who serves as his inside source. He realizes that what was kept from Katherine may be of even more use than what she actually knows, and his instinct proves bang on. In the opening scene, AlariKlaus comes off as delightfully twisted — promising her hundreds of years of torture before letting her die and getting started on it right away by having her stab herself over and over. The way he derides Alaric's life and personal style while occupying his body and home is cruel (but very funny). It produces the same good twin/bad twin comedic effect as when Katherine comments on her "dull as dishwater" doppelgänger. It's a strange feeling for the audience to invade the character's privacy, looking into Alaric's closet, cupboards, and drawers for the first time without him there to allow the snooping. Matt Davis has never been creepier or smirkier; his dance through the crowd of high school students was a particular highlight.

Perhaps thrown off by how confident Bonnie is that she can kill him, AlariKlaus is preoccupied with impressing the gang with his villainy, a need that weakens Maddox's otherwise clever plan to provoke Bonnie to death. AlariKlaus openly reveals his key advantage: he can take on another body if Bonnie kills Alaric's and the real Klaus won't even be hurt. This revelation, in turn, leads Damon to rethink the game plan. Though Damon is determined not to let Klaus win the night, it's a strange turn of events that such youngsters could possibly gain the advantage over the oldest vampire in the history of time, and even stranger for Damon, who appreciates good villainy when he sees it, to be so unimpressed by Klaus. Even the compelled Dana thought his name was stupid. Did Klaus underestimate them, or are they now underestimating Klaus?

"The Last Dance" begins with Elena very pointedly making Damon promise to do things her way and not keep secret plans from her, to which he reluctantly agrees (after hilariously refusing to "obey" her). While Stefan adheres to the new rule over the course of the evening, telling Elena about Bonnie's plan to die saving her, Damon makes a case for breaking it. If there's a way to keep Elena safe, to gain an advantage over those out to kill her, Damon has the will to do it — even if there's collateral damage, even if he has to lie to Elena or crush her with grief. His "whatever it takes" attitude saves the day in "The Last Dance" and just might prove to be what ultimately saves Elena, as he tells Stefan in their classic butting-heads conversation. What works best for Elena may be a combination of Damon's and Stefan's strategies. Stefan's not a bad strategist himself, as he demonstrates early in the episode when he's already thought of and rejected the ideas that Damon comes up with. He respects Elena's right to know what the hell is going on, her right to make decisions about her own life, and he's there for her when something awful (inevitably) happens. Damon, on the other hand, can not only brighten Elena's spirits on the dance floor in a way that Stefan doesn't, he's willing and able to be the "bad guy" — to kill when necessary, to clean up messes and dispose of bodies, to think of and enact plans that his brother may be too straight-edged to conceive or carry out. And Elena gets it. The truth of what Damon and Bonnie did doesn't upset her: she's grateful. As Damon says, "Here's to duplicity."

Bonnie and Elena have had their rough patches over the past vampire-filled year, but as Bonnie said in "Children of the Damned," she and Elena are "bonded for life" and she'd die for her best friend. Now that she has the opportunity to live up to her word, Bonnie doesn't hesitate to be Elena's protector. Like Damon, she thinks that being honest with Elena (or completely forthcoming with Jeremy) about the consequences of using the witches' power will only complicate things. With or without the Gilberts' permission, Bonnie will do whatever it takes. She first demonstrated this in "The Sacrifice" when she channeled Luka in an attempt to take down the tomb seal, even though it caused her physical harm and even though the spell had killed Grams in "Fool Me Once." And just as Bonnie promised Jeremy that she'd be fine in "The Sacrifice," she makes an empty promise to him outside the dance, downplaying the danger to ease his mind.

Once Jeremy spills the beans and Elena confronts Bonnie, the friends find themselves in another one of this episode's impossible binds. As Bonnie points out, Elena would make the same choice if their roles were reversed. But Bonnie can also imagine how Elena would feel to have her best friend die to save her. And Elena suffers through that (albeit temporarily), feeling at fault for Bonnie's death and believing she died in vain. Even more fiercely determined not to let Bonnie die after going through the trauma of her faked death, Elena expresses her resolve to Damon. But his commitment to saving her life is total, and to him, Bonnie is expendable, which means that it's up to Elena herself to come up with another way to kill Klaus. Luckily that alternative

is gathering dust in the basement. By pulling the dagger out of Elijah, Elena gives her side another potential advantage unknown to the enemy. Bonnie isn't dead and soon Elijah won't be either. Elena's plan is not without its own risks: though Klaus is a foe to both Elena and Elijah, she tricked and betrayed Elijah, breaking their bargain and her word. And she's seen the consequences of betraying Elijah: Trevor lost his head. How will Elena convince Elijah she's worthy of an alliance with him against Klaus?

COMPELLING MOMENT: Elena's grief at Bonnie's death. Give Nina Dobrev any convoluted supernatural scenario and she will make it achingly real.

CIRCLE OF KNOWLEDGE:
- No Tyler or Jenna in this episode.
- In a common ploy for *The Vampire Diaries*, AlariKlaus tells Katherine that he wants the dagger to stay in Elijah in the opening scene of the episode, foreshadowing the final scene where Elena takes it out.

- Klaus really is old: making Katherine stab herself in the leg over and over is a punishment that seems pulled straight out of Greek mythology, like Prometheus whose liver was pecked out each day and grew back each night.
- Poor Alaric, no one thinks it's unusual that he has zero knowledge of the class curriculum. But the idea that the oldest vampire makes a *terrible* history teacher is hilarious. It all kind of mushes together for Klaus.
- In a rather snippy tone, Stefan reprimands Elena and Bonnie, saying that school wasn't as safe as they thought it would be; seconds later, AlariKlaus walks into his "safe house." Eat your words, Salvatore.
- Maddox's plan for AlariKlaus to provoke Bonnie to death is the inverse of Katherine's schemes where the provoker is the one killed. She used that trick on Jimmy, compelling him to attack Mason until he is killed ("Kill or Be Killed"), and on Matt and Sarah compelling them to attack Tyler ("Masquerade").

THE RULES: In Alaric's body, Klaus is still able to use his compulsion (on Katherine, Dana, Chad and the boys) but is otherwise limited to human capabilities. He can enter Elena's safe house, because Alaric's body is not subject to the threshold rule. He has no access to Alaric's memories or knowledge. Bonnie explains to Jeremy that the Gilbert rings only protect humans from supernatural death, not a supernatural entity. With the power of a hundred witches, Bonnie is able to cast a spell on herself that allows her to die temporarily.

THE DIABOLICAL PLAN: By questioning a compelled Katherine about what she knows and what secrets she suspects might have been kept from her, AlariKlaus identifies the threat Bonnie poses to him. After AlariKlaus (rather conveniently) revealed to Bonnie that he could possess another body if she killed Alaric's, Damon comes up with a new plan: fake Bonnie's death so they gain back the element of surprise that AlariKlaus had stolen from them. With no diabolical plan whatsoever, Liz Forbes asks Matt to buy her some thinking time by playing the happy, clueless boyfriend with Caroline.

HISTORY LESSON: With the Decade Dance, 1960s references are rampant: the Beatles formed in 1960 and by '64 had 12 hits on the Billboard Hot 100. The Cuban Missile Crisis, a standoff between the U.S., Russia, and Cuba, took place in the fall of 1962. *Apollo 11* landed on the Moon on July 20, 1969. Elena's right about her history: the Watergate scandal broke in 1972, causing

Nixon to resign in 1974. Matt dresses as John F. Kennedy, president from '61 to '63, and, though Caroline says she's dressed as "Jackie O," Jacqueline Kennedy didn't get that nickname until her marriage to Aristotle Onassis in 1968. English fashion model Twiggy became the "face" of the late 1960s. But Klaus hates the '60s, preferring the Jazz Age of the 1920s.

BITE MARKS: Klaus compels Katherine to stab herself repeatedly all day long. To demonstrate her new power, Bonnie throws Damon across the room with just a flick of her hand. Chad and his friends beat up Jeremy for a little extra credit (and because they're under compulsion). Damon gets a stake in the shoulder. Stefan knocks out two of the boys attacking Jeremy, and Damon clocks a third. Bonnie throws AlariKlaus against the lockers and then down the hallway into a glass case. In their cafeteria battle, she breaks his fingers, dislocates his shoulder, buckles his knees, and as many other painful things she can think of. Elena slaps Damon.

PREVIOUSLY ON THE VAMPIRE DIARIES: Dana returns in this episode after making her debut in the classic "Not now, Dana" moment from "The Descent." In "There Goes the Neighborhood," Elena refused to live "every moment in fear that someone's coming after her"; here she expresses the same sentiment that she doesn't want to live like a prisoner. AlariKlaus tells Katherine that killing her would be a kindness she doesn't deserve; in "Masquerade" Damon felt the same way, telling her death would be too kind. AlariKlaus calls Elijah a "buzzkill"; Damon famously called Stefan "Buzzkill Bob" in "A Few Good Men" and Trevor called Rose a buzzkill when she refused to let him snack on Elena in "Rose." In "Unpleasantville," the 1950s Decade Dance episode, Caroline says that her ensemble took two hours to put together and she was going to stay at the dance for at least half that long; the writers have AlariKlaus echo that line, telling Katherine that since he chased her for 500 years, her death will take at least half that long. Also in "Unpleasantville," Stefan offered Elena the option of backing out of the plan to go to the dance in the hopes of luring out the vampire Noah, something he also offers as they get ready for the '60s dance. In both instances, Elena is resolved to go — what else can she do? On the dance floor, Damon humorously recaps the showdown at the '50s dance between Elena, Noah, and the Salvatore brothers, which took place in the cafeteria, like Bonnie's does with AlariKlaus here. Elena always goes for the slap when she's angry with Damon: she slapped him in "Friday Night Bites," he blocked her hits in both "Haunted" and "The Sacrifice," and she lands a good one on him in this episode. In order to fool Katherine, Stefan and Elena faked their breakup in "Memory Lane," keeping the truth from those closest to them because everyone had to believe it in order for the plan to work, a lower stakes version of what Damon and Bonnie do in "The Last Dance."

MEANWHILE IN FELL'S CHURCH: Of Klaus, Vickie Bennett says, "No one can fight him and live" (*Dark Reunion*). In that same novel, Klaus sends a message through a retro song, "Goodnight Sweetheart," as he does with his song dedication at the '60s dance. Like Bonnie in this episode, Stefan is prepared to lose his life in a battle against Klaus in *Dark Reunion*, and he lies to his friends to prevent them from stopping him. Says good old Matt Honeycutt, "He thinks he's going to go and stop Klaus even though he gets killed himself? Like some sacrificial lamb?" As Bonnie and Damon work well (and dance well) together in "The Last Dance," in *Dark Reunion* Bonnie and Damon team up to battle Klaus and have a moment of connection: "They weren't a centuries-old hunter and a seventeen-year-old human girl, sitting here at the edge of the world. They were just two people, Damon and Bonnie, who had to do the best they could."

OFF CAMERA: Gino Anthony Pesi, who plays Maddox, originally hails from Belle Vernon, Pennsylvania. He liked having the powers of a witch: "It's kind of fun, because I basically hold up my hand and people go flying off walls." As Kevin Williamson explained to the *Hollywood Reporter*, "Originally, we had planned to kill [Bonnie] for four episodes and let Elena be the one who hid her away and surprised everyone with it, but we said the audience would hate us. They'll never forgive us. Then we thought we could do this for one episode and bring her back next week. Then we thought no, better to do it at the end of the commercial break. We finally came down to a commercial break was all we could get away with."

MUSIC: Patrick Stump's "Spotlight (Oh Nostalgia)" plays as the Mystic Falls high schoolers prepare the decorations for the dance. The dance kicks off with Kula Shaker's "Hush," a cover of a 1967 song first recorded by Billy Joe Royal and more famously by Deep Purple in '68. Klaus sends his special shout-out to Elena with The Mamas and The Papas' 1967 hit "Dedicated to the One I Love," which was previously a single for The Shirelles in '61. Trent Dabbs covers "Last Kiss" (originally recorded in 1961, perhaps most famously covered by Pearl Jam in 1999), which plays as Elena dances with Stefan and then with Damon. The Birthday Massacre's version of "I Think We're Alone Now," a hit for Tommy James and the Shondells in 1967 (and for Tiffany in 1987), provides the soundtrack for Damon to cut the rug with random MFHS girls. The Manhattans' 1965 single "I Wanna Be (Your Everything)" plays in the background when Jeremy encounters Chad and his boys in the hallway. Elena searches for Stefan and talks to Caroline to The Dollyrots' "Dream Lover," a Bobby Daren song from 1959.

QUESTIONS:
- Did Bonnie cast a spell that brought her back from the dead, or was it a spell that made her merely appear to be dead — like Juliet drinking the poison in *Romeo and Juliet*? Either way, it's a powerful spell. Does Bonnie have the power to raise the dead?
- Does Katherine have an escape strategy? She seemed to be paying very close attention to AlariKlaus's conversations with Maddox, but she's been compelled not to leave the apartment.

❀

> *Klaus: Love is a vampire's greatest weakness and we are not weak, Elijah. We do not feel and we do not care.*
> *Elijah: We did once.*
> *Klaus: Too many lifetimes ago to matter.*

2.19 *Klaus*

Original air date: April 21, 2011
Written by: Kevin Williamson and Julie Plec
Directed by: Joshua Butler

Elijah explains to Elena what has really been going on for the past 1,000 years. Damon and Stefan come to blows.

In quite a feat, *The Vampire Diaries* writers managed to pull the rug out from under us, with a massive mythology fakeout, without cheapening the episodes that led up to "Klaus," where the Sun and the Moon Curse was the most important narrative motivator. Elijah's revelation that he and his *brother* Klaus faked the whole thing — Aztec drawings and all — is exciting rather than a rip-off because the critical element remains the same: Elena has to die in the impending sacrifice.

With the true curse and its backstory, the show manages to get rid of the awkward questions surrounding the Aztec curse (vampires roamed freely in the 1300s? An Aztec shaman somehow got the blood of a Bulgarian girl?) and open up a fascinating new world of story possibilities. Elijah tells Elena that there are nine members in his once-human family: a vengeful father who never liked "Niklaus," a mother whose unfaithfulness was her "darkest secret," five children of whom we know nothing (yet), Elijah, and Klaus who comes from a werewolf bloodline. The potential for flashbacks and family drama in that setup alone is limitless. Add to that the still-unknown entity of the Original Petrova, who is somehow critical enough that the witches, "nature's servants," made it so that her doppelgänger's blood must be spilled and that the curse must be broken in the doppelgäanger's birthplace. What relation to the Original vampire family (who hail from Eastern Europe like the Petrovas) did the Original Petrova have?

As much as the episode sent us reeling with Elijah's revelations (about the Original family, Klaus, the purpose of the fake curse, and the content of the real one), what worked about the exposition-heavy scenes was that the information elegantly tied together multiple storylines that have been exploring the same themes: betrayal, love, trust, and respect. The writers managed to feed the mythology into the dramatic conflict rather than overshadow the characters who are, after all, the heart of the show.

Elena is so often the recipient of an apology, but in "Klaus," it is she who is making up for past mistakes. The resurrected Elijah does not blindly trust her and she must carefully rebuild her image in his eyes as a person of honor before their new agreement will work. Her word means nothing to him until she proves its value. Elena and Elijah need each other; the only way to defeat Klaus is in unison, sharing his knowledge and her resources. Stefan realizes the potential in Elena having pulled the dagger out: the only person who could convince Elijah to help them kill Klaus is Elena. As the doppelgänger she is a valuable commodity, but more than that, Elena knows how to gain a person's trust and she understands what's important to Elijah. Time and again, her strength has been in her ability to empathize and communicate with people, using her words to connect to them. The story of Elijah's family gives Elena information that could one day prove critical. He trusts her enough to reveal how the bond between him and his brother was broken, and that he once cared for Katerina enough to seek an alternative to her death in the ritual. In essence it was the doppelgänger who came between Elijah and Klaus (through no fault of her own) and now history repeats itself with another set of brothers at arms over a doppelgänger. The story of Klaus and Elijah brings Damon and Stefan's current battle into perspective.

Though by no means identical, the two sets of brothers are paralleled in many ways in the episode from the major details (divided over a doppelgänger) to the minor ones (in back-to-back scenes, women under compulsion bring Damon and Klaus their morning coffee). In the flashback scenes, the stoic Elijah shows more heart than his brother. He cares about the fate of a human and still has the capacity to love. Though he tells Katerina he does not believe in love, it's clear that he cares for her and that he loves his brother enough to help him break the curse despite his misgivings about her dying for his brother's gain. In the present day, Stefan is disturbed by Damon treating Andie like a plaything, rather than as a person deserving of respect and the right to self-determination. Damon rejects the idea that Elena could figure out a way to handle the Klaus situation herself, going so far as to physically restrain her from returning to Elijah. Damon's anger with his brother grows as Stefan repeatedly stands in his way, not allowing him to act the same way Klaus does, without consideration. Klaus's willfulness and disregard for anything but his own rules could be seen as a cautionary tale, a preview of who Damon has the potential to become in 900 years should he continue to play by his own rules alone with blithe disregard for others.

The critical difference between Klaus and Damon — that makes one a villain and the other an antihero — is their motivations. Though Damon can be more than a little unbalanced (as he is at the end of the episode), his actions are driven by love. He wants to save Elena because he loves her, *and* because his brother loves her. Klaus, on the other hand, has forsaken love "lifetimes ago," calling it a "vampire's greatest weakness." And as much as love has proven to be a weakness for vampires and humans alike time and again, it is also what makes a vampire's eternity worth living. It was the lesson that Lexi taught Stefan in 1864 that put him on the path he's on today: "Love, Stefan, that's the point." As a rosy-cheeked Katerina says to Elijah, "Life is too cruel. If we cease to believe in love, why would we want to live?" It's a

Joseph Morgan as Klaus

"You always need your villains to have multiple layers and to be able to kill you with kindness as much as they can kill you with violence. I think Joseph really represents that." That's what Julie Plec told the *LA Times*' Showtracker blog about casting Joseph Morgan as Klaus, a part for whom they saw more than a hundred actors. Speaking to the *Hollywood Reporter*, Kevin Williamson was equally enthusiastic: "Joseph Morgan came in and he nailed it. He had the sense of humor that I wanted Klaus to have. The way we always described [the character] is 'Klaus can out-Damon Damon.'"

Born May 16, 1980, in England but raised in Wales, Joseph studied drama and began his professional acting career in his early 20s in London. As the actor explained to Hitfix.com, it was trial by fire on his first gig: "[Working for acclaimed filmmaker] Peter Weir, that was my first job. I came straight out of drama school and went to Mexico for five months to do *Master and Commander* [2003] and then I did a few TV things in between and then I worked with Oliver Stone [on *Alexander*]. On *Master and Commander*, people were giving me little tips. I didn't know what a mark was. When people shouted, 'Check the gate' at the end of a take [to ensure that the camera gate was clean], I was looking around for a gate. I didn't know what was what." Once he'd got the basics of acting for camera down on major motion pictures, he continued to work on interesting projects, among them *Hex*, *William and Mary*, *Mansfield Park*, and *Ben Hur* in the title role.

He made his move to America two years ago. "I really started to feel, towards the end of last year, like I wanted to branch out into American television, specifically because you get to develop a character for a longer period of time and you get to develop a relationship with the audience. You really get to grow and evolve with the character, and that was something that was fascinating to me — the possible longevity of playing a part like that." That possibility arose when he was cast on *The Vampire Diaries* as Klaus, a role he took a great deal of time and care in researching, reading L.J. Smith's book series and taking to Twitter where he engaged with fans in a way that only built up anticipation for his onscreen debut. In an interview with *Starry Constellation*, he explained, "I started asking questions of the fans [on Twitter] and people were just so responsive and really helped me with where I needed to go with Klaus, and what kind of things people responded to, and what people found frightening about those things. It really helped me build the character and put it together." Arriving in Atlanta to film, Joseph observed the dynamic between cast and crew and realized that he was in for a treat: "I came and I watched some of the '60s dance. That was the first thing I watched, and just to see even Nina standing and talking to the camera guys and everyone high-fiving after the shots, I thought, 'Okay, this will be good.'"

Joseph describes his character as "sociopathic. I feel like there's no line between wrong and right with Klaus. He does what he wants. That's something that's terrifying about him. He just fulfills his needs and desires." At the same time, as he explained to *Collider*, "You never want to play too vampiric or generically evil, so you look for emotions or character traits that you can relate to. The directors and producers of the show always encourage us to be as natural and as real as possible, and play the reality of what we're doing. That was a way of justifying Klaus's behavior and making him more three-dimensional."

Fans responded to Joseph Morgan's portrayal of Klaus, and to the seriousness with which he considered both his character in particular and *The Vampire Diaries* as a whole. Nothing warms a fan's heart more than hearing an actor quoting from an episode of the show that predates his character's introduction, as Joseph did in an interview with i09.com. "There's a line Elijah has way back in the series, where he says, 'I'm an Original, show me some respect.' As a human being, when you've been through something traumatic, or various life-changing events, it *feels* like you've been through something. And you feel stronger. I feel like Klaus has lived through a hundred, a thousand, of these experiences and has come out stronger. He has always come out in control of things. So yeah, there's a sense of that. There's also a sense that the other vampires — the Salvatores who are, like, 160 years old — these are pups to him. They're impudent little vampires who are running around, causing a little bother for him."

disturbing thought — a world where either Salvatore brother is immune to love, and instead hungry only for power like Klaus.

Rejected by his brother for his perceived betrayal (though in fact Elijah didn't help Katerina escape and was therefore never actually disloyal to Klaus), Elijah responds by forsaking his fraternal love for Klaus. The current purpose in his (looong) life seems to be killing his brother before his brother kills him. (What involvement, if any, the rest of the Originals have in Elijah's or Klaus's plans is unknown.) Elena reads Elijah correctly: she gives him the dagger as a sign of her trustworthiness and of her trust in him, and she realizes that he can't kill her for her betrayal because he needs her in order to kill Klaus. Elijah, like Elena, values the bonds of family and he seems to take an interest in her, watching how she works to prove herself and amusing himself by seeing the effect his story has on her. Their dynamic finds a parallel in the flashback to Elijah and a human Katerina, though in that interaction he is holding back information and deceiving her — she doesn't know that Klaus and Elijah are vampires — while with Elena he seems to be giving her the candid truth. He says he won't make the "common" mistake of caring for a doppelgänger again; will that position prove to be as hard to maintain as was his claim not to believe in love?

Both Elijah and Klaus characterize Katerina's actions in 1492 as a betrayal. But aren't Klaus and Elijah the ones who betrayed her? From what we know of the story, they befriended her under false pretenses and then revealed their intention to *kill* her in Klaus's ritual. And so she hightailed it out of there. Katerina never agreed to the terms of her enslavement, so she could never be disloyal to Klaus or Elijah. She didn't break the bonds of trust: they did by deceiving her. Klaus became vengeful because she ruined his plans, and Elijah blames Katerina for the breakdown in his relationship with Klaus. Katerina did mislead and betray Trevor, whose affection for her she knowingly took advantage of and whose love for her cost him his head in the end. But frankly, Trevor was the one who brought her to Klaus in the first place as a "birthday gift," knowing she was the doppelgänger and would be sacrificed. The bonds of trust and loyalty even among these vampires who live by a code of honor and swear by their word are complex and morally shaky, just as those bonds between humans can be.

The trust between Jenna and Elena was already broken coming into this episode — they hadn't spoken since Jenna found out about Isobel — and now Jenna knows the secret that has been kept from her for so long. As when Matt found out, Jenna is shown the truth in a frightening situation — her sorta-boyfriend wielding a knife and Stefan displaying his speed and fangs, growling at her to get out. Not exactly the scenario Elena would have preferred for her aunt. Elena freely admits to Jenna that she should have told her the truth and that this mistake is hers. Besides being scared and shocked, Jenna seems hurt by the fact that she's the only one who didn't know, and that her ignorance prevented her from fulfilling her duty to protect Elena and Jeremy. Instead they were trying to protect her. This moment has been a long time coming, and Sara Canning once again rises to the occasion, making this crucial point in Jenna's arc an honest and heartbreaking one.

Elena's decision to lie to Jenna was a betrayal because underlying it was a basic lack of respect for Jenna's right to know the truth and for her right to make her own decisions, something Jenna explained to the girls in "The House Guest." That's the same basic issue that Stefan tries to get his brother to recognize when Damon wants to overrule Elena's choices, saying she's "lost it." And it's also this issue that makes Damon's relationship with Andie so completely disturbing. By taking away her fear, he's robbed her of full knowledge of her situation and her willpower; she has become his smiling puppet, his "distraction," something less than a person. What Damon actually wants is a real connection, which he admitted in "Fool Me Once" when he told Elena that he didn't compel her on their road trip to Georgia because he wanted it to be real. When Andie tells Damon she cares about him, the words must sound hollow to him. He knows that if she were truly herself, she wouldn't be hanging out in her lingerie to comfort the vampire who snacks on her for breakfast and manipulates her personality to suit his preferences. Damon brings Andie, the battered girlfriend, to Katherine, another prisoner, to see if Katherine's "deserving" of freedom; it's twisted that Andie, who also needs vervain to prevent further compulsion, doesn't seem to want any. The final scene between Andie and Damon echoes Stefan's dark turn in "Miss Mystic Falls" when he compels Amber Bradley to fear him and run. But in that episode, Stefan chased her and attacked, just as Damon did to Jessica in "The Descent." Now Damon has the self-control to at least let her leave the room without killing her, while he kneels on the floor in shame, blood on his chin and tears in his eyes. Damon's treatment of Andie has been a fascinatingly dark turn for his character, one that zigs and zags Damon's progress toward becoming a viable love interest for Elena and a true hero of the story.

Stefan condemns how his brother treats Andie, and in their final altercation he hits Damon with what really matters to him: Damon may love Elena, but by behaving the way he does, Damon is actually ruining any chance he has with her. Damon's violent reaction is fueled not only by the fact that his brother has been pissing him off all day by letting Elena do things her way, but because when Stefan says Damon will never have Elena's respect, Damon fears that it's the truth. The brothers fight like mad dogs, called apart with one command from Elena. In a fury, and despite the possibly dire fallout, Damon refuses to give Elijah the apology he asks for. Will he come around, as Stefan rather hopefully tells Elijah? Or is he heading off the deep end? Stefan considers it an advantage that Damon loves Elena — he is as dedicated to protecting her as Stefan is — but does Damon believe, as Katerina once did, that love is not real unless it is returned?

COMPELLING MOMENT: Katherine's bourbon-fueled dance party. In an episode with this much information and so much heavy stuff, a dance break to a great song is just what is needed.

CIRCLE OF KNOWLEDGE:
- No Caroline, Matt, Tyler, Bonnie, or Jeremy in this episode.
- Stefan tells Alari/Klaus he appreciates vampires in literature, mentioning Bram Stoker (1847–1912), author of *Dracula*.

- The Gilbert kitchen knives, which saw plenty of vampire action last season, get more love in season 2. In last season's "You're Undead to Me," Elena cuts herself while chopping garlic causing Stefan to vamp out. In "There Goes the Neighborhood," Jeremy slices his hand open to tempt Anna. In "Founder's Day," Katherine takes John's fingers clean off his hand. This season, in "The Return," Elena wields one against an unseen Katherine. In "Plan B," Jenna stabs herself in the gut. And in "Klaus," AlariKlaus threatens Jenna after a soothing session of chopping vegetables.
- It was pretty rich of Damon to scold Katherine for double-crossing them with Isobel, while he's in the midst of going rogue and breaking away from the team himself.
- For a different take on the centuries-long battles that can result from one adulterous fling and the mixing of vampire and werewolf species to create a hybrid, watch the 2003 film *Underworld*.

THE RULES: A vampire inside a residence he hasn't been invited into feels as though he's suffocating; other side effects include disorientation, slamming into walls, and contortions. An Original can't be killed any of the usual ways (by sunlight, fire, or a werewolf bite); the only ways to kill an Original are with the dagger and ash, or with a powerful enough witch. Klaus, as a vampire-werewolf hybrid, cannot be killed by the dagger and ash — that weapon would harm the vampire part of him, but the werewolf part would heal — so the only known way to kill Klaus is with a witch. In order to maintain the balance in nature, every creature must have a weakness. A truly immortal being cannot exist; witches are the "servants of nature" tasked with maintaining that balance. The curse on Klaus must be broken in the birthplace of the doppelgänger and on a full moon.

THE DIABOLICAL PLAN: Fittingly the Originals have the most elaborate diabolical plan of all: Klaus and Elijah invented the curse of the Sun and the Moon in order to have all werewolves and vampires on the hunt for a doppelgänger and the moonstone, and they faked artifacts in "any culture or continent" they felt like. Elena successfully finds another strategy to kill Klaus: she and Elijah make a new agreement to work together. Because Elijah has a way (yet to be revealed) to protect Elena from permanent death in the sacrifice, their new plan is to let Klaus go through with the sacrifice. While Klaus is transitioning into werewolf form, he will be at his most vulnerable — as Tyler's was in "By the Light of the Moon," Klaus's first transformation will be long and horribly painful — and in that weakened state Bonnie can kill him using some of her borrowed dead-witch power. Klaus dies; Elena and Bonnie live. How they plan to deal with the vampire and werewolf also needed in the ritual, or Klaus's two powerful witches, Maddox and Greta, is yet to be determined.

HISTORY LESSON: Klaus has been trying to break the curse for the past 1,000 years. Presumably the Originals have been vampires for about that length of time. In season 1, the unreliability of historical documents was an idea raised when Giuseppe and Johnathan lied in town records; small potatoes compared to how Elijah and Klaus have been creating documents to further their own purpose. As it turns out, what Damon said to Rose in "The Descent," that legends are notoriously unreliable sources, was correct, he was just talking about a different legend.

BITE MARKS: Elijah feels like he's suffocating inside the Salvatore house, newly Elena's. Stefan grabs Damon, telling him to back off. When AlariKlaus threatens Jenna with the knife, Stefan slams him against the wall and presses the knife into his neck, cutting him. He knocks him out and gives him a few hard kicks for good measure. Stefan grabs Damon again when Damon physically restrains Elena from leaving the house. In the library, the brothers finally come to blows. In the flashback, Klaus slams Elijah into the wall. Damon bites into Andie and throws her to the floor. Alaric passes out after Klaus returns to his own body.

PREVIOUSLY ON THE VAMPIRE DIARIES: In the flashback, Klaus says, "*Zdravei*, Katerina," when he meets her at his party, just as AlariKlaus did when he saw her again in "Know Thy Enemy." AlariKlaus makes food for Jenna and "opens up" in a twisted echo of the scene where Stefan cooks for Elena and opens up in "You're Undead to Me." Katherine wanted the Salvatore boys to chase her in the "Lost Girls" flashback, a game similar to the one she plays with Elijah in the garden, wanting to be chased. Elijah's moment with Katerina is interrupted by the arrival of his brother, just as Stefan's moment with Katherine was when Damon returned home from the war in "Lost Girls."

MEANWHILE IN FELL'S CHURCH: In *Dark Reunion* Klaus is described in a manner that very much suits Joseph Morgan's Klaus: "*He looks like the devil. If the devil was handsome and blond.*"

OFF CAMERA: Greta Martin is played by Lisa Tucker, perhaps best known as a contestant in season 5 of *American Idol.* Her acting credits include *Zoey 101* and *The Game.*

FOGGY MOMENTS: At beginning of the episode, Andie leaves for work, but after Stefan gets the call from Jenna and leaves, she's back in the living room ready to go rogue with Damon. That was a short shift!

Now that we know what the real curse is, the rationale behind Klaus killing Katerina's entire family makes less sense. When it was the Sun and Moon Curse, killing off the Petrova line eliminated any possibility of another doppelgänger — meaning no one could break the curse, which didn't put Klaus at any disadvantage. He got to exact vengeance on Katerina in a way we now know has personal resonance (since his wolfy birth father and his family were killed by his vengeful stepdad). But since it's actually a curse that only affects him, does it make sense that Klaus would destroy the odds of there being another Petrova doppelgänger? Was he so blind with the need for vengeance that he shot himself in the foot? Or did he know about Katerina's "secret shame"?

While planting fake artifacts about the curse across centuries and cultures is a genius way to get vampires and werewolves looking for the doppelgänger and moonstone, how could Klaus be assured that he would be informed when the necessities for the sacrifice were discovered? Particularly if a werewolf had them, since Klaus is, presumably, on the vampire side of the age-old war, at least for now.

How did Trevor know that Katerina was a doppelgänger? Did Klaus use his mad artistic skills to make a portrait of the Original Petrova?

In the flashback to 1492, Klaus and company were still in England the day before the full moon but in order to do the sacrifice they had to be in the birthplace of the doppelgänger, Bulgaria. How did they plan on getting there in time?

Elijah says that Originals cannot be killed by sunlight, but he wears a lapis lazuli ring, which appears to be for daylight protection. Why?

How did Klaus's body get into Alaric's apartment without an invitation? When he emerges from his traveling case, he doesn't seem to be suffocating the same way Elijah was in the Salvatore cell. Is Klaus about to start gasping? Or is he immune because as a vamp-wolf hybrid, and even with one side dormant, the threshold rule doesn't apply to him?

MUSIC: Katherine twirls around on a stool to "Helena" by Foster the People (who also had a song in "The Dinner Party"). Doves' "Compulsion" plays while AlariKlaus chops vegetables and freaks out Jenna in the Gilbert kitchen. Katherine dances to Lykke Li's "Get Some."

QUESTIONS:
- Elijah asks Elena where she got the dagger. Katherine and Isobel provided it to John, but where did it come from originally? Did Katherine have it stashed away somewhere or did Klaus provide it to Isobel in an effort to have Elijah killed?
- Why didn't Elijah mention that he had a way to save Elena from the sacrifice the first time they made their deal? Was it because he no longer cared about the life of a human, especially not a doppelgänger?
- Rose said that Katerina was the first Petrova doppelgänger — was she? Now that we know Klaus has been trying to break the curse for 1,000 years (not the 600 of the Sun and Moon Curse), is it possible that there was a doppelgänger in the 500 years before Kat?
- In the flashback, Elijah says to Klaus, the witches "believe" they have found a way to save the doppelgänger — should we be concerned about that word choice or does Elijah have a surefire way of Elena surviving the sacrifice?
- What is the rest of the Original family up to? Are they on Elijah's side or Klaus's or neither? Does the tension between Elijah's father and Klaus still exist?
- Elijah is rather confident about how one can and cannot kill an Original. Has one of the family members already been killed? Is that how they knew to burn the white oak tree?
- How did Klaus get to be the brother in charge? Is it because he's a hybrid? Hated by Papa Original, one could imagine his status in that family being a kind of Cinderella, not the most powerful.
- Who else knows what the real curse is? Does Katherine? Did Trevor or Rose? Do Klaus's witches or did the late Martin witches? In order for the

Sun and Moon ruse to work, it must be a rather closely guarded secret that very few outside of the Original family know.

- Klaus mentions to Katherine that he has the moonstone and the doppelgänger is standing by. He has Maddox and Greta to perform the magic. Who will he chose to be his werewolf and vampire?
- After Emily possessed Bonnie in "History Repeating," Bonnie was shaken but otherwise okay (until Damon chomped on her). Will Alaric also be okay now that Klaus has left his body?
- Klaus says that vampires are the oldest "creatures of the night," second only to werewolves. His statement implies there are more creatures of the night than those two. What else is lurking out there?
- Elijah says Klaus will be able to sire a race of hybrids. Can Klaus procreate like a werewolf or would he create hybrids like one turns a human into a vampire?

❁

> Damon: *That's not a risk I'm willing to take.*
> Elena: *But I am. It's my life, Damon. My choice.*
> Damon: *We can't lose you.*

2.20 *The Last Day*

Original air date: April 28, 2011
Written by: Andrew Chambliss and Brian Young
Directed by: J. Miller Tobin

Damon force-feeds Elena his blood to ensure she'll survive the sacrifice — and come back as a vampire.

First rule of any supernatural showdown: always have a backup plan. Just as Katherine had her plans A through Z and Klaus believes in having a second set of creatures for sacrifice just in case there are any pesky heroics, Damon can't live with Elena's plan, which has no backup contingency. If Elijah were telling the truth, if his no-expiry elixir worked, then she would be resuscitated post-sacrifice. If not — she would be forever dead. From Elena's perspective, there is no choice but to have faith in Elijah and their plan, because she is unwilling to consider the alternative — Bonnie killing Klaus and dying in the process. To trust that things will work out as planned, to keep calm and carry on, to enter into the sacrifice fully knowing the risks. Because *she* is the key to breaking the curse, Elena feels compelled to keep Klaus from harming those she loves and to serve the greater good by preventing him from becoming a hybrid on the loose. That Elena's willing to give her life is not a surprise, but that she would rather risk dying than be guaranteed to return as a vampire is the central emotional conflict of "The Last Day."

It is an understatement to say that the Salvatore brothers react in different ways to Elena's trust in Elijah. Stefan urges Damon to have faith in her instincts about Elijah; after all, Elena trusts in them despite what they are and what they've done in the past. Damon rather hilariously points out that Elena's faith in him shows questionable judgment. And then minutes later, he proves that trusting him can be a dangerous undertaking when he pulls one of his classic Damon act-without-thinking-and-then-immediately-regret-it moves. Though Damon feels as though his opinion doesn't matter to her, Elena wants him to understand her choice and to respect it. But for him, even the possibility of losing Elena isn't an option; it's not an acceptable risk. In that moment Damon would rather have Elena hate him for eternity than lose her forever. Despite it being an obvious solution to their problem, seeing Damon force-feeding Elena his blood, ensuring that she'll survive the sacrifice as a transitioning vampire, came as a shock. Damon's innate impetuousness is fueled by the ticking clock of the sacrifice's approach and the impending sense of doom that has settled over the Salvatore house.

The fact that the possibility of Elena becoming a vampire has barely been mentioned in nearly two seasons is a remarkable feat for a show that is so often described as a romance between a mortal human girl and a hunky, immortal vampire. As Stefan says at the peak of their climb up the hill together, it's something he's thought of a hundred times — both in the context of saving Elena from the sacrifice and when considering their future together. Prior to this conversation, Elena has said remarkably little on the subject. In "The Return," Elena didn't understand why Jeremy would *want* to become a vampire, a subtle moment signaling that for her, eternal life as a 17-year-old girl doesn't have any appeal. In "Katerina," she didn't seem to even consider the option that Katherine offered her — to drink her blood and render herself useless for sacrifice (particularly since that wouldn't save her family from Klaus's vengeance). Family in all its forms is hugely valuable to Elena, and hearing from Rose in "The Descent" that "the whole idea of family — it's not exactly compatible with being a vampire" could have only reinforced Elena's feelings about what she would be sacrificing if she ever turned.

Before shutting the conversation down in "Crying Wolf," Elena broaches the question of the future she and Stefan could share, and the two acknowledge that there is an "unopened box" (to use her image) that Stefan is ready to delve into whenever she is. With Damon's blood in her, instead of thinking she has precious little life left, an unwanted eternity now stretches before her. Stefan pushed her to talk to him at the end of "Katerina," but Elena felt that because admitting her anguish wouldn't change anything, there was no point in opening up. And he does the same thing here, convincing her after the day's climb by the beautiful Mystic Falls that unbottling her feelings may bring her some measure of peace.

Elena is conscious of how painful it will be for Stefan to hear her true feelings: that she would rather risk dying than spend an eternity as a vampire. In her beautifully honest speech, Elena tearfully admits incredibly hard things to him — that she isn't sure she yet understands what love is, that an eternity with him is not something she is certain she will want, and that she doesn't want to be what he is, a vampire. Though Elena is tough and resilient, handling the grief and horror thrown her way, she's still a teenager. She feels the potential in her youth — a lifetime of possibility before her — and wants to grow up and learn and make choices. But the life she envisioned for herself has been taken from her. Though she may be uncertain of many things at 17 years old, she is still wise enough to realize that as one matures, one changes. But a vampire is frozen in time; Elena mourns losing the opportunity to evolve past her teenage self.

On their walk, Stefan tells the inquisitive Elena that the two hardest things about being a vampire are the bloodlust and the heightened emotions. Stefan is just now learning how to manage his bloodlust, after denying himself human blood for so long, and though he still struggles with the extremes of emotion a vampire feels, he says the good outweighs the bad. He manages it. And that's evident in how he carries himself. Just like Damon, he wants Elena to be by his side forever, but he won't even bring up the idea of her turning because he knows it's not what *she* wants. He respects her right to decide for herself, and because he loves her, he can't be selfish with her. Even

when saying goodbye, when Klaus comes for her, though everything in him is fighting against letting her go, he does.

On the flip side is Damon, who has control over his bloodlust but is only learning to manage his humanity now that he lets himself feel the overwhelming explosions of emotion a vampire feels — rage, love, rejection, and hurt. There's some truth in Damon saying to Stefan, in their fight, that Stefan's angry because he wishes he had the balls to turn Elena himself — it's what both brothers want. But Damon lets his selfish impulse rule him, while Stefan is able to fight it off. Where Stefan has impulse control, Damon gives into a frenzy of passion in an act with dire consequences for Elena and for his relationship with her. It's telling that Damon immediately sees the error of his ways (as he did after snapping Jeremy's neck): he knows he screwed up, as he moans to Alaric over a glass of bourbon at the Grill, and is willing to die at Klaus's hand trying to fix his grievous mistake. And dying is a distinct possibility for Damon — with that throbbing bite from wolf-Tyler revealed in the episode's final twist.

Our heroine is in danger of becoming a vampire, our anti-hero is slated for a harrowing death, recently not-so-clueless Jenna is about to vamp out and then be sacrificed . . . and there are still two episodes in the season. *The Vampire Diaries* built a reputation in season 1 for blazing through storylines with its twists and cliffhangers, and season 2 keeps up that frenetic pacing as the finish line comes into sight. With practically every character in peril, this episode promises a serious conversation in Caroline and Matt's near future, should they survive their current trapped-with-an-attacking-werewolf situation. (As Damon says, that's "tomorrow's problem.") Presented with Liz's hollow argument that all vampires are evil versus compelling evidence that Caroline is still Caroline, Matt realizes that she's not the enemy and he fights to protect her, even though he has no idea what the hell he's getting himself into. Matt shows faith in Caroline: the voicemail he leaves her while at the Grill suggests that he was planning to open up about the secret he and Liz have been keeping. And even Liz is faltering in her long-held beliefs that vampires are demons, soulless creatures who put on a show of humanity to trick their victims. She's not entirely wrong: some vampires are exactly that. It's just as with any other group — humans, werewolves, witches, vampires, in Mystic Falls or in real life — a blanket characterization is never accurate and is often a very, very dangerous idea to subscribe to.

Both Matt and Jenna — so recently clueless, now in the know — prove themselves to be handy with weapons in "The Last Day," Matt taking down Maddox and Jenna pulling a crossbow on Alaric. (And the way Alaric proves he isn't Klaus anymore? *Hilarious.*) Jenna responds to the high stakes of their situation: problems are put into perspective. Though she wasn't on speaking terms with Alaric just yesterday, today she sets aside her feelings of betrayal to let him know she loves him. "The Last Day" carries a sense of finality across its various storylines as its title suggests it will. Caroline wants to clear the air between her and Tyler. Tyler returns to Mystic Falls with a sense of control and calm that he didn't have when he left, and that he certainly didn't have last season. Like Caroline and Jeremy, Tyler has grown up a lot thanks to loss, pain, and life-altering supernatural complications. His awkward conversation with Caroline outside the hospital leaves much unsaid, but with literally no way to escape a conversation in the tomb, and with sacrifice an imminent possibility, they both open up. Caroline asks incredibly vulnerable questions, and Tyler responds in kind, telling her why he left without saying goodbye. They take steps toward reestablishing their bond. While she was hurt, she could never hate him, and in her offer to help him through his transformation, she again proves willing to endanger herself for him. Perhaps, given the forgiveness between Tyler and Caroline and Jenna and Alaric, Damon can hope for the same from the perennially forgiving Elena.

While the rest of the characters are banding together, protecting each other and making sure the ones they love know they are loved, our two resident villains keep fighting for themselves. Klaus has a thousand years of determination and experience riding on this curse-breaking plot, and his calm menace is impressive and more than a little terrifying. Joseph Morgan's Klaus does not disappoint: he manages to be casual and familiar ("Thanks for the loaner, mate") while maintaining dominance with the threat of violence and a preternatural capacity for revenge. Equally impressive is Katherine's resolve: she'll stand in sunlight and burn if it increases her chances of escape. For Katherine, it's a competition — both to live and for love. She suggests the Caroline and Tyler combo so she's not the vampire sacrificed. She's willing to throw Jenna under the proverbial bus in order to keep her secret from Klaus that she's on vervain. And she's willing to betray Klaus's secrets so she can take out Elena as her eternal competition for Stefan's heart.

Elena shares that Petrova fire that Katherine passed down to her, but she uses it to fight to protect her loved ones. She's willing to die to ensure their safety and it looks like, one way or another, she *will* die. After a season long build-up, it's finally time for the sacrifice of the doppelgänger — and it's a testament to Klaus's villainy that he chooses Jenna as his backup vampire.

COMPELLING MOMENT: Stefan and Elena's goodbye.

CIRCLE OF KNOWLEDGE:
- No Bonnie or Jeremy in this episode.
- Elijah explains that Klaus has to kill a vampire and a werewolf, representing the two halves of his bloodline. Then he drinks the blood of the doppelgänger, to the point of her death. Could there be any clue in that detail as to how the original Petrova is connected to Klaus? Did she die at his hand? Does he have to be willing to kill her (or a replica of her) in order to take such great power? (Implying she is, in one way or another, a person Klaus once loved.)
- Elena asks Stefan to do one of his vampire jumping tricks to save them the climb, a wink to *Twilight*'s Edward and Bella who journey vampire-style through the forest of Forks. But Stefan isn't into the whole "spider

monkey" thing; he prefers the climb. After all, he's scaled Mount Everest, the world's highest mountain.

- Damon calls Matt "Boy Wonder," the nickname for Batman's sidekick Robin.
- Klaus tells Katherine that he needs her to do something (lure out Jenna) long before he knows that Damon has been bitten by a werewolf and is useless to him. Convinced that one brother would meddle with his ritual, Klaus had decided to turn Jenna as a punishment before he had any evidence that either one had done so.
- Stefan and Elena's goodbye echoes the season 2 finale of *Buffy the Vampire Slayer*, wherein Buffy and her vampire boyfriend Angel share a "Close your eyes" moment.

THE RULES: Elijah theorizes that the Gilbert ring will not work on Elena because as a doppelgänger her origin is supernatural (and the rings only work on humans). The elixir he had made originally for Katerina has the power of resuscitation; whether or not it actually works remains to be seen. Tyler's transformation from man to wolf is happening faster than it did on his first full moon.

THE DIABOLICAL PLAN: Maddox the witch lures Tyler back to Mystic Falls by injuring his mother. Damon doesn't trust Elijah or his elixir, so he ensures that Elena will not die permanently by feeding her his own blood. Regretting his impulsive action, he tries to force Klaus to postpone the sacrifice by killing his witch and freeing his werewolf and vampire. Klaus, wise in his years, has backups: Greta, Jules, and Jenna.

BITE MARKS: Maddox throws Carol Lockwood over the banister onto the marble floor below. Damon force-feeds Elena his blood. Stefan throws Damon away from her, and the two fight, Stefan punching the living daylights out of his brother and Damon staking him in the gut. Maddox and Greta take down Tyler and Caroline with the brain-pain spell. Greta also injects vervain into Caroline. To test if she's still under compulsion (which she is not), Klaus orders Katherine to stand in the sunlight without her daylight jewelry on, and she complies with agonizing results. Damon and Maddox fight; Matt shoots Maddox and Damon snaps his neck. Damon knocks out Matt. Damon tackles Tyler when he leaps to attack Caroline; he is bitten in the tussle. Jules is imprisoned by Klaus and company. Klaus somehow knocks out Damon (who needs some sips from a blood bag and a few slaps from Katherine to wake up after the commercial break). Jenna comes back to life, meaning she was fed vampire blood and killed off-screen.

PREVIOUSLY ON THE VAMPIRE DIARIES: Elena and Stefan's first weighty conversation took place as they walked on a wooden bridge by the falls in the pilot, as they do again (by different falls) here. Damon tells Elena she can wish him an "eternity of misery" as he did his brother, a phrase we first heard in the pilot episode and saw in flashback in "Blood Brothers." Like Elijah does in the library, Rose also told Damon he talked a big game in "Katerina." Damon calls out Katherine for giving Klaus the idea to use Caroline and Tyler for the ritual, the vampire and werewolf she created for that very purpose ("Katerina"). Greta tells Elena that her father and brother were wasting their time looking for her — she wasn't lost. That same turn of phrase is how Isobel described herself to Alaric, who had been searching for her since she went missing ("Isobel").

MEANWHILE IN FELL'S CHURCH: In Klaus, Elena, and Stefan's first scene together in *Dark Reunion*, Elena urges Stefan not to allow himself to get hurt unnecessarily, as she does when she says goodbye to him in "The Last Day." Klaus is described as being "as crazy as Katherine — and even crueler" (*Dark Reunion*). In the climax of *Dark Reunion*, Klaus unexpectedly kidnaps one of the gang (Caroline) as TV Klaus does here with Jenna.

OFF CAMERA: In an interview for cwtv.com by Candice Accola, Kevin Williamson said the biggest writing challenge for the season was figuring out how to get out of the "corner" they'd written themselves into by saying that the blood of the doppelgänger is what breaks the curse — that Elena has to die.

FOGGY MOMENTS: The punch mark on Damon's cheek doesn't seem to heal with normal vampire speed, when he's speaking to Elijah in the library after his fight with Stefan.

MUSIC: Tyler visits his mom in the hospital to Cheyenne Mize's "Not." At the Grill, Matt calls Caroline, and Damon and Alaric meet Klaus in the flesh while The Vaccines' "Wolf Pack" plays in the background.

QUESTIONS:
- How did Maddox make Carol call Tyler? Was that compulsion by proxy or was that a spell?
- Is Elijah right — will Elena never forgive Damon for taking that choice away from her?

❈

> *John: Whether you're reading this now as a human or a vampire, I love you all the same, as I've always loved you and always will.*

2.21 The Sun Also Rises

Original air date: May 5, 2011
Written by: Caroline Dries and Mike Daniels
Directed by: Paul Sommers

The curse on Klaus is broken.

In the culmination of a season's worth of mythology, backstory, characters' choices and growth, "The Sun Also Rises" felt like a finale. Never a dull moment, as Caroline says to Matt, and the episode's action sequences, high body count, and poignant moments make this one of the series' best.

Fittingly, in an episode where the villain wins the day, there was a recurring theme of failure. And though almost everything did go wrong, one element worked just as planned: Bonnie Bennett. In her every word and action, Bonnie displayed confidence in herself — working to find a way to save Elena from becoming a vampire, preventing Jeremy from coming to the sacrifice, offering to kill Klaus single-handedly so Jenna will survive, and being a total badass during her attack on Klaus. As we've seen before, battles are lost or won based on the power and ability of the witches, and yet the witches themselves are never the ones instigating the fight. Greta declares that her duty is to Klaus and the "new order" while Bonnie, one of the "good ones" as Lucy characterized her in "Masquerade," is determined to vanquish the threat Klaus poses not just to her loved ones, but to the world at large. It's an interesting dynamic between "nature's servants" and vampires, and one that is likely to be further explored in season 3 now that a supernatural imbalance has been unleashed in the form of Klaus as a hybrid.

Everything changes and rarely for the better when you're in the heart of vampire country: the lives of Caroline, Tyler, Jeremy, Bonnie, and Elena — not to mention those characters who've been familiar with the supernatural world for much longer — revolve around its secrets and dangers. Normal doesn't exist for them anymore. And for Matt, Caroline's love is not enough for him to give up his life. His existence may be hard and ordinary, but Matt doesn't want to be a part of the violent world he witnesses that night. Their relationship fails to withstand this test: though Matt loves Caroline, he feels they are no longer part of the same world. But will it be possible for Matt to stay out of her world? Just as Elena first decided not to be with Stefan in "You're Undead to Me" but later came around, Matt may find himself unable to stay away, especially since his entire friend group is deeply involved in the supernatural. In the meantime, a distraught Caroline finds herself in the consoling arms of Tyler. These two get each other. They have lived through parallel experiences becoming "monsters" and learning how to deal with their new realities, and they've developed that bond despite the age-old feud between species. The distance that once stood between them is now closed. Caroline takes care of Tyler and, when he pulls her into a hug as she breaks down over Matt, he proves to be able to take care of her in return.

Both of Elena's parental figures feel they have failed in their duty to her — Jenna admits this to Elena directly, and John says it in his letter to her. Jenna and John each make decisions in "The Sun Also Rises" that put them in harm's way in an effort to protect Elena's life. John knowingly gives up his life for hers, while Jenna realizes she must not run but instead must attack Greta to stop the ritual from finishing. In her last act, Jenna is brave and clever. She hasn't been in on the supernatural secret for longer than a day, but she does her best to outwit Klaus (only with time does a vampire learn that neck snapping is always more efficient than neck biting). The bond between Jenna and Elena feels so real (thanks to Sara Canning and Nina Dobrev's talent and real-life closeness). The desperate reassurance that Elena gives her aunt — that no one but Jenna could have guided Jeremy and her through the difficult past year — reminds us of the very human struggles Jenna and the

Covington's cemetery played double duty this season, as Grove Hill's and Mystic Fall's cemeteries.

Gilbert kids have gone through together. Dragged into the sacrifice in an act of cruelty, Jenna is innocent in a way that the rest of the characters involved in the sacrifice aren't (even Elena), and seeing her killed for one man's selfish gain feels particularly villainous. Elena feels a sense of responsibility for Jenna — she tells her that *she* was the one who failed her. When Jenna is killed, with Elena powerless to do anything but advise her to turn off her fear, Elena's emotion seems to harden into rage aimed directly at the one responsible, Klaus. Not to give you any ideas, Elena, but as Elijah says, there can be honor in revenge.

Time and again, characters have placed more value on Elena's life than on their own, and John gives the gift of life to his daughter by making the greatest sacrifice he can. In that act and in his letter, which eloquently acknowledges all that held him back from having a connection with her,

John proves to be so much more than the weaselly uncle no one likes, to be much more than ordinary. He made his sacrifice quietly and honorably, doing the right thing without fuss, even going outside so Elena wouldn't see him die. He is unselfish and doesn't try to have a last moment with her, instead he uses the letter and the ring to make her believe his words — he sees the error of his ways and loves her no matter what. In "The Return," Elena told him that his hatred would end up getting him killed and in "The House Guest" she echoed that sentiment to Alaric, but in the end what kills John is love. Like Stefan expressed for himself in "Rose," for John, there is no better reason to die than to save Elena.

By his sacrifice, John secures for Elena what she was so terrified of losing: a lifetime of choices, of being human, of growing up. But with his death and Jenna's, as after Grayson's and Miranda's, Elena is forced to be more of a grownup. Even though Elena's life is hers again — she has resurrected as a human and her function as a doppelgänger has been fulfilled — she still doesn't have a normal 17-year-old's problems; she faces a stunning amount of grief, danger, violence, and darkness. And she does it with perseverance, dignity, and a forgiving spirit that makes John's description of her as an "extraordinary child" something that truly resonates. Elena's friends have always been hugely important to her but, as Stefan tells Damon at the funeral, now more than ever will she need them, having lost an aunt and an "uncle" as well as a mother figure and biological father in one awful day.

The series began with Elena and Jeremy in grief, and now the siblings once again find themselves where they were a year earlier — now with four graves to mourn. So much loss, but at least they still have each other. The crucial thing that's changed in Jeremy's character since the beginning of season 1 is that instead of shutting down when he's under pressure, he's not afraid now to reach out to his sister and to those around him to find strength and companionship and purpose. As heartbreaking as Jeremy's life has been and continues to be, the challenges have helped him grow up. He possesses the same inner strength that his sister does as well as the instinct to seek solace in those who love him.

The bonds between siblings are strong on *The Vampire Diaries*. Though Elijah promises not to fail Stefan and professes to be a man of his word, in the end he chooses to honor the duty he owes his family over that promise to Stefan. The tie that binds him to his other siblings and parents is more powerful. Klaus gives his brother his word, a vow that Elijah takes seriously and believes. How could Elijah kill his brother when there is renewed hope

that he could be reunited with the other seven members of his family? Will Klaus keep his vow to his brother or is his promise as long lasting and reliable as one of Katherine's?

By giving Katherine vervain, Damon gave her a choice, and she fails him by once again choosing to protect herself over anyone else. Damon's conversation with her echoed the dynamic between Stefan and Damon in season 1, showing just how much Damon has changed since then. Like Andie Star once wisely said, love changes us — and though Damon has faltered and made mistakes as he found his way, he is now capable of making choices that don't just further his own selfish interests, as Katherine and Klaus do. He has the capacity to consider others ahead of himself, with no desire for reward. He got his werewolf nip by intercepting Tyler's attack on Caroline. And he hides his impending madness and death so as not to further burden Elena in her grief, despite his desperate need for her forgiveness. (Even his decision to feed Elena his blood was made for both his brother's sake as well as his own.) It's this doing good for its own sake, this selflessness, that Stefan and Damon talked about in the season 1 finale, and that Damon is finally coming around to. The brothers are once again united — their animosity from "The Last Day" set aside — as Stefan resolves to find a way to save Damon. Stefan tried to save Jenna and failed, but he has faith that there is a cure for a werewolf bite and that they can find it. As the sun rises on the day after the sacrifice, there's a lot to grieve, but there's also that speck of hope that keeps Stefan fighting.

COMPELLING MOMENT: Not a moment this episode, but a character gone too soon. Rest in peace, Jenna Sommers.

CIRCLE OF KNOWLEDGE:

- The phrase "the sun also rises" comes from *Ecclesiastes*: "One generation passeth away, and another generation cometh; but the earth abideth forever . . . The sun also ariseth, and the sun goeth down, and hasteth to the place where he arose." Most famously, *The Sun Also Rises* is a novel by Ernest Hemingway, published in 1926, which uses the Biblical quote as one of its epigraphs. Narrated by Jake Barnes, an expat American living in France, the novel travels from the cafés of Paris to the Spanish countryside to Pamplona where its characters, members of the post–World War I "Lost Generation," drink and bicker over their jealousy (all the men are in love with the same woman, Lady Brett Ashley) against the backdrop of the precise violence of bullfighting. Hemingway considered his characters "battered but not lost," a description that could be used to describe the resilient nature of *TVD*'s characters as the sun rises after the sacrifice.

- Damon shares his brother's heroic instincts. He wants to offer himself to Klaus as Stefan does, but because of Tyler's bite, he's not a viable substitute for Jenna.

- In "Katerina," Stefan says that Klaus is known to be the oldest vampire, but Elijah is Klaus's older brother. Whether Klaus actually became a vampire before Elijah (making him the older vampire, though not the older brother) remains to be revealed.

- It's strange how many of the main characters have died and not stayed dead: Katherine, Damon, Stefan, Alaric, Jeremy, Bonnie, Caroline, Elijah, Elena . . . not to mention those who are now permanently dead but experienced a resurrection like John and Jenna.

- What would have happened if John had kept his Gilbert ring on? Just a theory, but it could have taken the "life force" or "soul" back from Elena when the ring's magic resurrected him, killing her again. At the very least, the risk of something like that happening prevented John from keeping his ring on and trying his luck.

- Though almost every episode features death, Jenna and John's is the first funeral shown on *The Vampire Diaries*.

THE RULES: Found in Emily's grimoire, Bonnie performs a spell that transfers John's life force to Elena, so she comes back to life as a human not a vampire. Bonnie also puts a spell on Jeremy, knocking him out with a kiss.

Jules is under a spell that slows down her transformation into a werewolf (and causes her great pain). Greta also binds each sacrifice victim in a magic circle ringed with fire. Klaus breaks the curse binding him, becoming a true hybrid, by killing a werewolf and vampire (using their blood in the most witchy-like makeshift cauldron we've seen on *TVD*) and then by drinking the blood of the doppelgänger, each sacrifice timed with the progression of the moon.

THE DIABOLICAL PLAN: Stefan offers himself as a substitute for Jenna, but Klaus refuses, portentously saying he has other plans for him. Elijah, hell-bent on getting revenge on Klaus for killing the rest of his family, makes an eleventh hour reversal, opting to have faith in his brother's word. Stefan vows to find a cure for Damon's werewolf bite. And Damon points out that they are without a strategy for defeating an "all powerful wolf-vamp and his two-faced older brother."

BITE MARKS: Matt shoots wolf-Tyler twice. Using her magic, Greta throws Elena to the ground. Greta cuts herself to let Jenna feed from her. Jules is in extreme pain under a spell that slows down her transformation. Damon slams John into the wall, after John tries to attack him. Klaus rips out Jules's heart. Klaus stakes Stefan in the back, breaking the stake so he can't reach back and remove it, and then knocks him out. Jenna attacks Greta, and Klaus stops her attack by staking her in the side. Klaus kills Jenna with a stake through the heart. He drinks Elena's blood, killing her. Bonnie puts Klaus through extreme pain and contortions throwing the power of a hundred witches at him. Elijah reaches into Klaus's chest and is on the verge of yanking out his heart. John dies, his life force drained in a spell that resurrects Elena.

PREVIOUSLY ON THE VAMPIRE DIARIES: The exchange between Elijah and Klaus seeing each other for the first time in 500 years echoes Damon and Stefan's first encounter in the pilot episode: "Damon." "Hello, brother."

MEANWHILE IN FELL'S CHURCH: In *Dark Reunion*, Meredith says to Tyler, "But sooner or later the sun will come up," a glimmer of hope that's reflected in this episode's title. Meredith, Bonnie, and Matt come upon the showdown between Stefan and Klaus from the top of a bluff, looking down on the action; in this episode it is Stefan who appears at the top of the bluff. Stefan's first demand is that Klaus "let the girl go" in *Dark Reunion*, and his intention is similar here: to rescue Jenna. In that fight, Klaus uses fire and lightning, which are part of Bonnie's arsenal in "The Sun Also Rises." A description fitting of many characters' willingness to sacrifice themselves, Bonnie writes in her diary of Elena, "She was strong and loving and loyal to her friends, and in the end she did the most unselfish thing anybody could do" (*The Fury*).

OFF CAMERA: This episode was shot during an actual full moon. After the episode aired, Mike Daniels, who wrote John's letter, tweeted, "Thanks for all the 'Uncle John's letter' love. Happy to have made you all cry! Wait, that sounds weird . . ." For the 2011–2012 TV season, Mike Daniels has left *TVD* to work on the new show *Pan Am*. This episode was actor Joseph Morgan's favorite to film. He told *Starry Constellation Magazine*, "It was about a week of night shoots, and that kind of creates a camaraderie with working through the night and being up and doing something incredibly exciting when everyone else is asleep. When I was a child my parents used to wake me up really early to go on holiday . . . when it was still dark and [we'd] get in the car and we were so excited. It was the same sort of thing with that episode except I was waking up to go and potentially, you know, kill lots of people."

Director of photography Paul Sommers directed this episode, his first, and he felt incredibly supported by the cast and crew through the process. The prop department even gave him an onscreen shout-out: in the scene where Damon walks away through the graveyard, a headstone to his left reads, "Paul Sommers Rest in Peace."

FOGGY MOMENTS: In "Klaus," Elijah says that the only way to kill Klaus, a hybrid upon whom the dagger and ash won't work, is with a powerful-enough witch. But in "The Sun Also Rises," he intends to finish the job himself by pulling out Klaus's heart. Does that mean that if Klaus was somehow restrained, anyone could kill him by removing his heart?

MUSIC: The funeral for Jenna and John is set to Birdy's cover of the Bon Iver song "Skinny Love."

QUESTIONS:
- What will happen to Katherine? How will she escape or is she Alaric's permanent house guest?

The quarry, first seen in "Blood Brothers," makes its return for the sacrifice.

- What does Klaus want with Stefan?
- What did Klaus do to the rest of his family? Presumably they are just as fearsome as Elijah: are there more weapons out there that temporarily kill Originals, like the ash and dagger? Why would Klaus go after the rest of his family? He has motive to take out his father (for killing his birth father and family), but what of the mother and other siblings? Did he kill them all as revenge on Elijah because Katerina fled the sacrifice? Or did they oppose his transformation?
- How will the deaths of Jenna and John be explained to the world at large? With Elena not yet 18, who will become her and Jeremy's legal guardian?
- Does Bonnie get to keep the witches' super power or does it lessen as she uses it (like a battery)?
- If the doppelgänger was created as a way to undo the spell, now that the spell is broken, will there no longer be more doppelgängers? Or does the doppelgänger just keep appearing in perpetuity?
- Will Damon survive his werewolf bite?

❖

Damon: You should have met me in 1864. You would have liked me.
Elena: I like you now, just the way you are.

2.22 As I Lay Dying

Original air date: May 12, 2011
Written by: Turi Meyer, Al Septien, and Michael Narducci
Directed by: John Behring
Guest cast: Kayla Ewell (Vicki Donovan), Ashlyn Henson (Warehouse Girl), Malese Jow (Anna), Bianca Lawson (Emily Bennett), Chris Whitley (Deputy), Mark Wilson (Deputy #2)

While Damon descends into madness and considers his lifetime of choices, Stefan gives himself over to his inner ripper to save his brother's life.

And so it ends. It's incredible to think how much has happened — how many lives lost, characters transformed, and game-changing moments have occurred — since "The Return," let alone since the pilot episode. This finale, which follows the action-packed, curse-breaking "The Sun Also Rises," was much more of a denouement than last season's, but "As I Lay Dying" not only resolved some lingering emotional threads, it set up the direction for season 3. And it was frightening. In a good way.

By beginning in the quiet grief of the Gilbert house, there's a glimpse of what is "normal" for Elena and Jeremy. Atlanta has burned, as Caroline says, and they survived — now it's time to put their lives back together and mourn those lost in the battle. Jeremy has placed a photo of Elena and Jenna beside his bed, and a mug still sits on Jenna's bedside table, details that make the Gilbert kids' situation feel incredibly real and raw. Like Damon says to Elena in his respectful request for forgiveness, Elena knows how the grieving process works; she and Jeremy have been through this before when their parents died. But now they are without the guardian who guided them through that loss. Elena takes on that role for Jeremy, wanting them to begin going through the motions of living. In Mystic Falls, "normal" means a picnic in the square and the town gathering to watch *Gone with the Wind*. Before Elena finds out that Damon is dying, her focus is on helping her brother deal with his grief. And once she's in danger, Jeremy refuses to sit idly by, but insists he has to find his sister. The bond of family is the most important thing to the Gilberts, as it's shown to be so in this episode for both Stefan and Elijah. Each has paid huge costs to honor his familial duty. Unfortunately for Elijah, Klaus has different ideas about family — he thinks they're best carted around in coffins. Did Elijah make a mistake not killing Klaus when he had the chance?

In "The Sun Also Rises," John asks Alaric and Jeremy to take care of each other, and Alaric steps up to that task by episode's end. Though he's drunk and bitter and grieving at the Grill, he immediately comes to Damon's side when he hears he's dying. His relationships with Damon and Jeremy are the closest things we've seen to Alaric having family. He's accepted Damon as his friend, despite his part in Isobel's change and Jenna's death, and he knows his friend well enough to bring a bottle with him — as well as vervain. At the witch house, he's incensed that Jeremy's life could be taken from him when he's just a kid, innocent; by the end of the episode he's realized that Jeremy, kid or not, doesn't want to be alone, and he takes up, at least temporarily, the role of guardian. Another small detail speaks to Alaric's grief and respect: he chooses to sleep on the couch, not in Jenna's room. How will he fit into the Gilberts' lives in season 3?

Though there is an implication of innate goodness to the term "nature's servants," we have learned over the past two seasons that witches are not without personal agendas. In the awesome channeling scene (so creepy to hear Bianca Lawson's voice coming from Kat Graham), Stefan calls out Emily Bennett on her personal desire to punish Damon. Emily refuses to reveal the cure for a werewolf bite because of Damon's past actions. With Bonnie, the witches warn her not to abuse her powers. We've seen witches work for their own gain or for evil, and this episode reminds us that Bonnie has to be mindful of the balance she maintains. Earlier this season, she tested the limits of her own power. She took power from Luka without his consent, and she has now angered the spirits of a hundred witches by coming back to them too many times. Regardless of her good motivations (to save a loved one or vanquish Klaus), Bonnie has pushed the boundaries of her abilities and asked for more than the spirits are willing to give, and there are more than just physical consequences to pay for that perceived greediness. Perhaps because Emily once cared for a Gilbert man herself, she does grant Bonnie the power to save Jeremy, but that incredible source of power seems to be now off-limits to Bonnie. Nothing comes without a cost on *TVD*, and Bonnie pays, just as Stefan has to pay a hefty price for Damon living beyond "his time."

Being sheriff in a town overrun with vampires, werewolves, witches, and a hybrid is a tough gig. Especially when the "evil monsters" include your friends and your daughter. Though Carol Lockwood's sudden insistence that something be done about the vampire problem seemed to be motivated only by the writers' need to get Liz Forbes into action, the results were well worth

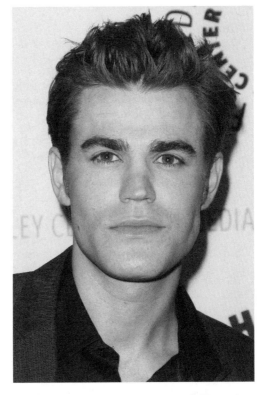

it. There are consequences to messing with things you don't fully understand, and Liz doesn't heed the warnings of Alaric or Elena. Instead she comes into the Grill gun blazing and accidentally kills Jeremy. Despite the fact that she's known about vampires her whole life, Liz shows she has no real understanding of the supernatural world. She thinks like a human in human circumstances, telling Alaric, Bonnie, and Caroline not to disturb the "crime scene" after she shoots Jeremy (what a horrifying moment that was). She doesn't know what Caroline's doing by trying to feed Jeremy her blood, and she doesn't get that she actually did kill Jeremy and is lucky Bonnie was able to raise the dead. Despite this, Liz is convinced by her daughter that there's one thing she can be sure of: Caroline is still Caroline, her "little girl." She is still who she used to be and, if anything, she's even more deserving of her mother's admiration since becoming a vampire. Vampire Caroline has spent this season fighting for her human relationships, and that hug was long awaited for both of them.

Gone with the Wind

Caroline referred to its "classic Southern elegance" and heroine in "Isobel," Damon had a first edition of the novel at his bedside in "The Descent," and, getting its third shout-out from *The Vampire Diaries* writers, *Gone with the Wind* is screened in the town square in "As I Lay Dying." Written by Atlanta, Georgia's own Margaret Mitchell, published in 1936, and made into a film that runs four hours (including intermission) in 1939, *Gone with the Wind* is an epic romance (as Elena calls it) set in Georgia in the Civil War era. It tells the story of Scarlett O'Hara (played by Vivien Leigh in the film), the daughter of a wealthy plantation owner whose pretty life as a spoiled Southern belle is destroyed by the ravages of war and the heartache of not being with Ashley (Leslie Howard), the man she loves. A fighter who learns to love her homeland, Scarlett lives alongside Ashley's good-natured wife Melanie (Olivia de Havilland), witnessing the violence and destruction that signals the death of the Old South, and she has a romance with Rhett Butler (Clark Gable), a rogue who seems to understand who Scarlett truly is beneath her airs.

Scarlett loses her identity as the world she knows ends in violence, horror, and poverty. Though still on the same land she was raised on, after Atlanta burns in 1864, Scarlett finds herself in a foreign world, having to fend for her survival in a physical and visceral way alien to how she was raised. She makes the resolution to "never to be hungry again" (at the end of the film's first part), and thus becomes ruthless, driven by the need to make money and to protect herself, her family, and her land at any cost. She enters a loveless marriage, runs a lumberyard and uses convicts for labor, knowing they'll be starved and beaten, and denies kindnesses to those she should call friends. Scarlett has the potential to be good, loving, and moral, and her constant companion Melanie sees that side of her and believes in her even when others do not. Despite the bad choices she makes, Scarlett is a compelling heroine whose sorrows and victories the audience shares.

The Salvatore boys grew up in the same era as Scarlett, and Damon served as a Confederate soldier. Like Scarlett, the boys saw the world they once knew taken from them during the Civil War. Damon was no longer a roguishly charming young man, the son of a wealthy landowner, but a vampire who had to fend for his survival himself. Instead of taking a virtuous path like Stefan tried to do (with some spectacular stumbles along the way), Damon made darker choices, shutting down all his feelings except his love for Katherine. Scarlett believes she loves Ashley, a man who feels for her but truly loves his wife Melanie. Her inability to put aside her feelings for Ashley costs her true happiness with Rhett, a man who does love her and believes he can force her into loving him back. The foursome — like our Katherine, Damon, Stefan, and Elena — are intrinsically connected; what each man lacks can be found in the other, as with the women whose personalities feel like two sides of the same coin.

In "As I Lay Dying," Caroline compares their current situation to Atlanta burning — Klaus won, just as the Yankees did, lives were lost, and the protagonists of our story are the losers. In "Isobel," Bonnie said Caroline "channels Scarlett daily," to which Caroline beams with pride, and while the two Southern girls share sassiness, determination, and a certain fearlessness, Caroline — faced with losing her identity as a pretty, popular girl when she became a vampire — chose a different path from her heroine. Instead of putting herself and her pride first like

Scarlett tends to do, Caroline is more like a badass vampire version of Melanie, helping those in need, aiding the wounded, and making amends with loved ones. Caroline does resemble Scarlett in how compelling a character she is, a woman who can easily be misjudged and underestimated based on her appearance, and she shares Scarlett's perennial hopefulness and fortitude. Even when in despair, Scarlett keeps her chin up: "Tomorrow is another day."

Like his brother Elijah, Klaus makes his promises carefully: he did tell the truth about his family — their bodies were not buried at sea — and he kept his word that he would reunite Elijah with them. He just didn't specify that Elijah would be dead when he did so. Tricky devil. Klaus describes himself as someone who rarely gets played for a fool, a description that applies equally to Elijah — except, apparently, when it comes to Klaus. Elijah's single-mindedness and code of honor became a weakness when he went up against someone who knows him as well as Klaus does. The vampire-brother parallels continue in this episode. Like Damon said of Stefan in the previous episode, Elijah also cleans up his brother's messes (as Klaus discovers his new werewolf side). Klaus commanding Stefan to go on a human-blood bender is a nicely twisted inversion of the act that started the Salvatore brothers' afterlives as vampires. Stefan forced the transitioning Damon to drink blood and complete his transformation. A century and a half later, Stefan still carries the weight of that with him. He tells Elena in the square that he owes it to his brother to seek the cure and he walks straight into the lion's den (also known as Alaric's apartment). As Damon says, Stefan is always "trying to right the wrongs of the past."

By forcing Stefan to drink (and drink some more), Klaus resurrects the monster inside him, the dark desires that Stefan buries every day. When Klaus presents Stefan with the "gift" of the girl for him to feed on, Klaus taking the first bite to draw her blood, the echo is made explicit: we saw Stefan do this to change Damon in 1864 ("Blood Brothers"). To prove himself as more than "just shy of useless" to Klaus, Stefan must kill the girl in a symbolic act of honoring the deal he's made with Klaus, his oath to be a "hell of a wing man" and a ripper. Killing this victim is about more than satisfying the innate thirst of a vampire for human blood; it's about the pleasure of the hunt and the kill. With each blood bag that he drank at the apartment, Stefan became more animalistic, until Klaus stood over him, feeding him like a wild growling dog on the floor. Klaus's corruption of Stefan is seemingly complete as Stefan gets into "the spirit of it." The man Damon called "always the hero" kills the girl in the warehouse and is once again a murderer.

A witness to the deal Stefan makes with Klaus, Katherine quite rightly describes it as him sacrificing everything to save Damon. The cost of Damon's cure is the life Stefan has built in Mystic Falls, his friends, Elena, and his identity. He's a vampire who strives to be as human as possible and respectful of human life, refusing to take it for his own sustenance and placing value on the sanctity of life (as seen in his remorse over any "collateral damage"). But now Stefan is trapped in his devil's bargain: if he decides to break his deal and refuse to do Klaus's bidding, he would all but guarantee that his brother, Elena, and everyone else he cares about would be lambs for the slaughter at the hands of a vengeful Klaus. Even before he became a hybrid who can't be killed, Rose said of him, "People do not escape from Klaus. Everyone who tries ends up back in his grasp and anyone who helps them dies" ("Katerina"). With that kind of new boss, any attempt Stefan could make to run for it is potentially more dangerous for his loved ones than him embracing his new life as a ripper. "The Dinner Party" gave us a firsthand glimpse of Stefan's dark past, but there was an implication that after Lexi helped him find his way, his days of being a monster were over. Apparently not: he was such a legendary ripper, wiping out a village more than 40 years after meeting Lexi, that the baddest of all the baddies had heard about his appetite for destruction. With that kind of legacy, it is entirely possible that Stefan won't want to give up on his "decade-long bender" with Klaus. Maybe Stefan's found a new best friend.

Ironically Stefan's need to do right has time and again caused him harm. His sense of guilt about and obligation to his brother, his need to fix the situation whatever the cost, turned him into a terrible negotiator, telling Klaus straight off the top that he will do whatever Klaus wants in exchange for the cure. And what Klaus wants is all Stefan has to give: everything that he cares about and has fought to be. In "Daddy Issues," Stefan pleaded with Tyler to be peaceful in order to protect what he values most dearly: "I came back to this town because I wanted a life. I wanted to exist where I could have friends, where I could build a family. I have that here; we can both have that." Klaus is not only literally taking him away from that (as they plan to leave Mystic Falls that night) but he is destroying Stefan's connection to his humanity by making him more monster than man. Has Stefan made the wrong choice in this deal with Klaus? Is Damon's life worth the destruction Stefan will unleash as Klaus's servant? Is it even conceivable that Stefan, always the hero, would make any other choice than to save his brother?

A common refrain on *The Vampire Diaries* is that there is always a choice, which Rose dealt with on her last day in "The Descent," and it's a realization Damon comes to regarding his love for Katherine. At the beginning of the episode, Damon is ready to die: he seeks forgiveness from Elena as his last act before trying to kill himself (well, his last act second to having a swig of the good stuff he keeps at the back of the liquor cabinet). Stefan refuses to accept that choice, as he refused to accept Damon dying in 1864, and he locks up Damon to stop him. As Stefan searches for a cure with help from Bonnie, he hopes for the best and expects the worst, sending over Alaric and Elena to watch Damon, to have a chance to say goodbye, and to give Damon hope that there could be a cure.

As with Rose in "The Descent," Damon's illness and suffering gives him time to ruminate on a century and a half of choices, to consider the hurt he's caused and the path he's taken as his subconscious muddles up memories with what he's finally come to understand in the present. Damon considers what Alaric must think of him, as he holds himself responsible for Jenna's death and turning Isobel. With Elena, Damon apologizes for all the hurt he's caused her. And perhaps most significantly for the vampire who was created and driven by his love for Katherine for nearly his entire existence, Damon realizes it was his own choice to love Katherine the way he did. She openly wanted both brothers, and he still chose to chase her. He takes ownership of his choice to drink her blood; the first step in the process of becoming a vampire was a decision he made himself, not Stefan's fault. In Damon's first hallucination, Elena appears to tell him that Katherine was toying with him, that he was free to say no to her. Interestingly, in Damon's mind Elena represents clarity and perspective on his past. As in reality, she pushes him, more than Stefan does, to think about who he is and who he wants to be. And he loves her for it. Though Damon regrets making wrong choices in his past, he also sees in his dying moments that if he hadn't followed the path he did, he never would have met Elena. In the town square, Damon's dementia makes him mix up past and present, Katherine and Elena, and he bites Elena, drinking her blood.

The oft-rewound scene of whispered confessions on Damon's bed was heartbreaking and perfect: he just wants Elena to know that he loves her, and she does know it. Twice already Damon's poured his heart out to Elena: the first time it turned out to be Katherine, and the second he compelled Elena to forget his confession. All season long, Damon has been trying to be who he thinks Elena wants him to be — a better man — and she could say nothing that would mean more to him than what she does: that she likes him just the way he is.

As he lies dying, in those moments that both he and Elena believe will be their last together, wrongs are forgiven and the distance between them is closed. Believing it's the end gives them permission to be with each other without barriers. With no time left, they have no choice but to say what they feel. Elena kisses Damon, and his "thank you" makes it feel like a goodbye, something Elena knew would mean the world to Damon and something she was willing to give him. But is it also more than that for Elena? It's a moment that completes the journey from the beginning of the season when Damon believed Elena had kissed him and she said she would never to that. Here Elena, for the first time, gets to say a proper goodbye to someone she loves who is dying. Everyone else she's lost has gone quickly and usually violently, giving her no opportunity for real closure. . . .

And then in waltzes Katherine with a cure that Stefan secured for his brother by sacrificing everything. The Salvatore Elena thought she was losing is saved, and the one she didn't say goodbye to is gone. With Katherine in the room, Elena immediately puts some distance between herself and Damon, hustling off that bed, but Katherine has seen the connection and tells her doppelgänger it's okay to love them both. It must sting a little for Katherine to see their heartfelt moment after Damon telling her in "The Sun Also Rises" that she doesn't deserve a goodbye.

With Stefan a ripper once again and Damon coming back from near-death, how will the relationships between the core three characters evolve next season? With Katherine's obligation to Damon paid by delivering the cure of her own free will, will she leave Mystic Falls and go back on the run from Klaus? Or does her choice to show a "friend" kindness signify a change in Miss Katherine? Will she stick around and further complicate an already very complicated situation between brothers and doppelgängers? (Or will Nina Dobrev finally get a break after an insane season of playing two characters?) As the witch spirits told Bonnie, there will be consequences. What fallout will come of Damon and Elena's kiss?

In a truly unexpected and spooky scene, the consequence of bringing Jeremy back from the dead is revealed. He senses (first hears, then sees) Anna and Vicki, his two dearly departed vampire girlfriends who were both killed violently. And there they are, in the Gilbert house. The shock of seeing two beloved characters thought lost forever back onscreen serves as a great cliffhanger. Their appearance raises questions about what exactly Anna and Vicki are — unquiet spirits? — and promises a wealth of mythological goodness in season 3. What is certain is that Jeremy has come back from the dead a changed man. He feels "different" because he is: he's no longer simply human, he's connected to the supernatural universe, and the past that has shaped him is now a literal part of his present.

The game has changed for season 3: Klaus brought the devil out of Stefan. Elena has undeniably complicated feelings for Damon. Caroline's heart is broken over Matt but she's found comfort in the arms of a werewolf. Bonnie loves Jeremy enough to piss off the spirits of a hundred witches, but now his two dead exes are back on the scene. And there are *eight* Originals lying dead in their coffins ready to be resurrected. There can be honor in revenge. . . .

COMPELLING MOMENT: The ripper is back.

CIRCLE OF KNOWLEDGE:

- No Tyler or Matt in this episode.
- When Damon puts his ring back on, he's symbolically agreeing to fight for his life again. In "Know Thy Enemy," when Katherine borrows Elena's outfit to impersonate her, she takes the vervain necklace Stefan gave Elena too. When Katherine wakes up in Alaric's apartment, she touches her neck realizing it's missing. Elena's necklace has symbolized both Stefan's protection and his love. It was fitting that it was absent as Elena's character began to have more agency in the late part of this season; she became the one calling the shots (whether or not Damon obeyed her). But with Stefan gone rogue and her new connection with Damon, the fact that the symbol of her and Stefan's love is missing feels rather laden with meaning. Is the necklace gone forever or is Klaus holding on to it?
- There are three clips from *Gone with the Wind* (see page 218) shown in this episode, all from the first half of the film. Caroline says that waiting to hear about Damon is ruining Scarlett for her, while onscreen Scarlett searches for a doctor to deliver Melanie's baby among the hundreds of injured and dying soldiers. Damon wanders through the square woozily while Scarlett navigates the chaos of citizens evacuating Atlanta as Sherman's army approaches. Elena finds Damon and he confuses her with Katherine and bites her while, in the climax of the first half of the film, Rhett tries to steer his carriage (carrying Scarlett, Melanie, her newborn baby, and Prissy) past an ammunitions factory on fire and about to explode.
- Caroline called Stefan a blood-oholic in "Plan B" and the language of alcoholism is used again by Klaus who refers to Stefan being "on and off the wagon" and going on a decade-long "bender."
- Katherine is able to get into the Salvatore house to deliver Klaus's blood despite never receiving an invitation from Elena. But as the doppelgängers remind us in their little exchange, Elena did die. Since Elena hasn't been reinstated as owner of the Salvatore house post-resurrection, *any* vampire could likely get into the Salvatore house. And by that logic, any vampire could also get into the Gilbert house, since the two surviving residents of the house, Elena and Jeremy, both died.

THE RULES: As a hybrid, Klaus can change into wolf form at will. He is also able to use a dagger on Elijah without dying himself (unlike a regular vampire who would die using the ash-and-dagger on an Original). The cure for a vampire suffering from a werewolf bite is drinking Klaus's blood — the blood of a hybrid. Bonnie is able to contact the spirits of the dead witches for help, first for information about a cure for Damon and then for the power to resurrect Jeremy from the dead. The witches warn Bonnie that there will be consequences to that spell, and we see a glimpse of that: Jeremy sees the dead.

THE DIABOLICAL PLAN: Spurred on by Carol Lockwood, Sheriff Forbes decides to "get some results" and goes after the already demented Damon Salvatore, unsuccessfully. With Stefan offering to make a deal with him in exchange for Damon's cure, Klaus decides to revive the ripper, feeding Stefan blood bag after blood bag until he is drunk on blood and willing to kill. Klaus's ultimate purpose for Stefan is yet to be revealed. Klaus stays true to his word to Elijah, "reuniting" his brother with the rest of his family whom Klaus carts around in coffins inside a giant shipping container. Diabolical.

HISTORY LESSON: Klaus reminds Stefan that in 1917 he slaughtered a migrant village in the coastal city of Monterey, California, then the "Sardine Capital of the World" and the Depression-era setting for local John Steinbeck's novel *Cannery Row*.

BITE MARKS: Damon sizzles in the sun, intending to kill himself. Stefan tackles him, throws him against several walls, and then into the Salvatore holding cell. Newly hybrid Klaus has been on a two-day killing spree with an unknown body count. Klaus kills Elijah with a dagger. He smashes Stefan against the wall, and then stakes him with surgical accuracy, just grazing his heart. Damon chokes Alaric, who responds with a vervain dart in his arm. Damon smashes Liz against the cell wall. Klaus bites Katherine, and then feeds her his blood to demonstrate the healing properties of hybrid blood. Liz shoots Jeremy in the chest, killing him. Klaus cuts his hand to fill the vial with his blood. Bonnie gets a nosebleed trying to resurrect Jeremy. In flashback, Katherine cuts her neck for Damon to drink her blood. Damon feeds on Elena in present day, thinking she's Katherine. Klaus bites the neck of the girl at the warehouse, and Stefan kills her.

As I Lay Dying

William Faulkner's 1930 Southern Gothic novel lends its title to the season finale of *The Vampire Diaries*. Consistently hailed as one of the best works of fiction of the 20th century, Faulkner's tale of the Bundren family, narrated by its seven members as well as eight additional characters whom the family encounters on their journey, has a simple plot but is complex and haunting in the telling of it. At the outset of the story, Addie Bundren, mother of five and wife to Anse, is the one who lays dying, watching her eldest son Cash build her coffin right outside the window where she can see him. She has made her husband swear to bury her with her people in Jefferson, as opposed to near where they live in New Hope (a request, which we learn in the chapter that she narrates posthumously, she made out of spite). On the journey, whatever can go wrong does — a mix of bad luck and idiotic choices — their departure delayed, bridges knocked out by flooding, broken legs and slain horses, buzzards circling overhead the coffin that sits in the back of the wagon on the hot July days, and an act of arson that almost absolves the Bundrens of their obligation to bury Addie in Jefferson. Beyond the questions of mortality, identity, and faith that the novel explores through its various narrators, Faulkner offers the idea that some heroic acts, or choices made out of a sense of duty, are downright wrong — pointless, destructive, reckless, or motivated by self-interest masquerading as righteousness (in the case of Anse, who has his own reasons to want to get to Jefferson).

The sense of obligation the sons, particularly Jewel, feel to do anything in order to see their mother buried according to her wishes, is mirrored in Stefan's resolve to find a cure for Damon's werewolf bite, no matter the cost. His heroic act, in seeking out Klaus, is reckless and costs him all he holds dear. Much like Darl, the second eldest Bundren son, is carted away to an insane asylum, laughing like a madman, in the final moments of *As I Lay Dying*, the finale of *The Vampire Diaries* ends with Stefan having lost himself too, given over to the darkness that lurked inside him. Darl is punished for setting fire to the barn that housed Addie's coffin as the family rested overnight; committing arson was wrong but Darl did it in order to do right by his family, which was being destroyed and made further destitute by the fool's journey they were on. Stefan is also separated from his life and family because of the choice he makes to do right by doing wrong. Though Stefan would vehemently deny that his brother is a "burden" just as the Bundren family repeatedly deny that of Addie's corpse, the death (or potential death) of a family member can destroy the living.

As strange as it may seem that Faulkner's dirt poor Mississippi farming family has anything in common with our mysterious first family of vampires on *TVD*, there are parallels that go beyond a predilection for carting around the dead in coffins. The middle child of five, Jewel Bundren is unlike his brothers and sister — a head taller than the tallest of them, willful, proud, unruly, and at odds with the patriarch Anse Bundren. In the chapter Addie narrates, we learn the secret that explains that difference: she had an affair with the Reverend Whitfield, and Jewel is not his father's son. But Klaus finds a counterpart in Jewel — both foreign to the family and yet a part of it. Jewel, like Klaus, is aggressive and violent but bound to the Bundrens against his will because of his mother. Able to get away with close to anything, Jewel was fiercely devoted to his mother, even in her death. Will Klaus turn out to have been his mother's pet just as Jewel was?

PREVIOUSLY ON THE VAMPIRE DIARIES: Klaus tells Elijah to "lighten up," just as Elijah told Alaric to in "The Dinner Party." The spirit of Emily Bennett possessed Bonnie in "History Repeating" when the girls did a séance and called to her. In "Blood Brothers," Stefan wanted to kill himself, was locked in the cell to detox, had flashbacks and dealt with his regrets, mixed up Katherine and Elena and the past and present. Events seen in that episode are what drive Stefan to give up everything for his brother in this one. In "Fool Me Once," Jeremy turned to the internet to search for information on vampires, just as he does here with the excellent search string "back from the dead." Bing likely doesn't hold the answers to this mystery, Jer.

MEANWHILE IN FELL'S CHURCH: In *Dark Reunion*, Stefan faces Klaus and both realize that as long as Caroline (who's being held hostage by him) is in danger, Klaus can make Stefan do whatever he wants, just as Klaus knows in "As I Lay Dying" that Stefan will do whatever he needs to do to get the cure for his brother.

OFF CAMERA: In an interview with PopWrap, Kevin Williamson talked about the final twist of the season and how the idea for it originated with his love for Kayla Ewell: "When we made the decision to kill Vicki [in "Haunted"], it wasn't an easy one, but something I felt was important to the show because it needed to have a different kind of life. A moment to make people sit back and say, 'This show is serious about genre storytelling.' And it worked. But I missed her. Right away I thought, 'She can come back.' But then I thought, 'Dead people have to stay dead or we're *Heroes*.' There have to be consequences. Especially when people die. In that moment I came up with Jeremy being haunted by Vicki, but that felt stupid. But when Anna came around, everyone fell in love with her too — I mean, the Twitter outrage when she died [in "Founder's Day"] alone proved that. Then we started playing off the idea that everyone in Jeremy's life was dying, so I thought, 'Now there's a story here!' I was waiting for the right time. It had to be earned. We've done werewolves, vampires, we've tried to keep it really grounded and now we're in a place after all the witchy-woo-woo of this year that I think the audience will accept this additional element to our world."

FOGGY MOMENTS: How was Elijah able to walk into Alaric's apartment? There seems to be an unusual cut in the scene between Klaus and Stefan in

Alaric's apartment. Right before the act break, Klaus slams Stefan against the wall; right after, they're in the middle of the room, Klaus is staking him, and Katherine is speaking out on his behalf. How did Klaus know that his blood was the cure for a werewolf bite? Was it the cure even before he became an active hybrid? In "The Last Dance," Bonnie died and then came back to life, but (as far as we know) she has no ability to see the dead like Jeremy now has. Is this because the spell she used on herself was to fake her death as opposed to raise the already-dead?

MUSIC: Damon takes off his ring and stands in the sun to Ingrid Michaelson's "Turn to Stone." Days Difference's "Speakers" is playing at the Grill when Alaric gets the call from Stefan about Damon. Caroline tells her mother that Jeremy's alive again to Girl Named Toby's "Holding a Heart." Damon lies dying in Elena's arms to "I Should Go" by Levi Kreis.

QUESTIONS FOR SEASON 3:
- Klaus and Stefan plan to leave the "tragic little town" of Mystic Falls right away. Where are they headed? What does Klaus really want from Stefan?
- Do all of the boxed Originals have daggers in their hearts? Did Klaus have a full dagger set made by one of his loyal witches? Is the dagger that Elena gave Elijah in "Klaus" still on the loose somewhere or was that the one Klaus stuck in his brother?
- Will Jeremy be able to see other dead people? (Like Jenna?) Will his connection be limited to those who were supernatural, or will he be able to see his parents? Are these spirits malevolent? Will the presence of two dead ex-girlfriends put a damper on his relationship with Bonnie? Will Jeremy share news of his ability or keep it to himself? If Jeremy has a connection to the supernatural world, does that make him in some way supernatural too?
- With the sacrifice over, what new threat will target Elena? Or are her days as a bull's-eye over?
- Aside from witnessing her introduction to Damon, Elena's path never crossed with Andie's. Does she know about the nature of Damon's relationship with Andie? Will she ever find out?

- Assuming that at some point someone pulls the dagger out of him, will Elijah show his vamp face in season 3?
- Will Elijah's resurrection elixir from "The Last Day" find a use in season 3?
- The curse was originally put on Klaus by witches powerful enough to do it. Does a force that strong still exist? Is there some lost knowledge of how to recreate that balance, since no creature is supposed to be invincible? Or does nature's requirement that there must be a balance mean that even as a hybrid, Klaus has a weakness — it's just not yet discovered?

Doppelgänger Hijinks Ensued: Doubles in Season 2

With Katherine's arrival in Mystic Falls at the end of season 1 of *The Vampire Diaries*, Elena was destined to come face to face with a "living, breathing double" of herself in season 2. Though there were issues of doubles and shadow selves in season 1 (in particular with the Salvatore brothers, and the mysterious Katherine Pierce), in season 2 the writers took the trope of doubling and brought it front and center, extending it far beyond literal doppelgängers to help illustrate (both visually and through the pairing of certain characters) the identity crises these characters face.

The term is derived from the German words for double (*doppel*) and walker (*ganger*) — and in folklore it was most often interpreted as a harbinger of death. In literature, thankfully, the character who is doubled won't necessarily drop dead. The tradition of "dualism" — whether there is a separate living double (a doppelgänger, twin, or shadow self) or an internal splitting of one character's identity into two (think Dr. Jekyll and Mr. Hyde) — was prevalent in the Romantic period and in Gothic fiction, as writers saddled their characters with issues of unstable identities. There's the "beast within" motif (as Linda Dryden describes it in her book on doubles, "the Hyde in each of us must be suppressed") as well as the "conflict within the soul" motif where one character experiences an internal split into two selves. While some fiction features literal doubles (like Edgar Allan Poe's 1839 story "William Wilson"), other authors have created a more subtle twinning, like Catherine and Heathcliff, in Emily Brontë's *Wuthering Heights* (1847), who can be interpreted as mirror images of each other, parts of a whole split in two.

Particularly in the early 19th century, the characters who found themselves confronting a double were frequently orphans. Described by Dryden as "the literature of solitude," these "double" narratives featured lone children facing isolation. Those features are also present in *The Vampire Diaries*: the show is littered with orphans (Damon, Stefan, Katherine, Elena, Jeremy, and arguably Bonnie and Matt), and most characters struggle with their feelings of isolation. Other traditions of the literature of doubling are also part of *TVD*:

- Characters often have a hereditary tie to the doubling (the doppelgänger "gene" runs in the Petrova/Pierce line, the Lockwood curse is genetic),
- The character is tempted by darkness (most notably Damon and Stefan),
- The character is an outcast of society (those involved with the supernatural feel separate from the rest of the townsfolk),
- The doubles are bound together and both feel the same pain (the spell tying Katherine and Elena made this idea literal in "Masquerade"),
- The likeness between doubles is unaccountable — it's out of the ordinary and it threatens the stability of the social fabric by enabling confusion and trickery with the presence of more than one of the same person (which sums up the experience of Elena and her friends once Katherine enters her world and toys with it), and
- The language in narratives of the double often employs verbal ambiguity; it's full of puns and double meaning (something the *TVD* writers love to play with).

Once the doubles have met, will they become enemies or partners? Which is the original and which the copy? Will the double destroy the original, or lead that character to become a more stable whole through the conflict between self and shadow self? The figure of a double calls into question the assumption that we all have a single, stable self — one identity that we carry through adult life, rather than a multiplicity of selves within a single person, often battling for dominance. And this is where the psychology comes in. Swiss psychologist Carl Jung (1875–1961) wrote about a "shadow self" — the darkness within each individual that is cut off from his or her conscious being — and it's a useful concept to consider in regards to doubles and doppelgängers. "We carry our past with us," said Jung in 1937. "[For someone to

be cured of a looming shadow self] it is necessary to find a way in which his conscious personality and his shadow can live together." The idea being, if one ventures into the "darkness" of the self and brings the self and shadow into a "precarious unity," then it's possible to assimilate the dark side rather than be overwhelmed by it (a likely result of denying and repressing it). "The hero's main feat is to overcome the monster of darkness," wrote Jung, referring to the victory of the conscious self over the subconscious urges. Does that bring to mind any vampires we know and love?

There is a multitude of dualism issues present in season 2 of *The Vampire Diaries* — from splits in personality (Damon, Stefan), to physical transformations (Tyler morphs from human to wolf, Caroline becomes a vampire), to mistaken identities and doppelgängers (Elena and Katherine). To begin with the physical doubles, Katherine's debut in Mystic Falls in "The Return" plays out like her character will be the archetypical evil doppelgänger: she's destructive, manipulative, sexual, violent, cavalier, and enjoys the dangerous fun in her "doppelgänger hijinks." She seems at first to be literally the harbinger of death, as she threatens to kill everyone Elena loves and she's later indirectly responsible for bringing Klaus down on them all. She's the antithesis of Elena; where Elena is virtue, Katherine is vice, a devil with instinctual, anti-social tendencies. Katherine fits into the tradition of a devil- or demon-as-double: she has great knowledge and power, she's older by centuries (as

---

Just to Clear Up Any Confusion . . .
- "I'm not Katherine." (Elena to Damon, "Friday Night Bites")
- "She's not Katherine." (Stefan to Lexi, "162 Candles")
- "We all know that you're not Katherine." (Isobel to Elena, "Isobel")
- "Elena is not Katherine." (Stefan to Damon, "Founder's Day")
- "I'm not Katherine." (Elena, repeatedly, to Rose, "The Descent")
- "You think I'm Katherine?" (Katherine, as Elena, to Damon, "House Guest")
- "Look at me, it's Elena. It's Elena." (Elena to Damon, "As I Lay Dying")

Damon likes to point out), she obstructs the double's plans (forcing the breakup with Elena and Stefan, and plotting twice to turn her over to Klaus), and she must be circumvented by cunning (see "Masquerade").

The femme fatale versus fair maid archetype doesn't stick around for long: as discussed in the preceding episode guide, Elena quickly adopts manipulative and strategic techniques more readily identified with Katherine. And in "Katerina," Katherine is humanized. Though she pretended to be an orphan when she arrived at the Salvatores in 1864 to elicit sympathy, it turns out that Katherine really is an orphan. She lost her parents just as Elena did, and both feel culpable for their deaths (Katerina for angering Klaus by fleeing, and Elena for being the reason her parents were on the road the night of the accident).

In Elena's fake fight with Stefan in "Kill or Be Killed," she says of Katherine, "It's like we're the same person. How could you hate her and be in love with me?" In that moment, Elena and the audience actually believe there's a world of difference between the two. But as the storyline develops and the lore of the doppelgänger is revealed — their existence is the result of a spell, and they are both doubles of a third, as yet unknown, Petrova — there is an undeniable bond between the two. And that is another hallmark of the doubles' tale: whether the double is an antagonist or a confidant, at some point in their narrative, the twins share a feeling of closeness and sympathy. Elena identifies with Katherine in "Katerina" (though importantly not with the decisions she makes), and the two are mirrored in their parallel affection for the Salvatore brothers. In the finale, Katherine very pointedly says to Elena that she should not be ashamed to love both brothers — after all, Katherine did.

A good-doppelgänger/bad-doppelgänger binary is too simple and boring for *The Vampire Diaries*, and by muddying the distinctions between Katherine and Elena — of what each girl is capable of doing and feeling — the writers have made these characters delightfully layered. As Katherine gets better at impersonating her younger twin, the two characters reveal more similarities. But beyond the literal double they have in each other, both Katherine and Elena have an internal split. There is Katherine, the vamp in both senses of the word, and there is Katerina, the girl who believed that a life without love was not worth living ("Klaus"). We know that the much-ballyhooed "emotions switch" for vampires is not real: Katherine is actively suppressing the feelings she has in order to survive at any cost. In the tomb with Stefan in "By the Light of the Moon," she says she knows she's done "terrible things" but she doesn't regret her actions, which were motivated by a fierce sense of self-preservation. Both Salvatore brothers give her a "look where that's got you" lecture (Stefan here, and Damon when she's trapped in Alaric's apartment), and in the finale, as if she has taken the criticism to heart, Katherine chooses to repay her debt to Damon, by saving his life instead of immediately fleeing. Not much in the grand scheme of things, but a huge step when you consider the villain who landed in Mystic Falls in "Founder's Day."

Elena's split identity in season 2 comes with the discovery that she is the doppelgänger. To some vampires, she is an object to be collected and destroyed along with the moonstone, her human life having no value greater to them than an old rock. Her new identity as "the doppelgänger," a supernatural entity, threatens to destroy her true identity as Elena Gilbert — a human with family, friends, and a future (and we see the significance of it to her in "The Last Day" when she mourns losing that life). In moments over the course of the season, Elena refers to "the doppelgänger" instead of speaking of "I" or "me," when talking about the sacrifice; she separates her two identities. While Katherine chose to save herself by fleeing the sacrifice, Elena chooses to save those she holds dear (a plan which fails spectacularly when Jenna dies, along with John) by going through with the sacrifice. Elena is rid of her supernatural identity: the doppelgänger has been killed, and in her resurrection she returns to her true self.

When Damon announced his presence in the pilot — "Hello, brother" — and Stefan very shortly thereafter tackled him straight out the window, the "hostile brothers" motif of *TVD* was established. While the audience became acquainted with the brothers, the battle was external — one good brother, one bad — but it didn't take long for the writers to take that tradition and layer it by giving each of Damon and Stefan internal conflicts that derive from and further complicate the relationship between the two. Their external conflicts reflect their internal struggles between self and shadow self.

Stefan sees in Damon (particularly in the killing-spree Damon who arrived in town) several aspects of himself that he is repressing. Instead of identifying as a vampire, Stefan tries his best to be human again by embracing his emotions and denying himself the sustenance and satisfaction his body craves — human blood. His vigilance in the present is contrasted with his violent past, which we learn about gradually over the course of season 1 and season 2, most fully in "Miss Mystic Falls" and in the flashbacks in "The Dinner Party" where Stefan "the Ripper" is revealed. Stefan sees a hard line within himself that separates the monster from the man. In his advice to Caroline in "Brave New World," he reveals how tempted he is by the monster's instincts. It feels good to give in, he says, but those feelings must be repressed. In the finale, Stefan's two selves come into direct conflict: in order to atone for his past wrong against his brother, Stefan feels he must find a cure for Damon's werewolf bite at any cost, and that cost is "the man" being devoured by "the monster." The boundary he painstakingly erected within himself over a century was torn away in one night by the more powerful Klaus.

While Stefan keeps constant vigil to repress his vampire instincts, he is either "man" or "monster." His brother, on the other hand, balances on the threshold between the two, teetering throughout the second half of season 1 and season 2. When we meet Damon, his "shadow self" is in control: he is a killer and he has thrown off the identity he had when he was human. His struggle to date has been to reconcile his "humanity" — his love for Elena, his love for his brother, his fervent wish to feel human again, and his instincts to do good (exemplified in his relationship with Sheriff Forbes) — with his desire to kill and to hunt. That conflict comes to a head in "The Descent" in his speech at the end of the episode, and from then on, Damon attempts a kind of amalgam of both identities: using Andie to indulge his vampire side by night, and fighting to save Elena from Klaus by day. He's a self-described "work in progress." By season's end, Damon is yet to resolve the two halves of his self: he is still by turns impulsive and selfish, considerate and selfless. Will Elena's deathbed validation — "I like you now, just the way you are" — help Damon resolve his identity crisis, or will he feel fraudulent because she is ignorant of his recent spate of violence (murdering Jessica, abusing Andie)? While Damon remains a character balanced on a moral threshold, he has a unique view from the precipice, a position that bridges both worlds and

Shadows in a Mirror

Mirrors are frequently used on *The Vampire Diaries* as a visual cue that a character is experiencing a touch of the split self or feeling a little duplicitous. The split within the character between their two selves is made literal onscreen as we see them and their mirror image. A few notable instances . . .

- In "Miss Mystic Falls," after Elena confronts Stefan about secretly drinking human blood, he goes into a restroom, looks in the mirror, and furiously smashes his reflection.
- In "Brave New World," Caroline stands in front of the mirror in her hospital room horrified by the vision of the new vampire self that is revealing itself by distorting her face. Later, in the school bathroom with Stefan, Caroline breaks down again looking at her monstrous reflection. Stefan turns her away from the mirror and acts as her reflection, showing her it is possible to control the vampire within.
- In "By the Light of the Moon," Elena is placed in front of two mirrors in her bedroom when she's talking to Bonnie and about to deceive her by taking the moonstone and attempting to leave the house, a visual cue to her split selves. Later in the same episode, we see her reflection in her full-length mirror as Elijah negotiates a deal with her; in that scene, she is acting as both "the doppelgänger" and as Elena, keen to save her loved ones from harm.
- In "Daddy Issues," both Elena and Damon are reflected in the mirror in the Grill's ladies room, as she urges him to be the better man, a moment that reminds us of the split between Damon's "good" and "bad" selves, and, arguably, of Elena's growing awareness of her power to manipulate Damon.
- In "The House Guest," the opening scene's doppelgänger mix-up makes use of mirror images: Stefan attacks Elena, thinking she's Katherine, as she looks in the mirror, and when Katherine reveals herself to be the one standing at his doorway, we see her image reflected in that same mirror as Elena recovers and Stefan is dumbfounded.
- In "The Last Dance," we see Matt's reflection in a mirror as he says to Liz that he can't keep up his duplicitous act; the formerly solid Matt Donovan is splintering under the burden of his secret from Caroline.

allows him to often adopt the role of narrator of events and of characters' development, as if he is aware of the story unfolding.

Last season, Tyler Lockwood was an otherwise normal jocky teen with rage issues, a guy who didn't always feel like himself, who could get so out of control that he'd beat the crap out of his best friend (after making out with that friend's mom). The "beast within" Tyler Lockwood is manifest in a literal way in season 2, when he learns of the Lockwood curse and (unintentionally) activates it. In werewolf narratives, the afflicted character is split between savage beast and regretful human, and Tyler's journey in season 2 falls into that tradition as we watch him physically transform from one self to the other and back. Unable to rid himself of that part of his identity (a family legacy), he is cursed to a lifetime as a lycanthrope, living with the secret and the potential for extreme violence once a month. As a wolf, he twice attacks Caroline, who is arguably the person he cares for most, next to his mother. His dark self attacks what his true self holds dearest. But with Tyler's "monster side" becoming so clearly distinct from his human identity, he is given the opportunity to control it in a way that wasn't possible when he was just an angry jock, and that isn't possible for a vampire, who lives day to day with temptation. By casting off his old self when he and Jules leave town ("Crying Wolf"), Tyler learns to manage his new identity. When he returns, he seems to have brought the two parts of himself into "precarious unity."

Tyler's journey was paralleled with Caroline's this season; both characters successfully navigate the transition from human to supernatural creature with minimal casualties and damage (RIP Carter and V5 deputies). The strength Tyler and Caroline draw from each other serves as a positive example of mirroring; far from being enemies (as they have been told they should be as werewolf and vampire), they find common ground and become allies (and, judging by that finale snuggle, potentially much more in season 3).

It's hard to find a character on *The Vampire Diaries* who doesn't fall into some form of doubling. Secret-keepers — like Alaric (teacher/vampire hunter) and Liz Forbes (mother/sheriff/vampire hunter) — constantly maintain separate selves, as does Matt when he deceives Caroline, and Bonnie who lives her life hiding that she's a witch from society at large.

In addition to doubles, there are multiples on *TVD*, where several characters represent a single concept. For Jeremy, his father figures are represented by a diverse array of men — his actual but deceased father Grayson, his uncle John (now also deceased), his teacher and buddy Alaric (who acts as his guardian in the finale), and Damon, who Jeremy tags along with early in season 2. For Elena, the concept of mother is embodied by Miranda, Jenna, Isobel, and perversely, as her oldest living relative, Katherine.

As we head into season 3, the fractured selves, monsters within, and literal doubles will still function as a powerful and meaningful narrative layer, one that adds not only more depth but a great opportunity for play, trickery, and those trademark *Vampire Diaries* jaw-dropping moments.

Interview with the Fandom

Chloe Dawn

My introduction to "TVD Chloe," as she was then known, was in her season 1 finale YouTube video wherein she freaked out about the awesomeness of that episode — "Oh my Salvatore!" Though she's not yet old enough to vote, Chloe Dawn has made her voice heard in important ways over the past year, spearheading charitable projects and raising awareness about pressing environmental issues — while simultaneously entertaining the heck out of the *TVD* fandom on Twitter and YouTube. Find her online at Twitter.com/TheChloeDawn and ScreamForADream.net.

How did you get into The Vampire Diaries — did you read the books, watch the show from the beginning . . . ?

I got into *The Vampire Diaries* fandom by watching the show. I had read the first three books before the show aired and never really connected with them the way I did with the show. In my opinion, the show has so much more added into it, and so many more twists and turns. Fans rarely like a television show or movie adaptation better than an original book series. *Vampire Diaries* is obviously a huge exception to that.

Chloe with Steven R. McQueen and Michael Trevino

Tell me about making your first vlog and the reaction people had to it.

My first vlog was kind of a spur of the moment thing. I was freaking out about the season 1 finale and I was like, "I need to share my feelings with someone." Who better than the internet? I grabbed my camera, jumped in my car, and started filming. I doubted anyone would watch it and contemplated not posting it. But sure enough, a couple of hours after it went up, Vee from Vampire-Diaries.net retweeted my tweet. Kevin Williamson, I'm assuming, saw it from them and then tweeted it and stated it was "The Best Review Ever." (That's the point where I started freaking out.) Then a couple of minutes later, Julie Plec tweeted it, then Nina Dobrev, Ian Somerhalder, Michael Trevino, and Matt Davis. The cast's and writers' comments were very positive. I couldn't believe that they had watched *my* video and actually thought it was entertaining! I'm pretty sure I didn't get an ounce of sleep that night. Honestly, looking back at it now, it's completely embarrassing! But if it weren't for the silly YouTube video, nothing I've been able to accomplish would have been possible.

What inspired you to start Vampire Support, now Scream For a Dream?

My inspiration behind Scream For a Dream, formerly Vampire Support, was Ian's passion about the BP oil spill disaster in the Gulf of Mexico. Seeing the pictures and video clips of the animals that had been affected broke my heart. I am a huge animal lover. I realized that I had been given a voice in the *Vampire Diaries* fandom because of my finale vlog and that I needed to use it to inspire teenagers to get involved. Our first project was putting on an auction of autographed memorabilia from *The Vampire Diaries*. Julie Plec and Kevin Williamson donated a pilot script signed by the entire cast, and that went for an amazing amount of $2,283, which was donated to the National Wildlife Federation. Many fan sites, fans, and others donated items, and the total amount raised from our auction was around $3,500. We also received a $5,000 Pepsi grant for their "Do Good for the Gulf" campaign. We were able to put together a T-shirt project for the Ian Somerhalder Foundation and raised $4,500. We also did many other smaller projects. Our grand total for our oil spill campaign was $24,000.

The second project that we have been working on is the "Save the Wolf" campaign with Michael Trevino. We have a Crowdrise page (Crowdrise.com/SavetheWolf) set up where we do signed-item giveaways for people who donate a certain amount of money. We also have been selling Save the Wolf and Team Tyler wristbands. All proceeds go to the Wolf Mountain Sanctuary. Wolf Mountain Sanctuary is "a non-profit, educational organization dedicated to the preservation, protection, and proper management of wolves in the wild and in captivity [whose] ultimate goal is to save these great noble animals from extinction." They are currently located in southern California and care for 14 wolves.

What kind of response to your projects have you had from the cast and creators of the show?

The response has been very positive. The cast and creators have been nothing but supportive of my efforts and projects. They tweet constantly about anything I am doing, donate items, and even talk about the projects in interviews. It's absolutely amazing that *The Vampire Diaries* cast and creators are so dedicated to their fans and the charitable projects the fandom has created.

You've been working with the Ian Somerhalder Foundation (isfoundation.com) since its beginning. What made you interested in getting involved with that project?

The Ian Somerhalder Foundation has been so inspirational. Kim Klingler, the executive director, has been nothing short of amazing working with Scream For a Dream and our campaign efforts. Scream For a Dream and the Ian Somerhalder Foundation look at a lot of issues in the same way. We have had a great relationship from the beginning, and I can't wait to see what we can do with ISF in the future.

Had you been involved with fundraising, charity work, or raising awareness before these fandom-related projects?

> I always have done little things around my community. Doing a walk or race for cancer research, sponsoring a child in Africa, etc. I have never done anything to the extent or level that I am doing now, because I never really had much influence on anyone. I'm very blessed and grateful to be able to help others and hopefully influence others to stand up for what they believe in.

A lot of people see the problems facing our world, but don't actually get up and do anything about it. What advice would you give to someone who wants to get involved?

> My advice is if you're going to talk the talk, you have to walk the walk. I know, not very original, but it's the truth. You always hear people in casual conversation with others about the problems in today's society, but they never actually do anything about it. My advice is to dream up the impossible and make it possible. People don't realize that the internet is an amazing tool and can bring so many people together in a collaborative effort to make a change in the world.

Let's switch gears to the show itself — what was your favorite moment from season 2?

> My favorite moment from season 2 would have to be Tyler's werewolf transformation scene [in "By the Light of the Moon"]. I am a huge Tyler fan and have been since the first season. No one understood why I liked him since he was such a jerk. I knew there was so much more to his character that we hadn't seen yet and that just drew my attention toward Tyler even more. I really wanted to know *why* he was such a jerk. The transformation scene was such a powerful moment, and I had been waiting for it for a long time. That scene was so full of emotion and truly displayed Michael Trevino's incredible acting skills.

What would you most like to see in season 3?

> More Tyler and Caroline, of course! I love the Romeo and Juliet aspect of their relationship. Michael Trevino and Candice Accola's

chemistry on screen is absolutely amazing, and I'd love to see how the writers can make a werewolf and vampire get along.

If you could write yourself a guest spot on an episode of *The Vampire Diaries*, who would your character be?

I've always joked that I could be some sort of crazed teen vampire researcher who does online videos about her findings in Mystic Falls. I'd love to see Damon have to come and find me, because I know too much information about the Salvatore brothers. Even if he had to kill me, I think that would be hilarious.

Describe *The Vampire Diaries* fandom with three adjectives.

Passionate, inspiring, and a little bit crazy. ;)

Spirits Talk:
Tiya Sircar

(Aimee Bradley)

How did you get into acting?

I began dancing at a very young age. That got me interested in musical theater, which I started doing when I was seven or eight years old. I started taking acting classes soon after and participated in community and school plays till I graduated from high school.

Before you were cast on *The Vampire Diaries*, were you already familiar with the show?

Not really. But once I got the job, I watched as many episodes and did as much research as I could, thinking I could familiarize myself with the plot and characters. I quickly realized that this was no ordinary show with an ordinary plot line! It was a bit overwhelming trying to cram an entire season's worth of relationships, betrayals, deaths, et cetera, into such a short amount of time before I started shooting, but the cast was very sweet to help me along the way.

Tell me about the casting process for the role.

I went in and auditioned for the casting directors. They sent my tape to the producers and in a few days, I got a call that I would be flying to Atlanta, Georgia, the very next morning!

Did you create any backstory for Aimee in building the character?

You know, it's funny, I just felt that I knew a few girls in my own high school that were just like Aimee that the backstory was already kind of there for me.

When you signed on, did you have any idea how long Aimee would survive in Mystic Falls?

Definitely not. On a show like *The Vampire Diaries*, any character's days can be numbered. Initially, there was talk that Aimee might have some sort of love story with Matt, then there was the hookup with Tyler . . . and then Katherine kills her off unexpectedly. Never a dull moment in Mystic Falls!

Tell me about filming the death scene.

My very first death scene! It was pretty intense. We were shooting in the middle of nowhere in rural Georgia on this beautiful estate that serves as the Lockwood mansion. My death scene was the last shot of the night so it was pretty late, maybe 2 or 3 a.m. We actually had to choreograph the whole thing, which proved to be rather difficult. Katherine is supposed to be holding me up with her super vamp strength, so we had to use some stage combat tricks to fake that as well as the vamp-strength punch to the spine that finishes Aimee off!

Aimee had a bit of thing for Matt. Do you think anything would have happened between them if Katherine hadn't killed her?

Yes! I was definitely looking forward to seeing what may have happened between Aimee and Matt and what problems that, in turn, would have caused between Aimee and Caroline. That could have been an interesting love triangle! Alas, thanks to Katherine, I guess we'll never know.

Of the *TVD* cast members you worked with, who would you say is most like their character?

Hmm, that's a tough one! Each cast member definitely brings a lot of their own personality to their respective role. For example, the charming, debonair side of Damon is very Ian. And that intense, piercing stare of his . . . also very Ian! And the sweet, bubbly, vivacious side to Caroline (you know, when she's not vamped out and ferociously attacking people), that's totally Candice. She's a sweetheart!

Do you have any favorite moments from filming on *The Vampire Diaries*?

I have to say that the entire experience being on and off set with those guys was a blast. They are a close-knit group of friends, both the cast as well as the crew, and they are so much fun to be around. As far as filming goes, maybe the dungeon scene where Aimee and Tyler make out after Caroline compels her. Those scenes can be uncomfortable to shoot, but Michael Trevino is a classy guy and totally made what could have been a scary experience very comfortable. Also, it was fun to be in that dank, dark dungeon. Working on a vampire show, you should get to be creeped out from time to time!

Any projects we should watch out for?

I do a cameo in the Justin Timberlake/Mila Kunis film *Friends with Benefits*. It's a hilarious scene with Justin and with Richard Jenkins, who plays Justin's dad. They were both so funny and really sweet in person. And the movie is hilarious! I also worked on a film called *The Domino Effect*, which was directed by Paula van der Oest, a Dutch director who was nominated for an Oscar in 2002. My first time working with a female director, which was a wonderful experience. I can't wait for the film to come out!

Living in Mystic Falls

What happens when your new favorite show happens to film in your hometown? If you're Covington residents Jessica Connell Lowery and her daughter Brannan, you turn a pastime of watching *TVD* film into a blog, a successful fan tour, and a way to give back through charitable campaigns. Meet the firecrackers behind VampireStalkers.com and MysticFallsTours.com.

How did you first get interested in *The Vampire Diaries*?

> **Jess:** My daughter and I both have a love for reading, and she was enthralled in the literary world of vampires and werewolves. So we, of course, had read The Vampire Diaries books long before there was talk of a TV show. Brannan and I were just lucky enough to love the books and have them film *TVD* here in our hometown.
>
> **Brannan:** It was one of the first vampire series I read after the Twilight Saga. I still remember coming home from school one day and Mama telling me that not only would they be making The Vampire Diaries into a show, but that it would be filmed in our town.

Tell me about your first time "stalking" the *Vampire Diaries* set — and how that eventually turned into Mystic Falls Tours.

> **Brannan:** Our first stalking experience was on a Friday. I came home and my nanny called me and said, "The hot one is filming!" Of course, at the time, I had no idea that "the hot one" was none

other than Mr. Ian Somerhalder. We went to our town square and sat and watched. After hours and hours, not only could I feel a new obsession growing, we got to meet Paul Wesley and watch Lexi [Arielle Kebbel] do her own stunt when she was being dragged into the alley by the cops [in "162 Candles"].

Jess: We had an immediate obsession with what was happening on the show before it aired. Can you say *spoilers*? Having a fun-loving cast that cared about their fans made it so much more fun to watch filming 12 hours at a time, in the heat or cold. After many days on set, after making friends with some of the cast and learning how hard they worked, we started blogging about the happenings of Mystic Falls. A lot of the fans were following us on Twitter and on VampireStalkers.com, so I decided to try and do tours and see how it went, so to speak. I can promise you I never thought I would spend my days giving tours of Mystic Falls and my nights stalking the sets — but I do. I am very lucky to have a successful business touring Mystic Falls and meeting all the passionate fans of *TVD*. The fact that I do it all with my 15-year-old daughter is a big bonus that every mother hopes for.

I took your Mystic Falls tour a few months ago and had a great time. Explain a bit about the tour for those who haven't made it out to Covington, Georgia.

Jess: Mystic Falls Tours is all about helping the fans experience what we are lucky enough to do every day of our lives. I take fans to all the outside sets used on *TVD*, while also providing a personal feel by telling all the awesome stories we have from stalking the sets or hanging out with the cast after filming. I try to make everyone feel like they're a part of Mystic Falls and hopefully even share some spoilers with them or have them see some filming while they're here. You never know who you will see or meet when you go out for ice cream in Mystic Falls!

Do you have a favorite "stalking" moment or a favorite story from giving a tour?

Jess: The craziest tour story — we had a fan-girl climb in a window of the Lockwood mansion flashback house, because she saw a wine glass that "Ian might have drank out of." Apparently her world would end if she couldn't take this wine glass home with her . . . ha ha!

Brannan: My favorite "stalking" moment was when it was about five degrees outside, freezing cold. We were standing in front of Gram's house, the only two people brave enough to endure the weather, to watch filming. And Kat came up in a truck and asked us to go to lunch with her. It was Nina's 21st birthday and, I have to say, getting to sit down with the entire cast and actually talk with them is something I'll remember for the rest of my life and a story I hope to tell my kids one day, because in my opinion, that's when all of our friendships started.

Jess, you're also one of the hosts of The VRO (TheVRO.com), which is *the* place for in-depth *Vampire Diaries* cast interviews.

Jess: I came in two years after the VRO had started. I was lucky enough to join something that I could be proud of. The "*TVD* Month of May" was started to bring the fans not only fun radio interviews with the cast of their favorite show, but also a way to interact with the cast. Most of our questions are submitted by the fans, for the fans, so when we interview the cast, we make sure we ask everything that the fans are dying to know. Sometimes we can even take live callers. There's nothing better than hearing a fan get excited, 'cause they're talking to their favorite cast member!

Do you have a favorite interview you've done with a *TVD* cast member?

Jess: Man, that's very hard to say . . . I have to say that I acted like a fan-girl big time when I booked Joseph Morgan, who plays Klaus. I actually jumped up and down! Ha, ha! Joseph was a fun interview, and we worked hard to get him and were lucky enough to be one of the first radio interviews he did after joining *TVD*, so that made it even more exciting. Ian Somerhalder would have to be a close second. I loved interviewing Ian because he is a friend and I am so proud of all he is doing with his foundation. Brannan and I both work for ISF and have since the beginning, so being able to give Ian a forum where he could spend the entire time talking about ISF, and nothing else, has to be a highlight of my VRO career. I have to say that Matt

Mother–daughter duo Jess and Brannan.

Davis is so surprising that he doesn't surprise me anymore — if that makes since? Matt comes on as "Ernesto Riley." He talks Illuminati and aliens, and it's slightly entertaining and it's important to him and his fans. David Anders surprised me some too; he's actually kind of sweet and liked to make fun of my Southern accent. I guess I had pegged him to be more tough than sweet, so that was a nice surprise.

How did you two get involved with fundraising efforts for ISF and other good causes?

Jess: Ian invited Brannan and me to join ISF in the very beginning. I had been helping with Vampire Support, now known as Scream For a Dream, for a while and we had been doing some great projects and fundraising. I think the fact Brannan and I knew Ian personally and that we are so heavily involved with the *TVD* fandom — as well as the fact we were working already with a charity — helped him and [ISF executive director] Kim want to include us. Before ISF was announced, we were behind the scenes donating our time and anything else we could to help. We are still very involved — from fundraising and brainstorming to helping with projects and getting ready for the first ISF event to take place October 2011 in Atlanta. It's very exciting for me to be able to show my children that you can't sit back and be silent. You have to step up and help now, if you want the world to be a better place for them and their children. ISF gives everyone a voice. I guess that's why I am such a strong supporter of it. Ian is taking his fame and using it to make a difference. How amazing is that? It's even more amazing to me that I can be a part of it.

As for *TVD* itself, what was your favorite moment of season 2?

Jess: Let's see, I am a Damon and Elena fan, so I loved the moments at the end of season 2 when Damon and Elena are in his bed. But I guess my very favorite moment was when Elena finally decided to take her life in her own hands, and she went to the basement and pulled the dagger out of Elijah [in "The Last Dance"]. That, to me, was an awesome moment, and I feel like it was about time that Elena said, 'Okay, it's my life and this is how it's gonna be!'

Brannan: Well, I am a huge Damon-Elena fan, so mine had to be in the end, where they were in the bed and he was dying, he finally told her how he felt with no vampire interference, and Elena kissing him. I can't say enough about that — I just wish I had my reaction on camera.

What would you most like to see in season 3?

Jess: I am looking forward to meeting the rest of the Original Family. If the rest of the family is half as entertaining to watch and hear (accents — oh my!), then I think season 3 will be one of the best. I am also looking forward to seeing Elena turn more and more to Damon while Stefan feels out his dark side. I think that Paul Wesley may actually be the breakout star of season 3. I am also dying to see what the consequences are for Bonnie and if the "ghosts of Jeremy's past" are just that — ghosts or vampires returned from the dead.

Brannan: I am looking forward to seeing Damon and Elena's relationship grow and become closer, and Stefan go and discover his dark side, and of course the lovely, bad brother Klaus.

Describe *The Vampire Diaries* fandom in three words.

Jess: Passionate, obsessive, and *loyal*.

Brannan: Passionate, crazy, and fun.

Spirits Talk:
Bryton James

(Luka Martin)

How did you land the role of Luka Martin?

I actually just went in on a Friday for a normal audition, and by Tuesday I heard I had been offered the part!

Were you already familiar with *The Vampire Diaries*?

Yes, I was familiar with the show, but only a little bit. I hadn't watched an episode before, but had for sure heard of it and its success.

You've been in literally hundreds of episodes of *The Young and the Restless*. How different is it to work on a show like *The Vampire Diaries* compared to Y&R?

Extremely different! For one, on *Y&R* we film an entire hour-long episode in one day. Whereas *TVD* takes about seven to ten days to complete one episode. Also, the amount of location shooting is much more on *TVD*. Getting used to doing so many takes of one scene is very different, since they have to film a take for every version of coverage [i.e., "covering" by filming from a variety of angles and distances].

You've been an actor your whole life, but was this your first foray into a supernatural genre show?

Yes, it was, and I really enjoyed it!

Bonnie — and the audience — learned a lot about witchcraft from Luka. Tell me about filming the "magic moments."

Really, the effects were the best part of doing a supernatural genre show for me. I mean, they actually made real sparks fly on the roof-top that night we shot the moonstone-floating sequence ["By the Light of the Moon"]. And as for the wind with the leaves flying around ["The Sacrifice"], that was done at about 7 a.m. in 40-degree weather with around five giant fans surrounding us, and we shot about 20 takes! But still, a lot of fun!

When you were cast, were you given an idea of how long Luka might be around Mystic Falls? Did you know why Luka and his father were working with Elijah or were you creating the character in the dark a little bit?

When I was first offered the role, I was told it was for only three epi-sodes, which ended up lasting about seven. And also in the cast we were lucky to get the script by the morning of shooting! Honestly, I learned about my character along with the audience as the story progressed from week to week.

Bonnie and Luka had a strange relationship brewing: they seemed to genuinely like each other, but at the same time they were always manipulating and betraying each other. Luka was also pushing back against his father's decisions. What's your take on Luka and his motivations?

I always believed Luka truly did have feelings for Bonnie, and that he hated being in the position he was in to obey his father for the sake of pleasing Elijah and saving his sister. I never thought of Luka to be evil, and really wished that he and Bonnie could have made up before my fiery exit.

Luka's death scene was intense — crazy-ass psychic witch attacks are a dangerous undertaking. How difficult was that sequence to film since your character was literally in two places at one time?

It was actually very fun! I mean, it really pushed you to have to act and make the audience believe what was going on, because many of the shots used were of the actors literally reacting to no one being there. And as for me catching on fire, I think the special effects, stunt doubles, and makeup department deserve all the credit, because they truly made it look amazing.

Was there a particular actor or character you were most excited to act opposite? A favorite scene or on-set moment?

Well, working with Katerina Graham was great. She's a very good actress who really is there for you in a scene always. And I think we had a lot of good chemistry. She's probably going to kill me for telling this, but there was scene that was cut of us walking back to my apartment door, after the rooftop moonstone-exploding scene, where she is thanking me for helping her. And she gives me a kiss on the cheek and then walks away as I watch her leave with a smile on my face. Well, in one of the takes, after the kiss, as I'm watching her go, she looks back at me with a smile while walking away and she ran into the wall on set. Luckily, the camera wasn't on her, because it was my close-up, but I just couldn't keep a straight face and I cracked up laughing!

Do you have any upcoming projects post-Luka?

Well I just re-signed with *Y&R* for another two years, so I'm excited about that! Also, I'm going to be voice-starring in a second and third Lego Hero Factory cartoon miniseries. So be on the lookout!

Thank you so much for your time!

Any time, thank you!

The Vampire Diaries Timeline

"We don't follow a true timeline for many reasons. Weather being one. Serialized storytelling being another." So tweeted Julie Plec. But below is an attempt to piece together the information provided in the first and second seasons of *The Vampire Diaries* into a semblance of a timeline. A question mark indicates that a date is only an estimate; a ○ marks a full moon.

c. 1000? — The Original family becomes vampires and the curse is placed on Klaus ("Klaus"). Klaus and Elijah begin faking documents about the curse of the Sun and Moon.

Dark Ages — Vampires punished those who threatened to expose their kind with 50 years in solitary confinement, according to Stefan ("You're Undead to Me").

1400s — According to Vanessa, the Sun and Moon Curse dates back 600 years to when the Aztecs were being plagued by vampires and werewolves ("Bad Moon Rising"); later Elijah reveals to Elena that the historical documents were fakes ("Klaus").

1450 — Rose is born ("The Descent").

1464? — Pearl becomes a vampire; she has "400 years on" Damon who is turned in 1864 ("There Goes the Neighborhood"). Presumably, Anna also became a vampire around this time.

1490 — Katerina Petrova gives birth to a baby girl who is taken from her ("Katerina").

1492 — Katerina meets Klaus at his birthday celebration; she and Elijah spend time together ("Klaus").

Night before the sacrifice, 1492 — Katerina escapes and becomes a vampire; Trevor and Rose begin running from Originals ("Katerina," "Rose").

Shortly thereafter, 1492 — Katerina discovers that her entire family has been killed by Klaus.

1659? — Lexi is born; she is 350 years old ("162 Candles").

1692 — The Bennett family moves from Salem to Mystic Falls ("Haunted"). They are among a larger group of settlers who moved to the area to flee persecution ("The Dinner Party").

1755 — The Saltzman family comes to America from Germany ("History Repeating").

1790? — A hundred witches are rounded up and burned at the stake in Mystic Falls ("The Dinner Party").

1792 — Mystic Falls cemetery is established ("Pilot").

October 9, 1810 — Giuseppe Salvatore is born ("Children of the Damned").

Early November 1847 — Stefan Salvatore is born ("Lost Girls," "162 Candles").

1860 — The town of Mystic Falls is founded ("Under Control").

January 23, 1864 — According to his tombstone, Giuseppe Salvatore dies ("Children of the Damned"). This date conflicts with many other details in the timeline and is likely a production error.

April 1864 — According to Vanessa (and to Isobel's research), Katherine arrives in Mystic Falls ("Bad Moon Rising").

June 1864 — Johnathan Gilbert begins writing the journal that Jeremy finds ("History Repeating").

September 1, 1864 — The beginning of the Atlanta Campaign fires, which Katherine uses as a cover story ("Children of the Damned"). Presumably, Katherine arrives at the Salvatore estate shortly thereafter. This date conflicts with Isobel's research ("Bad Moon Rising").

September 24, 1864 — The first Founder's Ball is held ("Family Ties"). Katherine confronts George Lockwood at the ball ("Memory Lane"). Damon is rebuffed when he visits Katherine in her bedroom after the ball; Stefan has just professed his love for Katherine ("Memory Lane"). Some time soon after the ball, Katherine reveals to Stefan that she is a vampire ("Lost Girls").

1864 — A comet passes over Mystic Falls ("The Night of the Comet").

The Battle of Willow Creek / The Vampire Purge — Mr. Tanner says that the Battle of Willow Creek took place in 1865 ("Pilot"), but the flashbacks suggest it was actually in late 1864. On the day of the battle, Katherine meets with George Lockwood to go over their plan to fake her death ("Memory Lane"). Damon is also with Katherine at some point on that day and sees her in possession of Emily's crystal ("History Repeating"). Stefan speaks to his father about the vampire situation and unwittingly drinks vervain, which leads to Katherine's capture ("Children of the Damned"). Damon makes a bargain with Emily for Katherine's safety ("History Repeating"). Stefan and Damon are shot trying to rescue Katherine ("Family Ties," "Blood Brothers"). Either one or both of the brothers watch the church burn ("History Repeating" conflicts with "Blood Brothers" on this detail). Before Katherine leaves Mystic Falls, having been released from the church before it was set afire, she gives George Lockwood the moonstone and she sweetly promises (the then dead) Stefan that they'll be together again ("Memory Lane").

The day after the Battle of Willow Creek — Emily gives the Salvatore brothers their rings; Stefan confronts his father and leaves him dying; Damon promises Stefan an eternity of misery ("Blood Brothers").

Shortly thereafter, 1864 — Stefan kills Thomas and Honoria Fell and Johnathan Gilbert (temporarily); Lexi and Stefan meet; Damon leaves Stefan in Lexi's care ("The Dinner Party").

1865 — Damon "made sure" vervain won't grow in Mystic Falls ("Family Ties").

1900? — The Salvatore boarding house is built ("Lost Girls").

1911? — Lexi tries to set up Rose on a date with Stefan ("Rose").

1917 — Stefan slaughters a migrant village in Monterey ("As I Lay Dying").

1942 — The start date for Anna's research into vampire attacks in the Mystic Falls area ("Bloodlines").

June 12, 1953 — "Uncle" Joseph Salvatore is killed at the Salvatore boardinghouse, presumably by Damon ("Family Ties," "You're Undead to Me").

1953 — Four people are killed by "animal attacks" in Mystic Falls ("Bloodlines"); that number likely includes Joseph Salvatore.

1962 — Five people are killed by "animal attacks" in Mystic Falls ("Bloodlines").

October 1969 — Stefan meets Sheila at an antiwar demonstration ("Bloodlines").

1974 — Three people are killed by "animal attacks" in Mystic Falls ("Bloodlines"). Slater is made a vampire and begins accumulating college degrees ("Katerina").

October 17, 1975 / January 18, 1978 — Isobel Flemming is born: the earlier date is on her driver's license ("A Few Good Men"), the later one on her tombstone ("Know Thy Enemy").

1980s — Elizabeth Forbes and Kelly Donovan go to high school together ("Lost Girls"); Kelly Donovan and Miranda Sommers are best friends ("There Goes the Neighborhood").

1983 — Anna sees Katherine in Chicago ("Fool Me Once").

Late 1980s? — Elizabeth Forbes and Logan Fell have known each other since he was six ("The Turning Point"). Kelly Donovan babysits Jenna Sommers ("There Goes the Neighborhood").

Spring 1987 — Lexi and Stefan attend a Bon Jovi concert; Katherine stalks Stefan ("Masquerade").

1989? — Damon meets Bree and asks for her help getting into the tomb ("Bloodlines").

August 20, 1991? — Vicki Donovan is born ("Lost Girls").

Early to mid 1990s — Jenna Sommers and Mason Lockwood attend high school together, along with Logan Fell ("Memory Lane").

1992? — Isobel leaves her hometown of Grove Hill; Elena is born ("A Few Good Men").

1994 — Jeremy Gilbert is born ("The Night of the Comet"). Stefan and Damon see each other for the last time before fall 2009 ("Pilot").

March 14, 1994 — Aimee Bradley is born ("Rose").

Late 1990s — Logan babysits Caroline ("The Turning Point").

2002 — Ten-year-old Tyler sees his uncle Mason; he doesn't see him again until after Mayor Lockwood's death ("The Return").

May 4, 2007 — The date of "death" on Isobel's tombstone ("Know Thy Enemy"), presumably her parents chose the date she disappeared, which conflicts with the timeline established in "Blood Brothers" that suggested Damon turned Isobel in **2008**.

May 23, 2009 — Grayson and Miranda Gilbert die in a car accident ("Pilot"); Stefan rescues Elena ("Bloodlines").

May–September 2009 — Stefan observes Elena and investigates her family history ("Bloodlines").

August 2009 — Katherine compels Jimmy to attack Mason; Mason kills him, which triggers his curse ("Kill or Be Killed").

August 31, 2009 — Mason writes in his journal about how different he's felt since killing Jimmy ("The Sacrifice").

September 6, 2009 — Damon kills a couple who is driving home from a concert ("Pilot").

September 7, 2009 — First day back to Mystic Falls High ("Pilot").

September 8, 2009 — Damon attacks Vicki during the party by the falls ("Pilot").

September 9, 2009 — The comet passes over Mystic Falls ("The Night of the Comet").

September 10, 2009 — Caroline wakes up with Damon; Stefan tries out for the school football team; Caroline and Damon crash Elena's dinner party with Bonnie and Stefan ("Friday Night Bites").

September 11, 2009 — Stefan gives Elena the vervain-filled necklace; Damon kills Coach Tanner ("Friday Night Bites"). (This date actually was a Friday.)

September 15, 2009 ○ — Mason turns into a wolf for the first time ("The Sacrifice").

September 24?, 2009 — The Founder's Ball is held; the date here is based on the original Founder's Ball, which was held on the 24th. Stefan captures Damon and locks him in the cellar ("Family Ties").

September 27?, 2009 — Three days after leaving Elena a cryptic voicemail message, Stefan tries to fix his relationship with her by making dinner for her ("You're Undead to Me").

September 28?, 2009 — The Sexy Suds Car Wash is held at the high school; Damon attacks Vicki and kills her friends; Elena figures out that Stefan is a vampire; Stefan asks her to keep his secret ("You're Undead to Me," "Lost Girls").

September 29?, 2009 — Damon turns Vicki into a vampire; Logan is killed ("Lost Girls").

There's a jump in the timeline here. Between "Lost Girls" and "Haunted" only a few days pass, but "Haunted" takes place at the end of October.

October 31, 2009 — Vicki is staked by Stefan ("Haunted").

Early November 2009 — Bonnie reveals her powers to Elena; Stefan turns 162; Damon kills Lexi ("162 Candles").

Mid-November? 2009 — Emily possesses Bonnie and destroys the crystal; Logan returns, now a vampire. Stefan has been asking Damon for "months" why he returned to Mystic Falls; Alaric mentions to Jeremy that they are halfway through the school semester ("History Repeating").

The following day ○ — With a full moon overhead, it's Career Night at Mystic Falls High School; Elena and Stefan have sex for the first time; she discovers the portrait of Katherine; Noah causes her to crash her car ("The Turning Point"). Damon rescues Elena from the car wreck ("Bloodlines").

The following day — Damon takes Elena to Atlanta to visit Bree; Bonnie falls into the tomb and Stefan rescues her ("Bloodlines").

The following day — Elena arrives back in Mystic Falls, and Stefan reveals that he rescued her from the car crash that killed her parents in May and that she is adopted ("Bloodlines").

December? 2009 — The 1950s Decade Dance is held at the high school; Caroline passes a Christmas display in a store window ("Unpleasantville").

Shortly thereafter — Stefan unearths the grimoire that was buried with his father; both Elena and Bonnie are kidnapped ("Children of the Damned").

The following day — The tomb opens; Duke has a party at the old cemetery where people are wearing winter coats and hats; Sheila Bennett dies ("Fool Me Once").

Winter 2010 — An ill-fated hiker tells Harper the year; the Bachelor Auction is held at the Grill ("A Few Good Men").

No indication of time of year for "There Goes the Neighborhood" or "Let the Right One In."

One month before Founder's Day ○ — Johnathan Gilbert returns to Mystic Falls; the kickoff to Founder's Day party is held on the night of a full moon; Stefan gives in and drinks human blood ("Under Control").

Three weeks? before Founder's Day — Bonnie returns to Mystic Falls; the Miss Mystic Falls competition is held; Elena and Damon lock up a blood-drunk Stefan ("Miss Mystic Falls").

A few days later — Stefan refuses to eat; Elena convinces him not to commit suicide; Isobel shows up at the Grill ("Blood Brothers").

The following day — The Mystic Falls High students prepare floats for Founder's Day; Elena meets her birth mother, Isobel ("Isobel").

The following day — Isobel gets the Gilbert invention from Elena and gives it to Uncle John ("Isobel").

Founder's Day — The tomb vampires, Anna, and Mayor Lockwood are killed; Tyler, Matt, and Caroline are in a car accident; Katherine impersonates Elena, kisses Damon, and attacks Uncle John ("Founder's Day").

The following day — Mason returns to Mystic Falls for his brother's wake; that night, Damon "kills" Jeremy and Katherine "kills" Caroline ("The Return").

The following day — Caroline completes her transition to a vampire; the school hosts a carnival ("Brave New World").

Full Moon ○ — Alaric, Damon, and Elena go to Duke University. Caroline gets a daylight ring from Bonnie. Mason turns into a werewolf. Tyler discovers the Lockwood secret. ("Bad Moon Rising")

The following day — Caroline wakes up to find Katherine in her bedroom ("Bad Moon Rising").

The following day — Assuming this is not the same day that Katherine wakes up Caroline, because Katherine's wearing a different outfit when she shows up at the Salvatore boarding house. Jenna hosts a barbecue; Katherine reveals to Stefan the real story behind the Vampire Purge of 1864. ("Memory Lane").

August 2010 / the following day — The day of the Historical Society Volunteer Picnic; that night, Sheriff Forbes is put in the Salvatore holding cell until vervain is out of her system ("Kill or Be Killed"). The flashback to "one year ago" in "Kill or Be Killed" is later revealed to take place in August 2009 ("The Sacrifice"), meaning the present-day events take place in August 2010.

Three days later — It takes three days for the vervain to leave Liz's system ("Kill or Be Killed"). The gang sets up for the masquerade ball; Mason is tortured and killed by Damon ("Plan B").

Masquerade Ball — Katherine kills Aimee; Tyler triggers the curse by accidentally killing Sarah; Katherine is captured and put in the tomb; Elena is kidnapped ("Masquerade").

The following day — Elijah kills Trevor; Damon and Stefan rescue Elena ("Rose").

The following day — The Martins arrive in Mystic Falls; Elena visits Katherine at the tomb; Rose and Damon visit Slater; Elijah compels Slater to kill himself ("Katerina").

It's not clear how many days, if any, pass between "Katerina" and "The Sacrifice," but since Slater's body is still undiscovered in "The Sacrifice" it's safe to assume the timeline is continuous.

That night — Late at night, Jonas steals various artifacts from Elena's room ("The Sacrifice").

The following day — Jeremy manages to get the moonstone out of the tomb; Stefan is stuck in the tomb with Katherine; Elijah kills three vampires ("The Sacrifice").

The following day — Tyler calls Mason as he gets ready for the full moon ("By the Light of the Moon"). Assuming this is a separate day since he's wearing a different shirt than in "The Sacrifice."

Full Moon ○ — Tyler makes his first transformation. Rose is bitten by Jules. ("By the Light of the Moon")

The following day — Jules wakes up in the bloodbath campground; Rose dies ("The Descent").

The following day — The werewolves kidnap and torture Caroline ("Daddy Issues").

The following day — Stefan and Elena go to the lakehouse. Tyler leaves town with Jules. ("Crying Wolf")

The following day — Assuming it's the next day, since news of Tyler's departure is just spreading. Elijah is killed (twice). Katherine is freed from the tomb. ("The Dinner Party")

The following day — The Grill burns down; Luka and Jonas Martin are killed ("The House Guest"). Jenna meets Isobel ("Know Thy Enemy").

The following day — Isobel kills herself; Katherine is kidnapped; Alaric is possessed by Klaus ("Know Thy Enemy").

The 1960s Decade Dance — Bonnie fakes her death to fool Klaus; later that night, Elena takes the dagger out of Elijah ("The Last Dance").

The following day — Elena spends the day with the newly resurrected Elijah, learning of the true curse ("Klaus").

The Sacrifice ○ — Damon force-feeds Elena his blood; Stefan and Elena go for a climb by the falls; Damon gets bitten by Tyler ("The Last Day"). Klaus breaks the curse, killing Jenna, Jules, and Elena, and transforming into a true werewolf-vampire hybrid ("The Sun Also Rises").

Next morning — Elena and Jeremy bury Jenna and John ("The Sun Also Rises").

The following day — Klaus "kills" Elijah. Jeremy dies but Bonnie resurrects him. Stefan and Klaus make a bargain. ("As I Lay Dying")

(By moon cycles, it is just over two months from Founder's Day to the events of the finale. By time markers within episodes, it is only 26 days.)

Season 1 Refresher

1.01 "Pilot" Stefan and Elena meet on the first day back to school at Mystic Falls High. Vicki Donovan is attacked by Damon in the woods.

1.02 "The Night of the Comet" Damon antagonizes his brother, dangling Vicki off a roof over the town square, as a comet passes over town. Stefan and Elena kiss.

1.03 "Friday Night Bites" Stefan joins the football team, but then Damon kills Coach Tanner, ending the football season prematurely. Caroline debuts her new boyfriend, Damon (and a penchant for neck scarves).

1.04 "Family Ties" At the Founder's party, Stefan manages to capture Damon by spiking Caroline's drink with vervain. Vicki leaves Tyler behind for Jeremy Gilbert.

1.05 "You're Undead to Me" It's the Sexy Suds Car Wash! Bonnie sets water on fire. Elena figures out Stefan's a vampire. Damon escapes from the Salvatore holding cell and attacks Vicki as she parties in the graveyard.

1.06 "Lost Girls" The first flashback episode brings us our first glimpse of Katherine and a heck of a lot of backstory on how Stefan and Damon became vampires. Bored, Damon turns Vicki — but not before their classic dance party moment.

1.07 "Haunted" Halloween in Mystic Falls marks the first death of a major character, as Stefan stakes Vicki, on the loose and hungry for Gilbert blood.

1.08 "162 Candles" Stefan's BFF Lexi comes to town on his birthday, the one day he isn't allowed to brood, and Damon kills her to cover up his own bloody tracks. Bonnie reveals to Elena that she's a witch in one of the series' most magical moments of magic.

1.09 "History Repeating" The girls hold a séance and Bonnie is possessed by her ancestor Emily Bennett, who destroys the tomb-opening crystal. Alaric Saltzman makes his debut.

1.10 "The Turning Point" Damon deals with Logan Fell, now a vampire, while Tyler and Jeremy come to blows at the school's Career Fair. Stefan and Elena sleep together for the first time. She discovers Katherine's portrait, takes off, and ends up in an accident, after a vampire in the road causes her to crash her car.

1.11 "Bloodlines" Damon takes Elena on a road trip to Georgia where she gets nice and drunk and saves his life from Lexi's angry ex. Stefan helps Bonnie get her powers back. Elena finds out she's adopted.

1.12 "Unpleasantville" It's the 1950s Decade Dance at MFHS. Uninvited vampires crash the party, but the Salvatore brothers kill Noah. Matt and Caroline kiss.

1.13 "Children of the Damned" Pretending to work with Damon, Elena and Stefan race to find the location of Emily Bennett's grimoire before he can. In flashback, we see the events leading up to Katherine's capture. Bonnie and Elena are kidnapped by Ben and Anna.

1.14 "Fool Me Once" The tomb opens — and Katherine isn't in it.

1.15 "A Few Good Men" Damon goes on a bender. A bachelor auction is held at the Grill. Elena finds out that her birth mother is Isobel, Alaric's not-so-dead wife.

1.16 "There Goes the Neighborhood" Caroline and Matt and Elena and Stefan go on a double date. Damon makes out with Matt's mom. Two tomb vampires attack the Salvatores.

1.17 "Let the Right One In" A storm moves into Mystic Falls. Stefan is kidnapped and tortured. Damon, Alaric, and Elena rescue him. Caroline discovers Vicki Donovan's body.

1.18 "Under Control" At the kick-off to Founder's Day party, Stefan tries to manage his thirst for human blood and fails. Tyler makes out with Matt's mom. Uncle John Gilbert arrives with a magic ring.

1.19 "Miss Mystic Falls" Caroline wins Miss Mystic Falls. Stefan attacks Amber Bradley.

1.20 "Blood Brothers" Starving himself in the Salvatore holding cell, Stefan flashes-back to the night he and Damon became vampires.

1.21 "Isobel" Elena meets her birth mother, Isobel, who demands the Gilbert device from her. Bonnie pretends to deactivate it.

1.22 "Founder's Day" As the town celebrates its sesquicentennial, the tomb vampires face off with the vampire-hating members of the founding families. Damon kisses Katherine, thinking she's Elena, and Katherine chops off Uncle John's fingers.

Sources

"Aconitum Vulparia (Lycoctonum)," Alchemy-works.com.

"Al Septien & Turi Meyer Interview: *Smallville*, *The Vampire Diaries*, and How to Make It in the Bizz," TheGorgeousGeeks.com. May 12, 2011.

Amatangelo, Amy. "Howling at the Moon," BostonHerald.com. January 30, 2011.

An American Werewolf in London. DVD. MCA Universal, 2009.

Anders, Charlie Jane. "Secrets of Klaus, the Baddest Ancient Vampire of Them All," io9.com. April 28, 2011.

Baring-Gould, Sabine. *The Book of Were-wolves*. Originally published by Smith, Elder & Co., 1865. Republished by Cosimo, 2008.

Barnhart, Aaron. "KC's Veteran Writing Duo Gets Sucked into *The Vampire Diaries*," KansasCity.com. September 6, 2010.

Bentley, Jean. "*The Vampire Diaries*: Taylor Kinney Helps Us Say Goodbye to Mason Lockwood," AOLTV.com. October 25, 2010.

Bernstein, Abbie. "Exclusive Interview: *The Vampire Diaries* Actress Candice Accola Is Young Blood," AssignmentX.com. February 17, 2011.

Bibel, Sara. "*Vampire Diaries*: Nina Dobrev Sinks Her Teeth into Dual Role," XFinityTV.Comcast.net. March 3, 2011.

Bierly, Mandi. "*Vampire Diaries* Exclusive: Michael Trevino Talks Tyler's Transformation, Scenes with Damon and Stefan, and Jules' Motives," EW.com. December 10, 2010.

——————. "*Vampire Diaries* Exclusive: Michaela McManus Talks Jules' Motives (and Damon's Shower Scene)." EW.com. December 17, 2010.

——————. "*Vampire Diaries* Scoop: Katherine's Diabolical Master Plan, Her History with Klaus, and Damon's Chest All Revealed Tonight," EW.com. November 11, 2010.

——————. "*Vampire Diaries* Set Cursed? Ian Somerhalder Talks Filming Tonight's Episode with Walking Pneumonia," EW.com. January 27, 2011.

——————. "*Vampire Diaries*: Could Jules Give Matt a Story Line? What's Elijah's Offer?" EW.com. November 24, 2011.

——————. "*Vampire Diaries*: Daniel Gillies Talks Elijah's Turn On and His Pick for Playing Klaus," EW.com. January 18, 2011.

——————. "*Vampire Diaries*: Dawn Olivieri Talks Playing Ian Somerhalder's Love Interest," EW.com. February 17, 2011.

——————. "*Vampire Diaries*: Joseph Morgan Talks His Inspiration for Klaus, and His Pick to Play the Father of the Originals," EW.com. April 28, 2011.

——————. "*Vampire Diaries*: Michael Trevino Talks Tyler's Transformation (and His First Leather Jacket)," EW.com. October 29, 2010.

——————. "*Vampire Diaries*: Where Were We?" EW.com. March 2, 2011.

——————. "Which TV Character's Bedroom Are You Dying to See?" EW.com. January 21, 2011.

"Bon Jovi: Slippery When Wet Tour." http://e1000bonjovi.creatuforo.com/slippery-when-wet-tour-tema1275.html.

Brigadoon. DVD. Warner, 2005.

Byrne, Craig. "Julie Plec Addresses Finale Spoilers & Possible Deaths," VampireSite .net. April 27, 2011.

"*Chez Tortoni*, 1878–80 (oil on canvas)," Bridgemanart.com.

"Common monkshood, Friar's cap, Garden wolfsbane," Poisonous Plants and Animals. http://library.thinkquest.org/C007974/1_1com.htm.

Compolongo, Gabrielle. "Daniel Gillies on Elena, Klaus and a *Vampire Diaries* Hook Up," TVFanatic.com. February 9, 2011.

——————. "Julie Plec on 'Dark Place' Ahead for *The Vampire Diaries*," TVFanatic.com. December 22, 2010.

——————. "Lauren Cohan on *The Vampire Diaries*, *Chuck*, and More," TVFanatic.com. February 1, 2011.

Cursed. DVD. Alliance Universal, 2005.

"The Daguerreian Era and Early American Photography on Paper, 1839–1860," The Metropolitan Museum of Art. http://www.metmuseum.org/toah/hd/adag/hd_adag.htm.

The Descent. DVD. Lionsgate, 2006.

"Destruction: Wolfsbane," Werewolves.com. October 2, 2009.

Diaz-Arnesto, Laura. "Byzantine Herbs and Drugs — The Poison Aconite or Wolfsbane," MyByzantine.wordpress.com. July 2, 2010.

Dobbs, Michael Ann. "What It's Like to Be a Young Writer Working with Joss Whedon and Kevin Williamson," io9.com. February 22, 2011.

Dryden, Linda. *The Modern Gothic and Literary Doubles*. New York: Palgrave Macmillan, 2003.

Ducky. "Interview with *Supernatural*'s Bela — Lauren Cohan," DuckyDoesTV.com. October 9, 2007.

Facebook.com/pages/Randy-J-Goodwin/

Faulkner, William. *As I Lay Dying*. New York: Vintage International, 1990.

Fienberg, Daniel. "HitFix Interview: Joseph Morgan Discusses Bringing Klaus to *Vampire Diaries*," HitFix.com. April 28, 2010.

"Ford Fiesta Inside the *Vampire Diaries* Video Series," CWTV.com.

Freeman, Jane. "On *Richard III*." Toronto Public Library/Stratford Festival lecture series. March 22, 2011.

Gelman, Vlada. "*The Vampire Diaries*: Caroline 'Recognizes that Tyler Needs a Stefan,' Says Candice Accola," LATimesBlogs.LATimes.com/ShowTracker. November 24, 2010.

——————. "*The Vampire Diaries*: Executive Producer Julie Plec Teases a Return, Klaus' Debut," LATimesBlogs.LATimes.com/ShowTracker. March 18, 2011.

——————. "*The Vampire Diaries*: Taylor Kinney on Mason's Journey and His Love for Katherine," LATimesBlogs.LATimes.com/ShowTracker. October 25, 2010.

Gilmer, Maureen. "Wolfbane and Other Garden Evils," HGTV.com.

Goldman, Eric. "*The Vampire Diaries*: Caroline Gets Ready to . . . Sing?" TV.IGN .com.

——————. "*The Vampire Diaries*: Nina Dobrev on Katherine's Next Step," TV.IGN.com. February 2, 2011.

Gone with the Wind. DVD. Warner, 2009.

Guiley, Rosemary Ellen. *The Encyclopedia of Witches, Witchcraft and Wicca*. New York: Checkmark Books, 2008.

Halterman, Jim. "Interview: *The Vampire Diaries* Co-Stars Candice Accola & Michael Trevino," TheFutonCritic.com. December 10, 2010.

Hamilton Boys' High School, HBHS.school.nz.

Hampson, Courtney. "Candice Accola: Interview with a Vampire," *CH2 Magazine*. October 2010. Accessed via Candice-Accola.net.

HarperTeen.com

Hemingway, Ernest. *The Sun Also Rises*. New York: Scribner, 2006.

Huxley, Aldous. *Brave New World and Brave New World Revisited*. New York: Harper Perennial, 2005.

"Ian Somerhalder Interview," JustJared.com. February 8, 2011.

"Isabella Stewart Gardner Museum Offers a $5 Million Reward for Stolen Masterpieces," ArtKnowledgeNews.com.

Jester, Alice. "C2E2 Report: Interview with *Vampire Diaries* Executive Producer Julie Plec," TVfortheRestofUs.com. March 21, 2011.

"Joseph Morgan," CurtisBrown.co.uk.

Knight, Nicholas. "Director's Cut: J. Miller Tobin," *Supernatural Magazine*. September-October 2010.

LaurenCohan.com

"Lauren Cohan," TV.com.

Lawrence, Will. "Paul Wesley," *Wonderland Magazine*. October 2010.

"Lexicon of Jungian Terms," New York Association for Analytical Psychology. http://www.nyaap.org/jung-lexicon/h.

"Live from C2E2: Candice Accola Dishes on Caroline Forbes (*The Vampire Diaries*) & Her Squishy Heart," GeekGirlOnTheStreet.com. March 20, 2011. http://www.youtube.com/watch?v=ESKfHL6t5KE.

LJaneSmith.blogspot.com

LJaneSmith.net

Loggins, Emma. "Interview: Candice Accola from *The Vampire Diaries*," FanBolt .com. January 26, 2011.

Machosky, Michael. "Belle Vernon Native Fights Aliens in *Battle: Los Angeles*," PittsburghLive.com. March 10, 2011.

MacKenzie, Carina. "*The Vampire Diaries* Joseph Morgan on Klaus and Damon: 'I had to make him play on my terms,'" Zap2It.com. April 28, 2011.

—————. "*The Vampire Diaries* Nina Dobrev: Is Katherine Coming Out of the Tomb?" Zap2It.com. February 16, 2011.

—————. "*The Vampire Diaries*: Damon's Demons Surface; Can Elena Forgive Stefan's Dark Past?" Zap2It.com. February 7, 2011.

—————. "*The Vampire Diaries*: Michael Trevino's 'Shining Moment' on Tyler's Darkest Day," Zap2It.com. December 9, 2010.

—————. "*The Vampire Diaries*: Zach Roerig and Candice Accola Talk Young Love, Butterflies . . . and Murderous Vampires," Zap2It.com. February 23, 2011.

—————. "*The Vampire Diaries*' Nina Dobrev: 'There's a Lot of Heart and Soul Coming Back,'" Zap2It.com. January 27, 2011.

—————. "*Vampire Diaries* Star Candice Accola: Will Caroline Forgive Tyler?" Zap2It.com. March 31, 2011.

Martinez, Rodolfo. "On the Dark Side: Paul Wesley Talks Acting and *Vampire Diaries*," *WWD*. December 2010.

Miller, Karl. *Doubles: Studies in Literary History*. New York: Oxford University Press, 1987.

"Monterey: History," City-Data.com.

"Moonstone," International Colored Gemstone Association. Gemstone.org.

Morales, Juan. "Daniel Gillies," *Interview*. July 2004. 36.

Mullins, Jenna. "*The Vampire Diaries*' Ian Somerhalder Tells Us What's Ahead for Damon, and It Involves Whiskey," eOnline.com. February 10, 2011.

Murray, Rebecca. "Daniel Gillies Talks About *Captivity*," About.com.

—————. "Trent Ford Talks About *How to Deal*," About.com.

Nahuatl Dictionary. University of Oregon Wired Humanities Project. http://whp. uoregon.edu/dictionaries/nahuatl/index.lasso.

Ng, Philiana. "Kevin Williamson Shoots Down Potential *Vampire Diaries*, *Secret Circle* Crossovers," HollywoodReporter.com. April 25, 2011.

—————. "Q&A: *Vampire Diaries* Boss on Creative Changes, the Post–*Dawson's Creek* Era and Spoilers," HollywoodReporter.com. April 21, 2011.

"Nina Dobrev — Katherine & Elena — *TVD*," CW Source. KTLA.com.

Oebel, Nicole. "Interview with Taylor Kinney," MyFanbase.de. 2010.

OfficialMaiaraWalsh.com

Prudom, Laura. "*The Vampire Diaries* Star Ian Somerhalder on Playing the Bad Boy With a Conscience," TVSquad.com. February 9, 2011.

Radish, Christina. "Joseph Morgan Talks *The Vampire Diaries* and *Immortals*," Collider.com. May 9, 2011.

—————. "Executive Producer Kevin Williamson Interview," Collider.com. January 26, 2011.

—————. "Taylor Kinney Exclusive Interview *The Vampire Diaries*," Collider .com. October 21, 2010.

"Randy J. Goodwin Profile," GBTAcademyOfTheArts.org.

"Randy J. Goodwin," tv.com.

Rogers, Robert. *A Psychoanalytic Study of the Double in Literature.* Detroit: Wayne State University Press, 1970.

Rose, Lacey. "*Vampire Diaries* Actress Joins Josh Schwartz's *Georgetown* Pilot (Exclusive)," HollywoodReporter.com. March 16, 2011.

Rosenfield, Claire. "The Shadow Within: The Conscious and Unconscious Use of the Double," *Daedalus* (vol. 92, no. 2). Spring 1963. 326–344.

Ross, Robyn. "*The Vampire Diaries*' Dawn Olivieri: Andie Star Won't Play the Victim," TVGuide.com. February 17, 2011.

"'Shadow' Carried by All, Says Jung," *New York Times.* October 22, 1937. http://www.nytimes.com/books/97/09/21/reviews/jung-lecture2.html.

Shakespeare, William. *The Tempest.* Oxford: Oxford University Press, 1994.

Showpatrolman. "Steven R. McQueen: Jeremy-Bonnie About to Heat Up *Vampire Diaries*," Blogs.RedEyeChicago.com. February 10, 2011.

Sicha, Choire. "Inside the *Vampire Diaries* Craze," TheDailyBeast.com. November 2, 2010.

Smith, L.J. *The Vampire Diaries: The Awakening.* New York: HarperTeen, 2009.

——————. *The Vampire Diaries: The Fury* and *Dark Reunion.* New York: HarperTeen, 2007.

——————. *The Vampire Diaries: The Struggle.* New York: HarperTeen, 2009.

"Soapography: Bryton McClure," Soap Net via http://youtu.be/8DyiXllHQyo.

"Social Aspects of the Civil War: Introduction," www.itd.nps.gov/cwss/manassas/social/introsoc.htm.

"(Spoilers) Exclusive Interview with *Buffy* S.9 Writer Andrew Chambliss," BuffyFest.blogspot.com. April 1, 2011.

St. Columban's Today newsletter. Spring 2009. www.stcolumbanshome.org.

Steinberg, Jamie. "Taylor Kinney: Total Transformation," StarryMag.com.

Steinberg, Lisa. "Joseph Morgan: Sinking In," StarryMag.com.

Sternberg, Alix. "From the Set: Exclusive Interview: Matt Davis (Alaric) from *The Vampire Diaries*," TheTVChick.com. January 28, 2011.

——————. "From the Set: Exclusive Interview: Sara Canning (Jenna) from *The Vampire Diaries*," TheTVChick.com. January 28, 2011.

——————. "From the Set: Interview: Julie Plec (Creator/Executive Producer) of *The Vampire Diaries*," TheTVChick.com. January 27, 2011.

——————. "From the Set: Interview: Kat Graham (Bonnie) from *The Vampire Diaries*," TheTVChick.com. January 25, 2011.

——————. "Interview: Michaela McManus (Jules) from *The Vampire Diaries*," TheTVChick.com. March 10, 2011.

——————. "Interview: Steven R. McQueen (Jeremy Gilbert) from *The Vampire Diaries*," TheTVChick.com. February 17, 2011.

Swift, Andy. "*Vampire Diaries*' Dawn Olivieri on Bath Time with Ian Somerhalder: 'I Really Enjoyed That Scene,'" HollywoodLife.com. February 10, 2011.

"Taylor Kinney as Luke Gianni," My8binghamton.com.

"Taylor Kinney Interview with E!," VampireDiariesGuide.com. October 23, 2010.

"Taylor Kinney," NBC.com/Trauma.

The Wolf Man — The Legacy Collection. DVD. MCA Universal, 2004.

"Tiya Sircar: *The Vampire Diaries* Interview," ClevverTV. September 30, 2010. http://www.youtube.com/watch?v=rDs9SMSoAUY.

Turchiano, Danielle. "From Damon & Stefan to Elijah & Klaus: *The Vampire Diaries* Brotherhood," Examiner.com. April 28, 2011.

Twitter.com

"*Vampire Diaries*' Candice Accola Visits *TV Guide Magazine*!" March 31, 2011. http://www.youtube.com/watch?v=VMwzd2GMWlU.

"*The Vampire Diaries*: Julie Plec & Steven McQueen Talk Season 2," NiceGirlsTV.com. October 12, 2010.

"*Vampire Diaries* — Michael Trevino," Show Patrol TV. March 19, 2011. http://www.youtube.com/watch?v=6qdCrohIU_c.

Vampire-Diaries.net

The Vampire Diaries — Stefan's Diaries Vol. 1: Origins. New York: HarperTeen, 2010.

The Vampire Diaries — Stefan's Diaries Vol. 2: Bloodlust. New York: HarperTeen, 2011.

The Vampire Diaries — Stefan's Diaries Vol. 3: The Craving. New York: HarperTeen, 2011.

The Vampire Diaries. TV Series. Executive Producers Leslie Morgenstein, Bob Levy, Kevin Williamson, Julie Plec. The CW. 2009–.

"Virginia Slave Law Summary and Record," Slavery in America. http://www.slavery-inamerica.org/geography/slave_laws_VA.htm.

Weinstein, Joshua L. "*Vampire Diaries* Star Paul Wesley Joins Eva Longoria in *The Baytown Disco*," TheWrap.com. May 13, 2011.

Wieselman, Jarett. "Dawn Olivieri: You Never Really Die on *Vampire Diaries*," NYPost.com/Blogs/PopWrap. March 24, 2011.

——————. "Taylor Kinney Answers Your *Vampire Diaries* Questions," NYPost.com/Blogs/PopWrap. October 21, 2010.

——————. "*Vampire Diaries* Creator Spills on the Past, Present and Future of Mystic Falls," NYPost.com/Blogs/PopWrap. December 10, 2010.

——————. "What Will *Vampire Diaries* Season Three Look Like?" NYPost.com/Blogs/Popwrap. May 16, 2011.

Wiki.Vampire-Diaries.net

Wikipedia.org

YouTube.com/CWTelevision

YouTube.com/TheCWSource

Acknowledgments

As always, thank you to my ECW family — David Caron, Erin Creasey, Troy Cunningham, Jack David, Sarah Dunn, Jennifer Hale, Michael Holmes, Jenna Illies, Rachel Ironstone, Jennifer Knoch, and Simon Ware — for your support of Calhoun endeavors. Gil Adamson, thank you for being the best editor a girl could ask for — full of good advice ("keep your stick on the ice") and marginalia comedy. Thank you to those who designed *Love You to Death* — cover and photo-section designer Rachel Ironstone, page designer Melissa Kaita, and typesetter Gail Nina — and to Chris Nicholls for granting permission to use his stunning photograph of Nina Dobrev (originally published in *Flare*) that graces this book's cover. My gratitude to Jennifer Hirte and Sylvia Gelinek at S&S for bringing season 2 of *Love You to Death* to German readers.

Thank you to Tiya Sircar, Bryton James, Chloe Dawn, and Brannan and Jessica Connell Lowery for their interviews. A world of thanks to all the journalists whose articles are quoted herein. Thanks to Sarah Dunn for *TVD* GTs and for her expert proofread. Mad love to Red and Vee — you don't know how honored I am to write for your site; it means the world to me to be part of the Vampire-Diaries.net crew. Thank you to all the people who comment on my episode posts there, who chat with me on Twitter, and to the *TVD* family at large — a passionate, wisecracking fandom if ever there was one. I'm very proud to be a member (and to be mistaken for a flight attendant). A special thanks to Bite On This, The VRO, The Televixen, The Salvatore Council, I Heart Vampire Diaries, My Entertainment OCD, and Vampire Stalkers for their support. Adam, you will always be my second favorite Forbes. Finally to my family and the Ace Gang — I love you to death.